The Villas & Riads of Morocco

Text by Corinne Verner

Photographs by Cécile Tréal and Jean-Michel Ruiz

The Villas & Riads of Morocco

Translated from the French by Laurel Hirsch

HARRY N. ABRAMS, INC., PUBLISHERS

CONTENTS

6 Introduction

Islam and the Home
10 INTERNALIZED SPACES
13 The Patio, a Paragon of Enclosure
21 A Decorative and Methodical Art

In the Medina
30 APPARENT DISORDER
34 A Declaration of Heritage, a Modern Construction
41 *Dars or Riads?*

Fès
52 THE HOLY CITY
52 A Retiring and Melancholy Nature
57 A Jewel of Hispano-Moresque Art

Portraits
72 GLAOUI PALACE: A GHOST TOWN
80 RIAD AL BARTAL: THE HOUSE OF BIRDS

Marrakech
90 ANDALUSIAN ART INFUSED WITH RURAL INFLUENCES
97 The Particular Charm of House-Gardens
107 The Garden, a Metaphor for Paradise

Portraits
112 DAR EL QADI: THE HOUSE WITH THE TOWER
120 RIAD LAMRANI: THE MAGNIFICENT GARDEN

Essaouira
130 A COSMOPOLITAN TRADING POST
130 A New and Eccentric Medina
138 Patios Made of Stone and Wood

Portraits
144 VILLA BAGHDAD: AN ALCHEMY OF AFRICA AND THE EAST

Kasbahs of the Oases
156 AN ARCHITECTURE UNIQUE TO NORTH AFRICA
163 Adobe and Raw Brick: An Outdated Structure
169 Rudimentary Interiors
180 A Heritage in Peril
185 The Restored Kasbahs of N'Kob and Skoura

Temples to the Art of Living
196 AGAFAY
196 A Kasbah of Lords
199 Usurped Objects
203 Theatrical Décor
208 DAR AHLAM
208 The Enchanted Kasbah
211 Contemporary Influences
214 A Universe of Sensations

INTRODUCTION

Ever since the days of its first embassies, Morocco has asserted itself as a sublime foreigner within the West. European travelers who let themselves be guided there by the whims of their meanderings have never ceased to partake of its art of living and celebrate its refined culture. The land there, however, is less buoyant: along the country roads a fiery wind scorches the plains and the mystery of labyrinthine cities seeps from the high walls, while homes remain protected, encircled behind their blind walls. An enigmatic country, Morocco cries out to be discovered. A poor country, there are unimaginable riches hidden behind its cracked walls. Visitors who manage to enter a house are struck by the magic of the place. In contrast to the austere exteriors, the interiors reveal a splendor of gems: carved plaster, floors of marble or mosaic, ceilings with marquetry or painted motifs. Bathed in subtle light, scented with the perfume of flowers and essences, graced with the chirping of birds and the murmur of fountains, the interiors celebrate a warm and tender art of living centered around an appreciation of intimacy.

Morocco also stands out as a country of great diversity. This westernmost land in the Islamic world, where the local Arabic dialect is called *Maghrib* ("where the sun sets"), is both Mediterranean and Atlantic, mountainous and desert, Arab and Berber. Houses in Fès are constructed with very high ceilings and illuminated by a central shaft of light. There is great attention to the sophistication of the décor. Trounced by the heat of the summer months, Marrakech homes had originally been built on one floor, with rooms and galleries opening onto a garden, a replacement for the ornamentation found in Fès. The kasbahs in the valleys of the pre-Sahara are armored with rough-hewn clay walls. But the art of living experienced there is oddly similar to elsewhere: whether the home is a palace, a fortress, or a house, there one lives outside of time.

Islam and the Home

The Moroccan home is different from a European house in ways far more profound than mere décor. Throughout the country all urban and rural homes adhere to a tradition passed down through the ages that expresses an ideal of unity faithful to the philosophy of the broad-reaching *Dar al-Islam* (House of Islam). From the outside, a passerby lost in the labyrinth of a medina would never surmise what lay just inside. Moroccan homes are almost hermetically sealed and their façades are devoid of adornment. Only some muted ornamentation on the street-side doors, designed to allow a laden donkey to pass through easily, hint at the refinement to be found within. Windows, often absent altogether, are situated only in secondary quarters, such as stairwells or service areas, in order to provide ventilation or light. The houses fall prisoner to their immense sightless, unhearing walls. A glance of the eye is neither caught nor cast.

INTERNALIZED SPACES

Press your ear to the wall, and silence is all you will hear. A taste for the cloistered, the serpentine, the hidden— are these Moroccan attributes? Committed to keeping their domestic space away from the gaze of others, whether in the city or the countryside, the first thing Moroccans will do after buying a plot is to erect an enclosing wall.

Whitewashed with lime in the north, scorched raw adobe in the south, the walls reflect the social order. They express the need to protect oneself against animals, thieves, or strangers. But even greater than this defensive role, they have a symbolic function: the wall divides the world into two distinct and opposing spaces—the private and sacred indoors, the public and profane outdoors. It intensifies the division of space in terms of the sexes that, according to Muslims, assures a balanced social structure. Traditionally, men's work takes place in the public, exterior sphere, whereas women undertake their activities in the interior, private space. The homes are shut, closed in unto themselves, to protect the wives and daughters who, in accordance with the principles of an ideal Islamic society, must remain in the house, living apart from men. In the Maghrib (Arabic for "where the sun sets" or "west" and commonly used to refer to Tunisia, Algeria, and Morocco), one never asks a husband about the health of his wife. The question is posed more modestly: "How is the house?"

However, while the walls express a desire for seclusion and withdrawal, modeled upon a patrilineal formula, they do not in the least hinder the life of the neighborhood. Friendships develop from one house to the next and hospitality is one of Morocco's most cherished institutions. Thresholds, demarcations, and passageways define all. Whether the home is rich or poor, the welcome is always the same—so gracious that to many outside the culture it seems excessive. Invited into the most lavish room in the house, replete with thick carpets, guests sit on sofas with clusters of embroidered pillows and are served tea graced with the scent of orange-flower water in the household's prettiest glasses; this is followed by an extravagant meal.

RIGHT:
The code of honor recommends that men live separately from women. Even when not working, they remain outside the home

The blind walls are an expression of the social order. The streets are public and profane spaces, while the home is private and sacred.

Meanwhile, expensive aromatic essences from Africa and the East burn in censers. Then there are the surprising ritual gestures—tender inquiries about your health, his hand clasping yours, then touching his forehead, heart, and lips. There are rules of propriety that call for shoes to be removed before entering a room and hands to be washed before sharing a meal from a communal plate. Hospitality is a matter of family honor and a requirement across all social strata. But the presence of a guest does not entail the conflation of spaces, for the oppositions of public and private, outside and inside, male and female remain in the home. The presence and movement of outsiders within the house is governed by the ancient Moroccan rules of etiquette known as *hashouma*, a kind of social and moral proscription that prohibits offending others.

Following tradition, the outsider who appears at the doorstep is shown in by a maid or the head of the household, never by the wife. A zigzagging entryway hides the interior courtyard—where women perform hired work or household chores—which the guest does not enter. A staircase leads upstairs to a reception area, called the *douiria*. In more opulent houses, *douirias* often have separate entrances accessible from the street. In the houses of the less wealthy, where there is no reception room, women take refuge in a shared room that is off-limits to the guest, so that the private life of the house is protected from the social life of the head of the household.

 The Patio, a Paragon of Enclosure

The wall marks the border between the chaotic, hostile, and soiled external world and the ordered, secure, and impeccable interior world. The nomad protects his encampment with a hedge; the peasant protects his village with a fortified enclosure; and the city-dweller protects his house with a wall. All these enclosed spaces

OPPOSITE AND ABOVE:
All doors are based on the same model. The leaf in which the small door is inserted only opens to receive goods and cumbersome provisions, or to let a laden beast pass through

PAGES 14–15:
The openings never give onto the street, but rather always face the patio and are protected with iron grilles decorated with spirals and scrolls

ISLAM AND THE HOME 13

have openings that lead only toward the interior, onto a central space from which radiate an array of other rooms. In the more modest city homes (*dars*), this central space is a patio, while larger bourgeois residences (*riads*) have refreshing courtyard gardens hidden behind the walls. A kasbah on an oasis, however, might merely have a dirt courtyard. Although the size of this space is highly variable, it is always square or rectangular. While usually open to the sky, it might have a roof fitted with an octagonal skylight.

In these Moroccan houses, where one lives removed from the world, the patio is an archetype of the sacred enclosure, defined not merely by its limits but, primarily, by its center. Historians believe that the origins of the house with its central courtyard are to be found in the ancient Middle East. Transported through migration and trade, this model appeared throughout the Mediterranean countries of the western Islamic world. There have also been, however, Saharan influences.

This idea of the sacred center, intimately linked to Islam, was already well established. It is invariably found in the design of public spaces (including mosques, caravansaries or *fondouks*, Koranic schools or *zaouïas*), as well as in the layout of cities. The establishment of a central locus is the point of departure for all inhabited spaces. It must be remembered that the Islamic world is centered upon the holy city of Mecca, where Muslims from around the world assemble once a year and, gathering in concentric circles, re-establish the unity of their community. Ideally, all houses would be built to face toward this center of the world, but the complexity of the medina makes such orientation impossible.

The first element of a residence to be designed is the patio or interior courtyard (*wust ed-dar*) and it is the main area of the home. It is from there that the other rooms radiate and it alone provides the source of light. It is there that all architectural embellishment appears, as it is here that the concept of a façade appears, reflecting both the family's social status and the refinement of the Moroccan art of living.

PAGES 16–17:
The somber ornamentation on the street-side doors rarely gives an inkling of the luxurious interiors of the homes. Here, the patio at Riad Kaiss

ABOVE:
Riad Berbère

ISLAM AND THE HOME 19

In the city or the countryside, houses always open onto a central patio from which radiate all other rooms.

 A Decorative and Methodical Art

Just as with the architecture, interior décor varies according to the family's affluence and the urban or rural setting. Interior courtyards are usually simple and austere in the valleys of the High Atlas Mountains, but in the cities they are more like intricate sculpted boxes: in Marrakech and the valleys north of the Sahara, clay, lime, and plaster dominate, but in Fès, a city with an educated and sophisticated population, artisans sculpt out of such

ABOVE LEFT AND RIGHT:
The interiors of the Riad Berbère have a variety of ogive arches, in wood or covered in plaster and lime whitewash

PAGES 22–23:
The Ben Youssef Madrassa is testimony to the refinement of Hispano-Moresque art. Floral ornamentations and epigraphic friezes carved into plaster are mixed with geometrical motifs made with zellij

ISLAM AND THE HOME 21

noble materials as marble, ceramic, and cedar. But it is impossible to contrast the Hispano-Moresque traditions of the cities with the raw Berber ornamentations of the countryside. The designs exemplify the same geometric principles that convey to the center and regardless of their sophistication, they all employ only three kinds of motifs—geometric, floral, and epigraphic.

A geometric motif is always devoid of any deviation. Constructed upon repetition and symmetry, the only room for play is with its size and proportions, with a preference for miniaturization. It is an art that entails interlocking, not dissimilar from geographic sketches. The curved sectors give birth to arabesques, while the rectilinear ones metamorphose into stars and swirling rosettes. Of the vast litany of motifs, the most dominant would likely be the *testir*—an interlacing geometric pattern developing around a central star. Only slightly less commonly found are *mouqarnas*, or the bees' nests design that is used for decorating the intrados of arches. These motifs are sculpted in stone, wood, or plaster, while the checkerboard structures are constructed in tile mosaics and bricks.

Seen almost everywhere, the floral patterns derive from the Arabo-Andalusian tradition. One of the principle motifs is the *touriq*, a botanical ornamentation composed of interlacing floral, foliage, and palmette patterns. The palm is a recurrent design in Moroccan art that appears singly, doubled, notched, and as a spiraling spiral that evolves into an arabesque. Floral design remains an abstract art. Far from imitating nature, it limits its interpretation to the acanthus leaf, the palm tree, and the pinecone. Except for the movement, there

ABOVE:
Floral decorations are introduced into a geometric motif based on symmetry and repetition

RIGHT:
The primary decorations are concentrated on the upper portions of the patio's façade

PAGES 26–27:
Nejjarine Fondouk in Fès

is no reproduction of reality and it is subordinate to the geometrical design in which it is inserted. In the epigraphic patterns, the cursive form appears most frequently. When it is sculpted in stone, however, the Kufic style, a monumental script par excellence, is preferred.

Although the decorative techniques are quite ancient, artisans—painters, ceramicists, sculptors, and woodworkers—do not form any general artistic culture. A sculptor who works in plaster, for example, would not be capable of carving a motif in wood. Each artisan has his own repertoire of designs drawn from the Spanish tradition (itself a descendant of the Hellenic Christian art), as much as the Eastern Islamic tradition. The Hispano-Moresque hybrid, born of the crossing of these influences, spread throughout eleventh- and twelfth-century Morocco during the Almoravides and Almohades dynasties.

Despite undergoing continual change dating back to the Middle Ages, a remarkable continuity prevails and is particularly apparent in the decorative work found in the interior courtyards, the bedrooms, and the salons. It adorns the floors, doors, and walls, columns and their capitals, and above all, the ceilings, as Moroccans enjoy stretching out on their fine woolen carpets and contemplating the polychromatic prisms carved into the fragrant cedar.

Constructing or renovating a Moroccan house takes quite a while. How many hours of hard work did these masterpieces of interior design require? Amid the patios, however modest they may be, one lives as if in a palace. This is exactly what seduced Europeans, who delighted at spending time living in a house in the medina or a kasbah in the south. Ever since the nineteenth century, countless artists and writers were thrilled to live there, even dreaming, perhaps, of never leaving.

Thanks to an 1832 diplomatic mission led by the count de Mornay, the Romantic painter Eugène Delacroix (1798–1863) produced a great number of sketches and watercolors that would inspire all his future work. Following the count and Delacroix, Edmondo De Amicis, Gabriel Charmes, and Charles de Foucauld would make their own journeys. The French novelist and naval officer Pierre Loti

(1850–1923) was also fascinated by the luxury and refinement of the palaces in Fès, which he reproduced in his Moroccan-style house in Rochefort, on France's Atlantic coast. The twentieth century saw visits from the historian and essayist André Chevrillon (1864–1957), the literary brothers Jérôme and Jean Tharaud (1874–1953 and 1877–1952), and the artists Henri Matisse and Raoul Dufy. The fashion designer Paul Poiret (1879–1944) created collections that were inspired by the interlacing motifs of the fountains in Fès. Jacques Majorelle (1886–1962) painted the kasbahs of the south and created a wonderful garden at his home in Marrakech. During this same period the jewelry designer Charles Jacqueau (1885–1968), working for Louis Cartier, created extraordinary accessories based upon the geometrical mosaic patterns. Moroccan homes, seemingly predisposed to reverie and artistic inspiration, beg a suspension of time.

In the Medina

A medina is a zone organized in accordance with the archaic rules of ancient cities in the Arab-Muslim world. Whether taking the form of a Bedouin camp or the great city of Baghdad, a circular district was the paragon of the medieval Islamic center. All medinas were enclosed within a rampart that was punctuated by crenellated towers and entered through monumental gates that were shut from dusk to dawn. Lines of communication adhered to the logic of the society. Principal axes emanated from the gates along the periphery and continued to the center of the town, which was customarily the site of the mosque from where the five calls to prayer sounded, creating the town's daily rhythm. Serving as an extension of the ancient caravan routes, these great axes were trading centers between the local residents, the rural populations, and the passing foreigners. Designed for commercial interests, they were lined with shops and artisans' stalls, and formed what came to be called a souk. These avenues then branched off into secondary streets that circumscribed the plots of land where residents lived amid an unlikely tangle of lanes and dead-end streets in traditional town dwellings—*dars*, *riads*, and palaces.

APPARENT DISORDER

The city serves as a beacon in Islamic culture. There intellectual life shines and religious activity takes place. The first impression of anarchy is nothing more than an illusion. The medina is arranged in different sectors, separating the economic life of the city from the private life of its residents.

Down the alleyways and the crooked culs-de-sac, within the quarters where concealed residences cluster, there are no business enterprises. Each quarter is a community unto itself with all the requisite elements—mosque, Koranic school, fountain, hammam (traditional steam bath), latrines, *soukia* (a small local souk), bread oven, and mill. Often the hammam marks the center of the residential quarter because as every town must have a mosque, so must it have a hammam where the faithful can perform their ritual ablutions near the place of worship. In the ideal Islamic society, if a private house does not have a hammam, the bath is the only venture outside permitted for women.

Unlike the main streets of the town, where everyone walks, neighborhoods are only frequented by their residents, their families, and their clients, as is evidenced by the names of the streets (*derb*), which often indicate the tribal or regional origins of the residents. Like the *kissaria* (a small independent covered market), the quarter can be closed at nightfall. The numbering system of addresses, which runs from right to left in keeping with Arabic writing and follows each twist and turn of the *derb*, often remains an enigma to the foreign traveler. It is quite possible that number 1 will be across from the last number on the street; the doors are rarely directly opposite or side by side. The massive doors, with their rough studs and heavy knockers, belie the owner's affluence. There are some, however, that are adorned with sculpted cornices and tympana.

Each *derb*, no wider than about ten feet (three meters), originates at the house located at the end of

RIGHT:
The urban fabric of a medina is centered around a religious building. Pictured here, the Ben Youssef mosque in Marrakech

PAGES 32–33:
Marrakech, the epitome of a medieval city, is ringed by ramparts that form one of the most vast walls in the western Islamic world

the cul-de-sac. This house, the most remote of all, is usually owned by an important member of the community. The cul-de-sac reinforces the separation of the sexes. Women and children roam freely in it and often the front door is left open to encourage visits and conversation. Although the house may serve to isolate, the social ideal remains one of community. Any pretext is valid in order to maintain the network of solidarity.

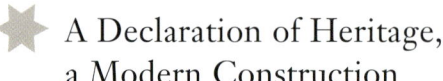 A Declaration of Heritage, a Modern Construction

Among the countries of the Maghrib, Morocco holds the record for conserving medinas. Fès and Marrakech, both declared World Heritage Sites by UNESCO, are endowed with irrefutable architectural riches. The only laws that protect them, however, date from the period of the

ABOVE LEFT AND RIGHT:
*The souks of Marrakech.
Each street specializes in
a different trade. Some
form a small covered
independent market
called a* kissaria

*The main streets of the medina house only businesses.
The residential quarters are secluded along small alleyways
and culs-de-sac.*

French Protectorate. In fact, it was Marshal Louis Hubert Lyautey, the first resident general of the French Republic in Morocco, who was responsible for placing the medinas under the jurisdiction of the heritage protection. Upon his arrival in 1912 Lyautey created the Antiquities, Fine Arts, and Historic Monuments Service that worked to safeguard, maintain, and promote indigenous art. Headed from its inception by the painter Tranchant de Lunel, this institution had the power to oversee all reconstruction projects of sites within the medinas. Specific regulations were instituted for each city, with acts applying to monuments as well as private residences. The latter could not be taller than the ramparts, must be constructed of traditional materials, and in keeping with the local style. In truth, the colonial administration enforced its control primarily over the arrangement of façades and roofs, the placement and height of doors, and the size and color of homes. Signs and posters that did not conform to the zone were not permitted. Even in the new towns, which were established as places for the colonialists to live far away from the locals, the construction of public buildings was controlled by an architectural ordinance.

In 1918 the program to safeguard the national heritage was extended to include the crafts industry, and the Office of Indigenous Crafts was assigned the mission of collecting, cataloguing, and exhibiting antique objects to ensure that the subsidized crafts workshops would not succumb to European influences. The arts were documented, museums were founded, and an expansive annual crafts fair was instituted. The Moroccan crafts industry experienced a great revival with artisanal objects and expertise being exported onto world markets.

However, this ideological fervor inspired by Lyautey dissipated even before the outbreak of World War II. With an increase in automobile traffic and health problems due to the overpopulation of the medinas, the regulations were deemed overly restrictive and the safeguarding measures became polemical. The rift between proponents of modernity and defenders of tradition grew deeper, as

LEFT:
At the dyer's souk, skeins of wool are hung to dry on the terraces

ABOVE:
A small street in the Fès medina

PAGES 38–39:
The numbering system of addresses, which goes from right to left, follows each twist and turn of the street

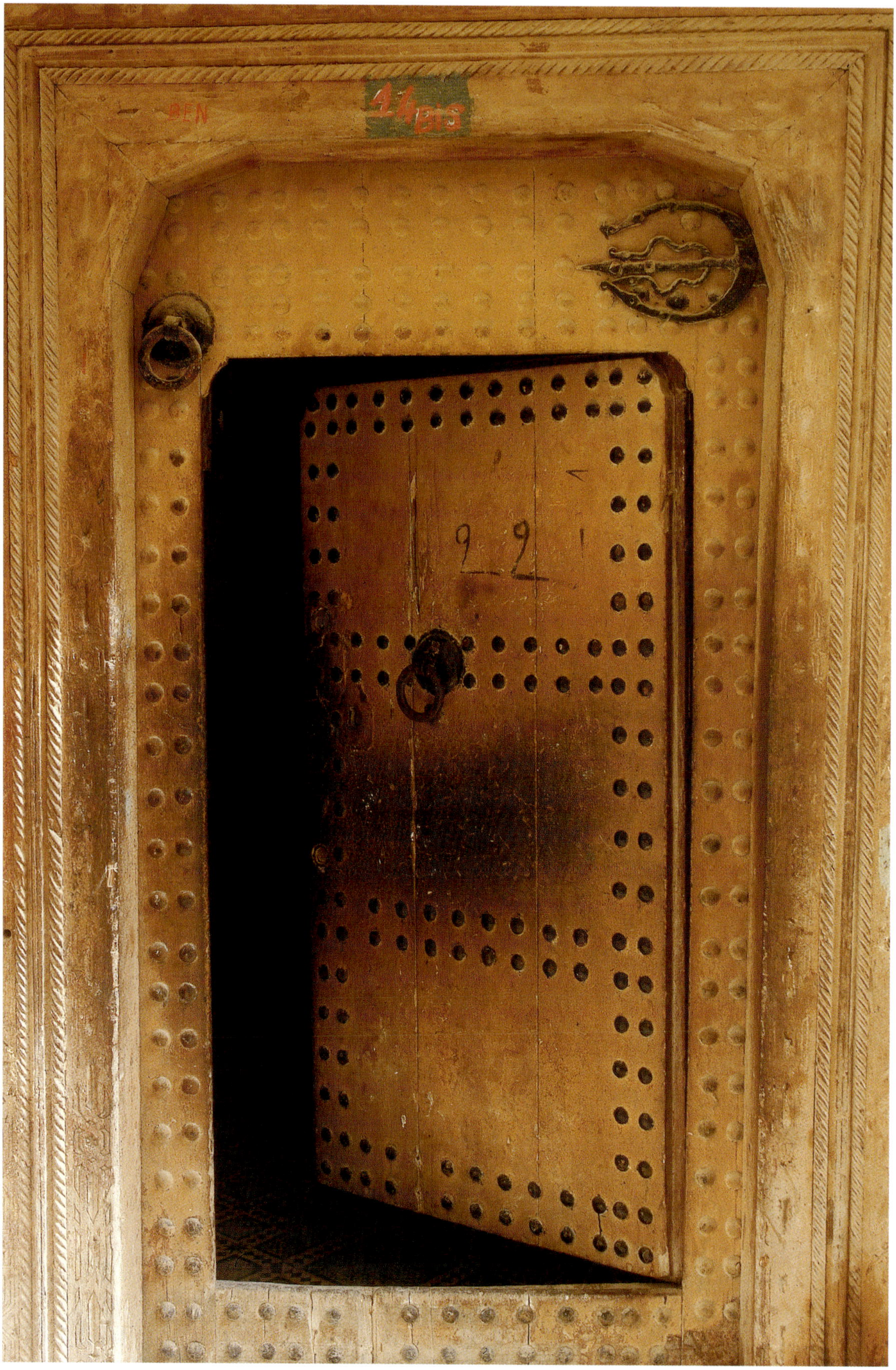

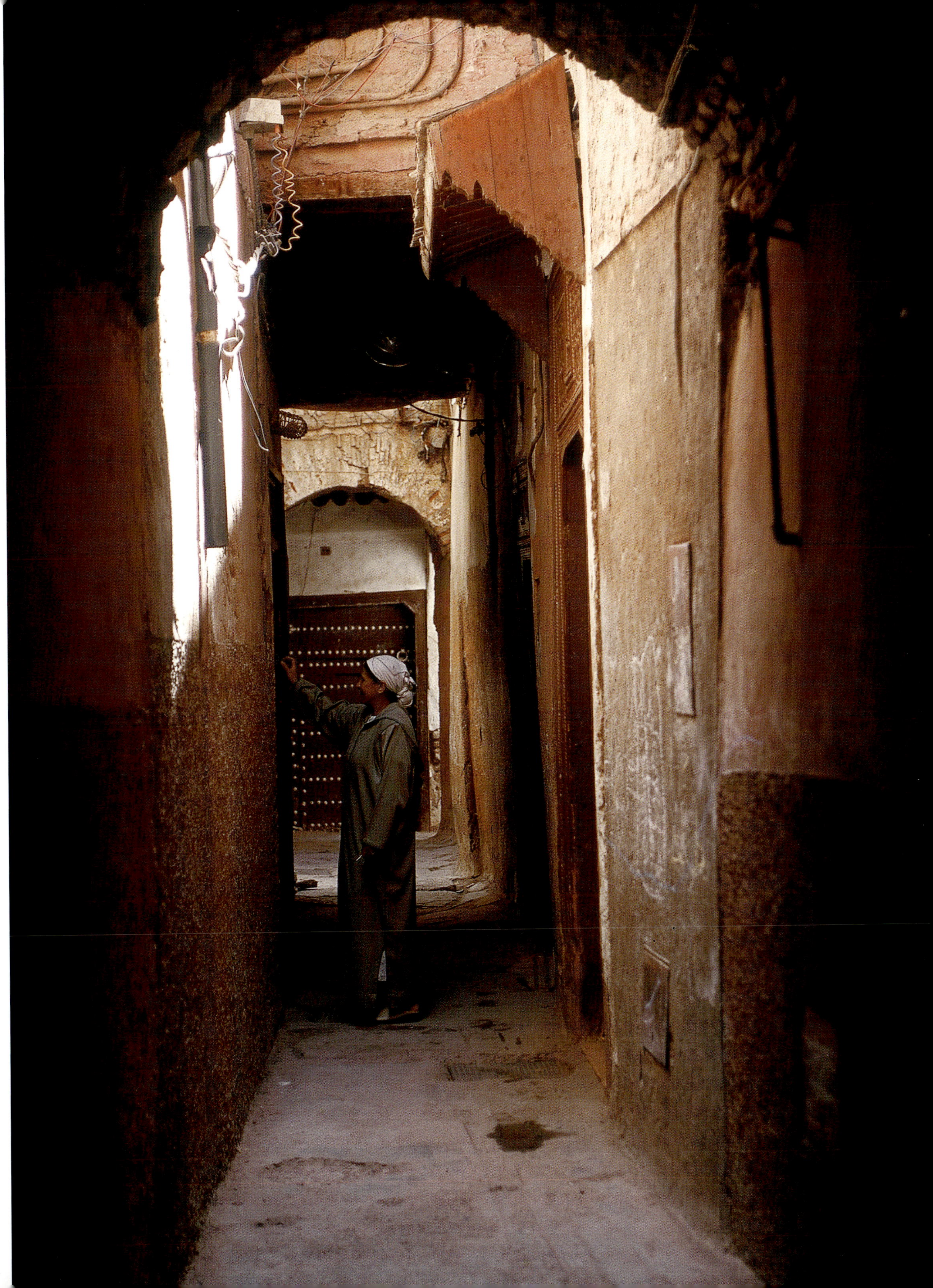

The medinas of Fès and Marrakech have been declared World Heritage Sites by UNESCO, but safeguarding them remains a difficult proposition.

economic and political crises prevented the colony from embarking upon large renovation projects.

The only measures that remain in force today are those promulgated during the colonial period, making questions regarding the preservation of the national heritage all that more urgent. Ever since the second half of the twentieth century, residents of the medinas have ignored these laws and as no other efficient system of control had been instituted, buildings have been refaced with inappropriate materials such as concrete.

✦ *Dars* or *Riads*?

The interior architecture of Moroccan houses surprises the foreign visitor, who most likely is not used to vertical perspectives and narrow rooms, nor to living under the open sky. The layout of the space answers to cultural imperatives that may evade the outsider. How could it possibly be familiar?

A *dar* is the most common type of home to be found in the medina. An archaic residence, the noun in Arabic is feminine and means a house, but the word is also used to indicate a circle, as if the plan of all Moroccan houses retained the memory of a circular nomadic encampment. The *dar* is arranged around a small, open-air patio that is rather square and without any real garden. Closed in by thick walls that are extraordinarily tall, the overwhelming summer heat does not penetrate.

Traditionally, two to four main rooms branch out symmetrically from the patio; in the houses of the community's elite there are often intermediary triple-arcaded porticoes. The oldest of these were constructed with simple, straight wooden lintels, while the most recent employ Moorish ogive arches with vertical springers. The rooms do not communicate with one another, and unlike Western homes, their function may change according to circumstance: a sitting room may become a bedroom, or vice versa. And if they tend to be long and narrow—no more than approximately thirteen

LEFT:
Despite laws prohibiting it, residents of Marrakech have added a story to their houses

ABOVE:
During the Middle Ages only prestigious buildings and the homes of judges were permitted to rise above the level of the terraces

ABOVE:
A riad *is an enclosed garden divided into four sectors around a central fountain*

OPPOSITE:
Dar Zorzor

feet (four meters) wide—this is because of the length of the joists and the fact that there is no tree broad enough to furnish beams. Sometimes a loggia (*behou*) has been constructed facing the door, enlarging the space. The arches at either end of the room may also form alcoves for a sofa or bed.

In keeping with the affluence of its owner, a *dar* might have an elaborately decorated guesthouse (*douiria*) with its own hammam heated by a wood-burning oven in the cellar. There may even be a second small *douiria* that is linked to the main residence by a zigzagging passageway, used to store the harvest of wealthy landowners or as servants' quarters.

Service rooms and stairways are always relegated to the corners of the buildings. Today most *dars* have a

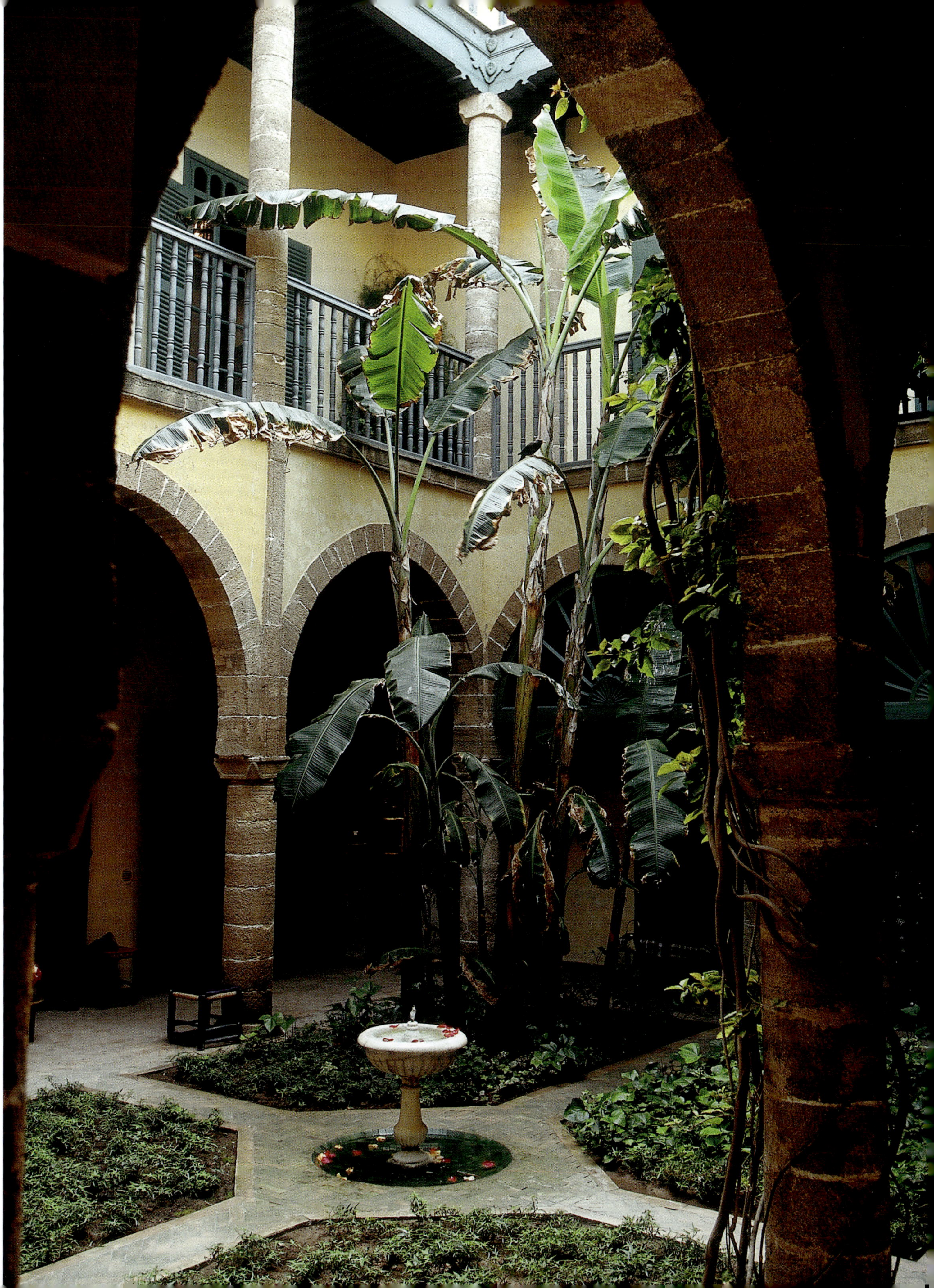

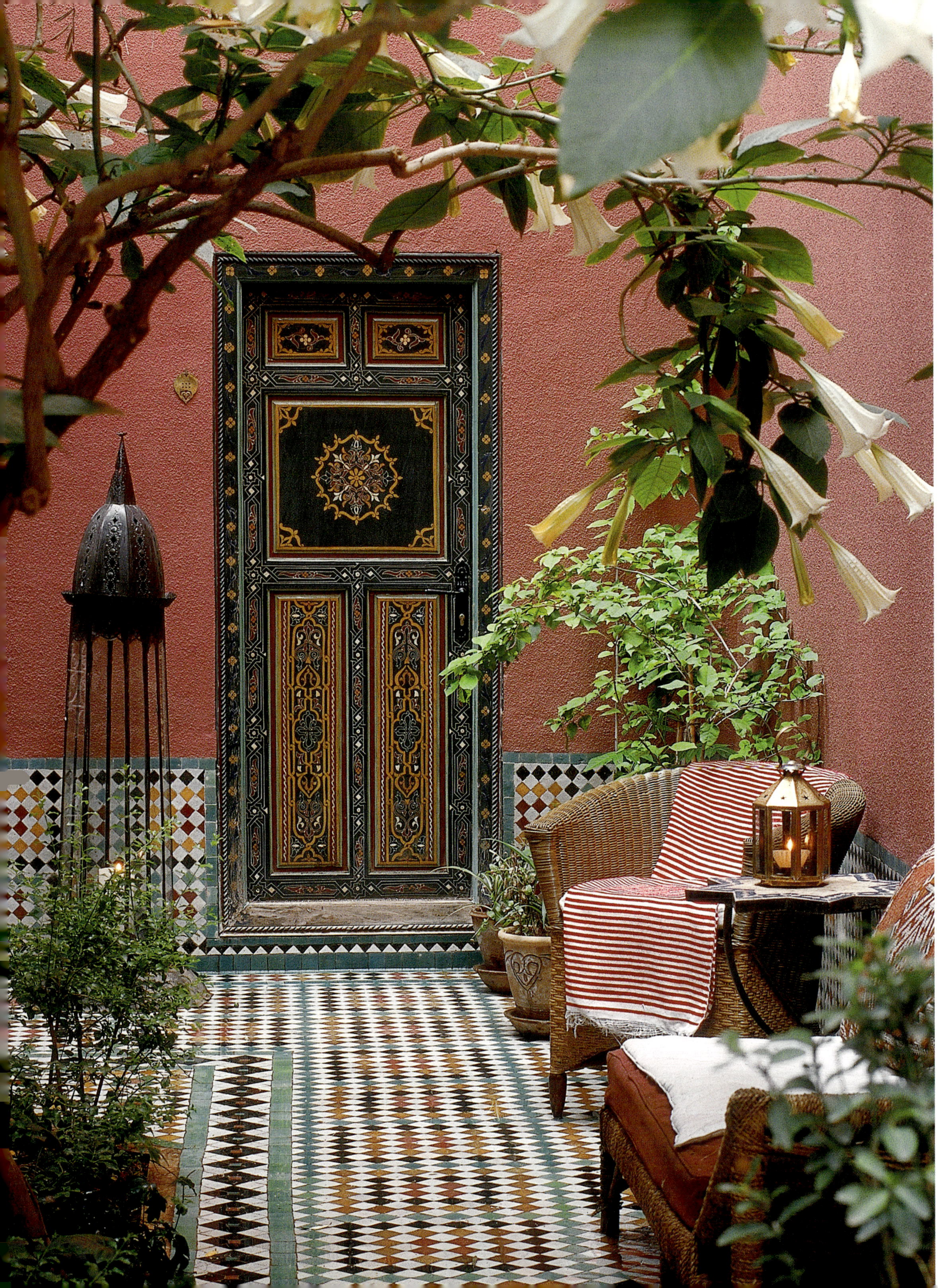

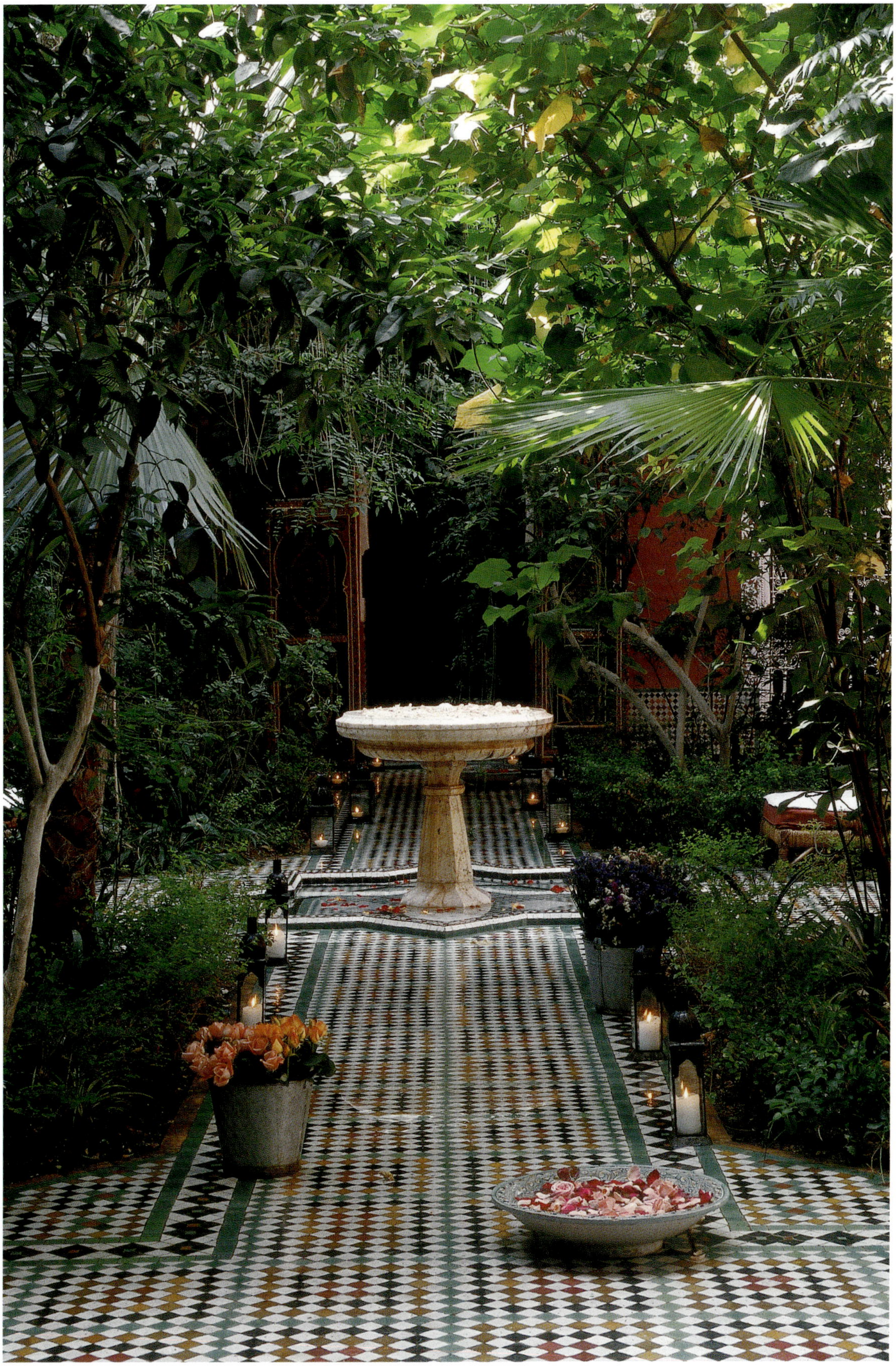

PAGES 44–45:
In the patio at Riad Kaiss, one's feet never touch the ground. The garden is crisscrossed by two medial paths covered in zellij

PAGES 46–49:
A large pleasure garden in Fès

second story that might either be fitted with balconies that protect the façade from sun and rain, or with a roof awning or a cornice. The roof is in fact a terrace that is accessed by a stairway that comprises two flights set at right angles. Very narrow—never more than twenty-four inches (sixty centimeters) wide—its steps are tall and reinforced with a hardwood rafter. In the past, the terrace was a social sanctuary for women, as according to an adage, a Muslim woman left her home only twice in her life: the first time to move into her husband's house, the second time to go to the cemetery. So it was on the roof that women kept in contact with their neighbors, all the while attending to small chores.

A *riad* is an enclosed garden divided into four verdant sectors, in the center of which is a fountain or a pool. Its appearance will vary depending upon the city. In Fès, for example, it bears the unusual attribute of an indication of power, a mark of prestige reserved for only a select few. A pleasure garden, the *riad* is only found within an array of the grand quarters of a manor house or a palace. In Marrakech it constitutes a house unto itself. Built on the model of a *dar*, the defining components are assiduously preserved: tall protective walls enclose a space organized around an open-air patio. However, this spacious patio stretches the length of the house and is bathed in sunlight as if it were declaring itself in direct contrast to the shadowed, serpentine medina. It answers a sudden need for space and order, another approach to life. Here nature is queen. Within the geometric stricture of the buildings a garden vibrant in wild colors and chirping birds has taken root. Blossoms cascade from the balconies, wafting the elegance of their scent. Water sings through the channels, reflecting in the central pool the subtle harmonies of architecture and nature. The trees, heavy with ripe fruit, cast their graceful shadows onto the façade of the patio. The arabesques carved into the décor converse with the flowers. In a door frame adorned with painted bouquets, the evening breeze sets aflutter the noble drapes accentuating the theme of a hanging garden. The jewel of the art of living in the Islamic world, the *riad*, in the image of the heavenly garden, is dedicated to sensual pleasures and the joys of meditation.

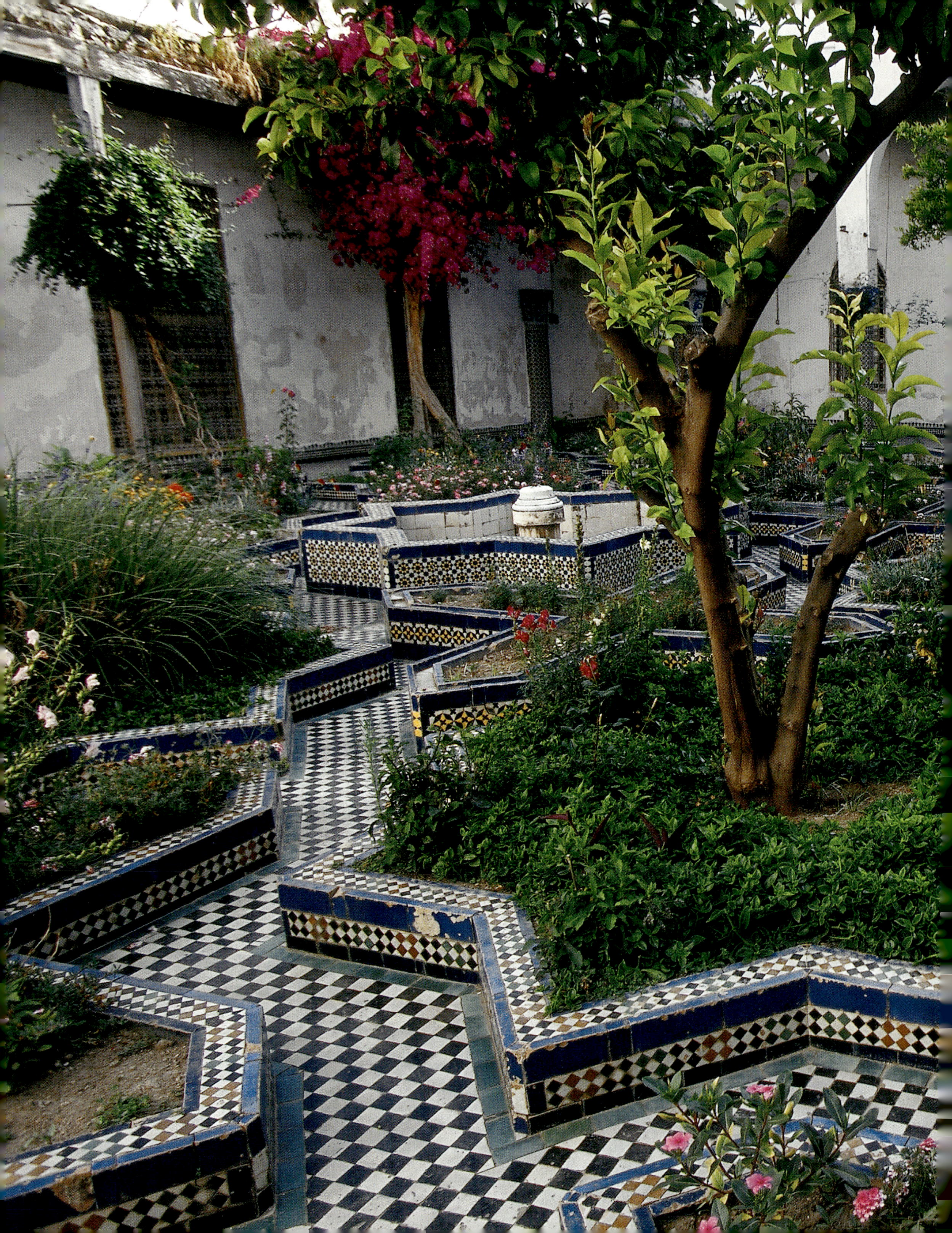

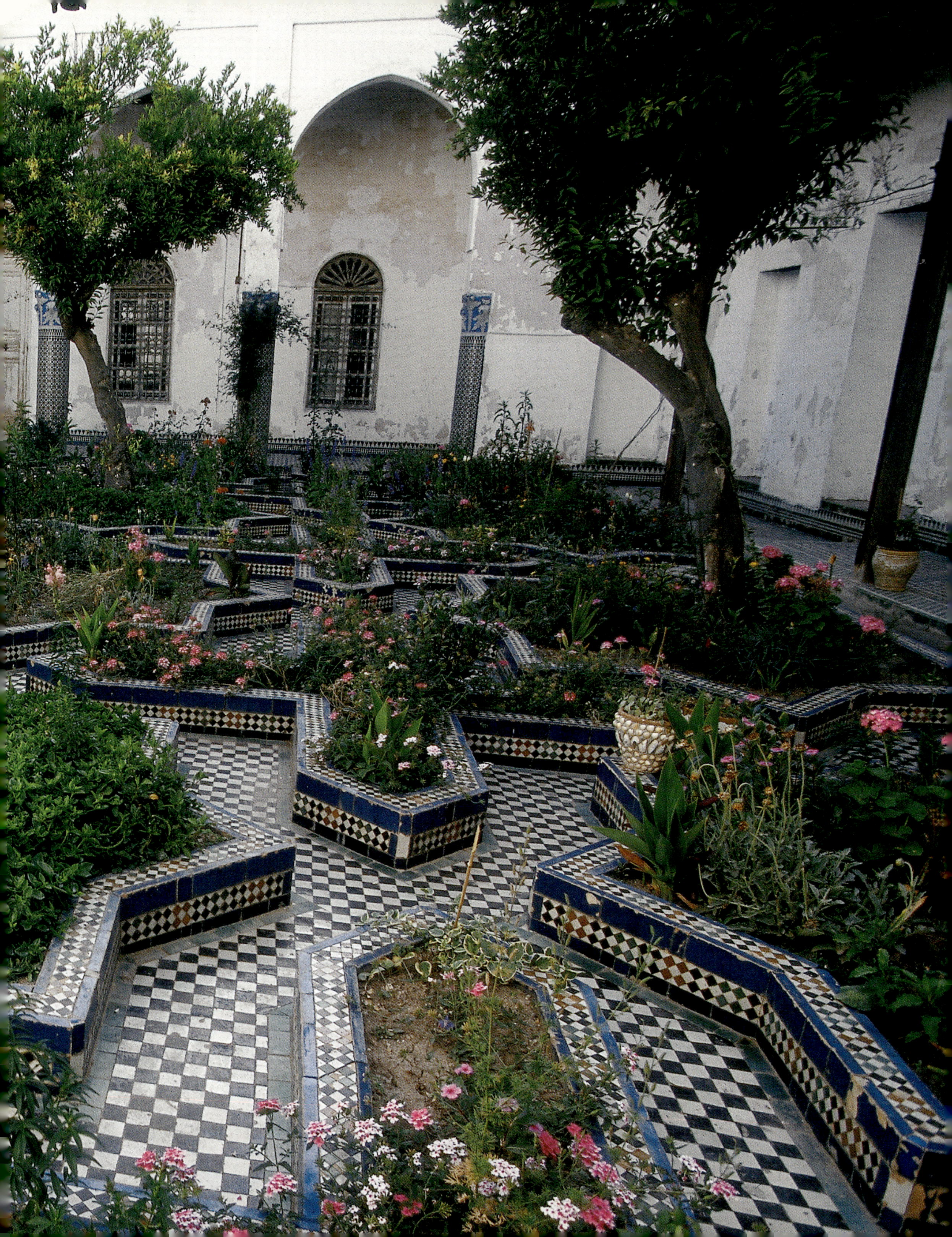

Fès

Situated in the verdant hills in the northwest of the country, Fès is composed of three cities, each with its distinct architecture. The most ancient, Fès al-Bali, was built in the ninth century by the Idrisside dynasty in the area surrounding the Kairouyine Mosque, a prestigious university that was said to be able to accommodate twenty thousand pilgrims from around the world and destined to assure the influence of the city throughout the medieval Islamic world. Worn away by time and bathed in chiaroscuro, Fès al-Bali has long been considered a mysterious city by European travelers; even a disturbing and impenetrable one that is wholly devoted to the practice of faith and the pursuit of knowledge. The defensive character that prevails in other Moroccan medinas is even more pronounced here. Residences rarely have openings. The vertical lines of the patios are accentuated. Windows, when there are any, are protected with iron bars. Doors are laden with studs, bolts, locks, and knockers and are reinforced beneath thick, low frames, forcing one to stoop in order to enter.

THE HOLY CITY

Populated from the outset by learned people and theologians, the city acquired its reputation as a center for the upper classes who, claiming direct descent from the Prophet, would form the country's elite. Thus Fès al-Bali abounds in subtle, refined palaces and grand homes that display the most sophisticated decorations in all of Morocco.

✦ A Retiring and Melancholy Nature

Set within its walls the color of sand, proud of its religious character and of its elite, Fès al-Bali presents itself as a maze of tangled little streets that go off in all directions. More than in any other city, the residents live withdrawn into their houses. The weather here is rather inclement—brutal winters are followed by scorching summers. However, as the region is rich in lumber, rooms are both larger and more comfortable than elsewhere. An atmosphere of saintliness seems to have shielded Fès al-Bali from the gyrations of history. The imposing Kairouyine Mosque remains the beating heart, setting the pulse throughout the bustling mercantile district. In accordance with a recurrent Islamic paradigm of city planning, the district was organized by trades. Spice merchants, coppersmiths, copperware merchants, tinsmiths, carpenters, tailors, weavers, clothes merchants, and tanners all formed their own small islands within the city, each with its own sounds, rhythms, and scents. The receding beauty of its many palaces presents a certain melancholic charm. Invisible behind their crenellated walls, they are reached by twisting paths and arched passageways. The various forms of construction subscribe to no technique in particular, but like the houses, the palaces are made of lime, sand, bricks, and plaster. Their protective walls, however, are far more numerous, as well as taller and thicker, and are adorned with crenellations that point skyward, as a palace must augment its enclosure not only in order to defend itself against a potential external enemy, but also to appear as an impregnable sanctuary and to assert its military character. In addition, their protection was entrusted to a special

RIGHT:
Founded in the ninth century during the Idrisside dynasty, the Kairouyine Mosque remains the beating heart of Fès al-Bali

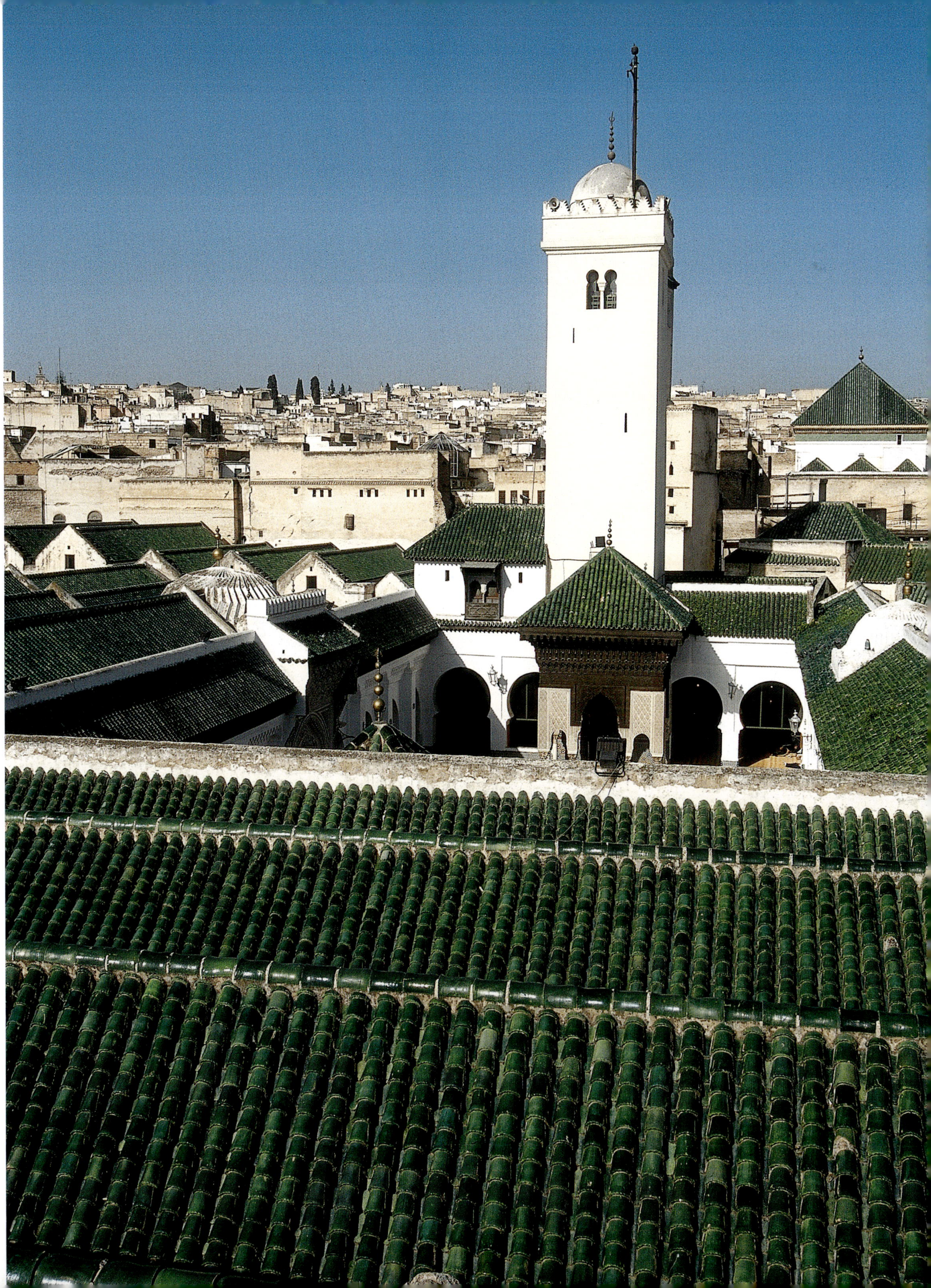

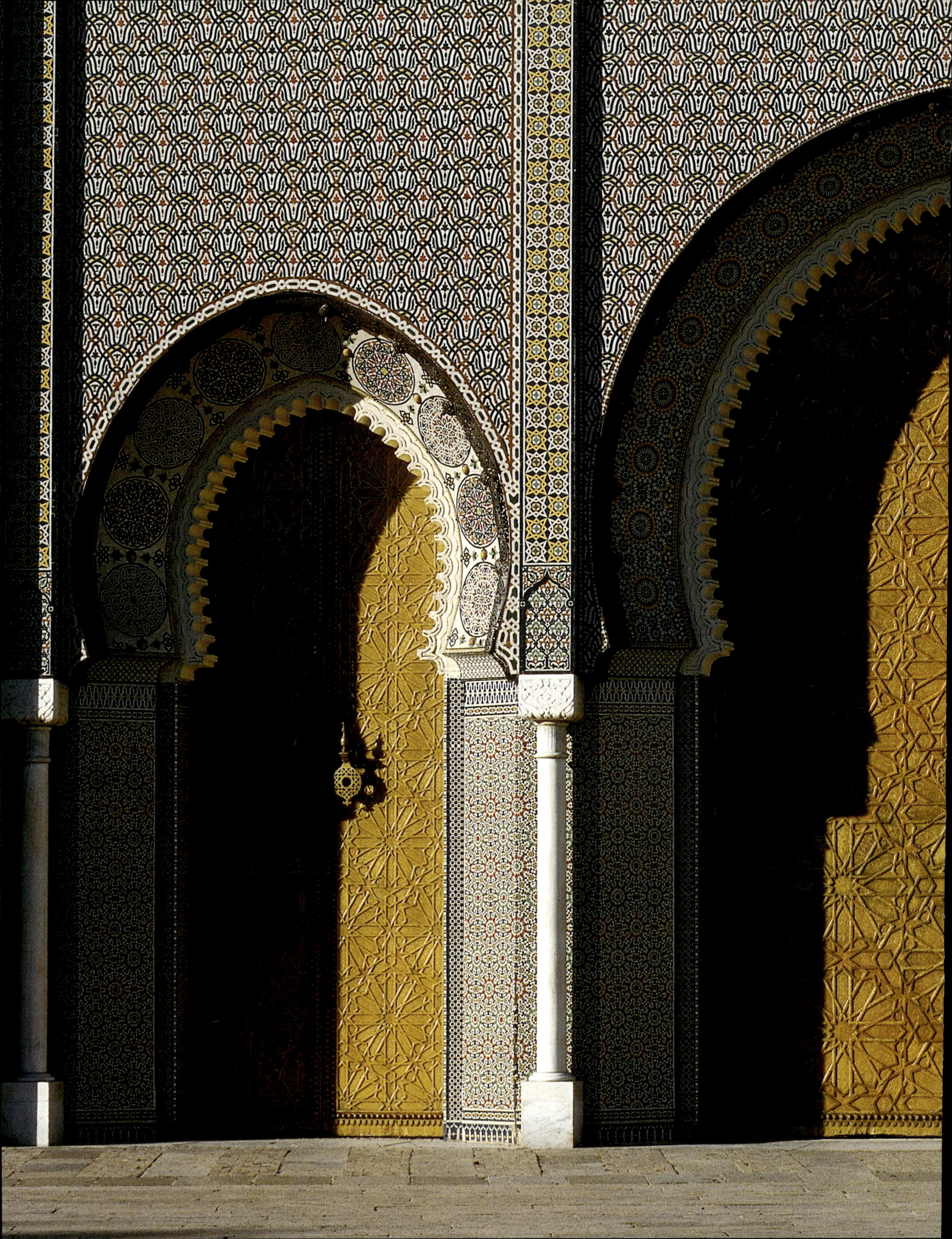

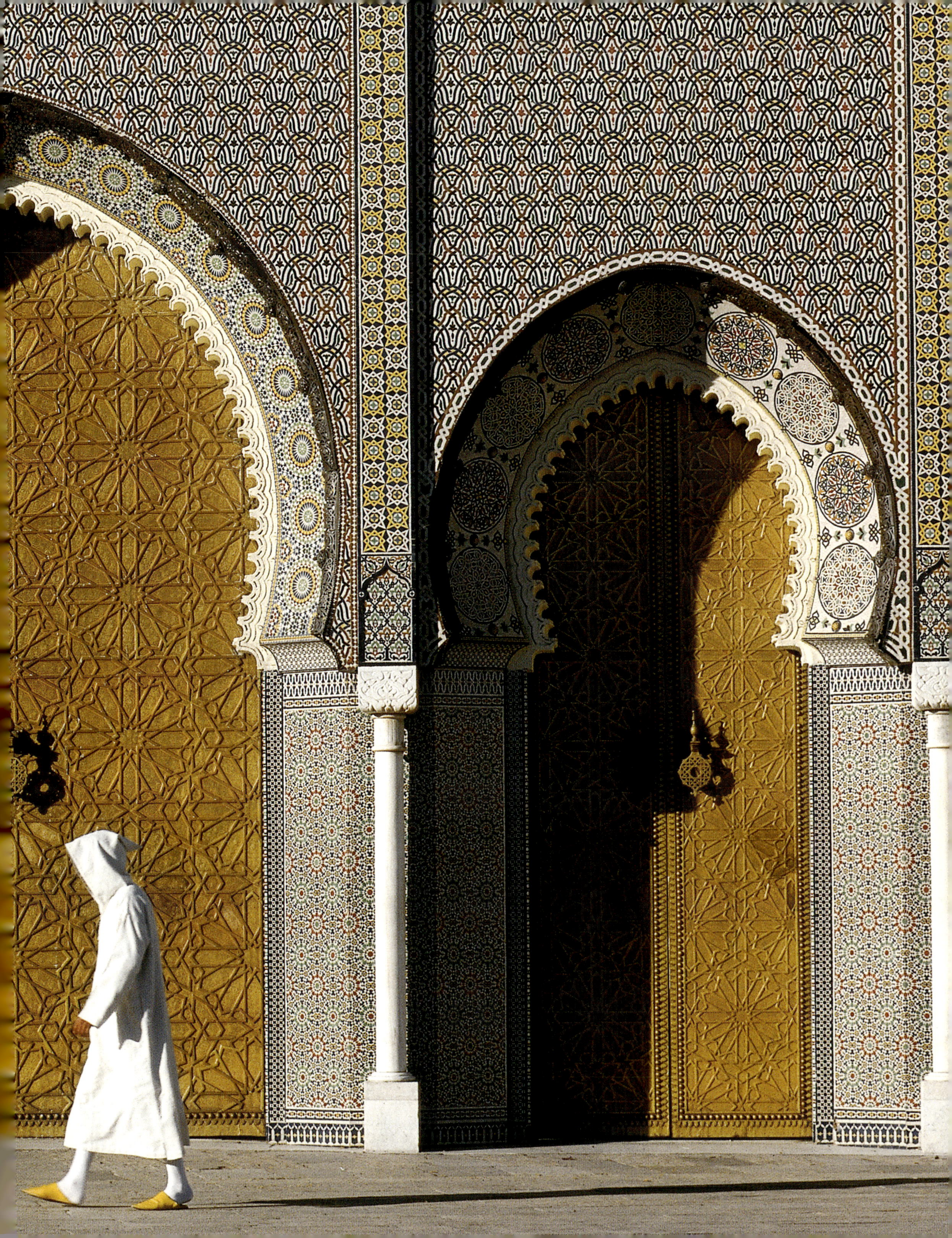

PAGES 54–55:
The royal palace is always prepared for a visit by the king

ABOVE LEFT:
The galleries at Dar Adyel are crowned with solid cedar lintels and protected by balustrades of turned moucharabieh

ABOVE RIGHT:
As all Fezzi houses were, Dar Batha was constructed with very high ceilings

OPPOSITE:
The Mokri Palace is paved in marble and laden with ornamentation. Its vertical perspectives are accentuated

corps of guards—eunuchs and a veritable militia (*mokhzenis*). Having since been abandoned by the notable Fezzi families, many of these palaces are today open to the public. Upon entering one discovers an array of screeching doors replete with bolts and locks, each opening onto an infinity of rooms, courtyards, and gardens, the arrangement of which is highly variable.

It was in the upper reaches of the palaces that the secret life of the harems took place. On terraces, off-limits to men, women would walk about and chat openly, leaning on the walls with their elbows. From there the secrets of the residence would take flight, passed from roof to roof. Travelers at the dawn of the twentieth century related how the boldest of these women would conduct clandestine love affairs, not hesitating to forge successive walls for an encounter with a beloved.

56

✷ A Jewel of Hispano-Moresque Art

The decoration found in Fès houses is copious—ceilings fashioned out of painted cedar with interlacing geometric and floral motifs, walls covered in multicolored mosaic (*zellij*), marble floors, and sculpted cedar cornices. Thanks to the cedar forests of the Atlas and Rif Mountains, the interior courtyards of Fès resemble carved chests. The wood ceilings of ceremonial salons, the main focus of attention, are illuminated paintings (*zouaqs*) decorated with floral patterns that appear to imitate European fabrics, Oriental faience, Chinese porcelain, and Persian carpets. The pride of a bourgeois house, these masterpieces require months of arduous work to produce. Not a single open space around the central motif is left blank, and thus the eye is not held captive by any one line, rather, the soul must meander and lose itself in the interlaced infinity. The decoration of the ceiling is complemented with large lintels, balustrades, and canopies of cedar that have been sculpted, carved, or turned in the *moucharabieh* style of screens, which waft their fragrance through the house. The door leaves, wooden shutters, and cabinets are decorated with painted flowers in colors of a past time that sing the charms of bygone springs. As cedar is a dry and rot-proof wood, it does not require treating or varnish, and remains in remarkable condition even when exposed to extreme weather conditions. It is impervious to both the larvae of wood-eating insects and the intense humid heat of hammams.

The decorations on the wood are further enhanced with luminous, brightly colored enamel. Known as *zellij*, these small terracotta tiles are cut after firing and then laid out in a mosaic of faience. Houses in Fès—the floors, the wainscoting—are covered with them. Unlike the motifs of Byzantine mosaics, the patterns are fixed and present only a limited number of combinations, all of which are perfectly symmetrical and kaleidoscopic in the intensity of their design. The repertoire of individual *zellij* comprise some two hundred shapes, each with an evocative name, such as soldier, olive pit, fig leaf, snail, or *dirhem*. A master craftsman knows all the traditional combinations, as well as how to set them in different-sized areas. The almost mathematical rhythm of the geometry of the motif must not be intruded upon. The master cuts the tiles with a heavy steel hammer that he frequently sharpens using a piece of marble. With stunning precision, he makes each cut with a single blow. He then lays out the pieces on a wooden board, the enameled side facing down. Once the panel of *zellij* is set, he sprinkles it with plaster and cement and then lifts up the board and affixes the panel to the wall. Some of the *zellij* are beveled at the level of the terracotta, just beneath the enamel surface. These cutout pieces, which are used in the epigraphic borders, require great virtuosity. They are enameled in black and decorated

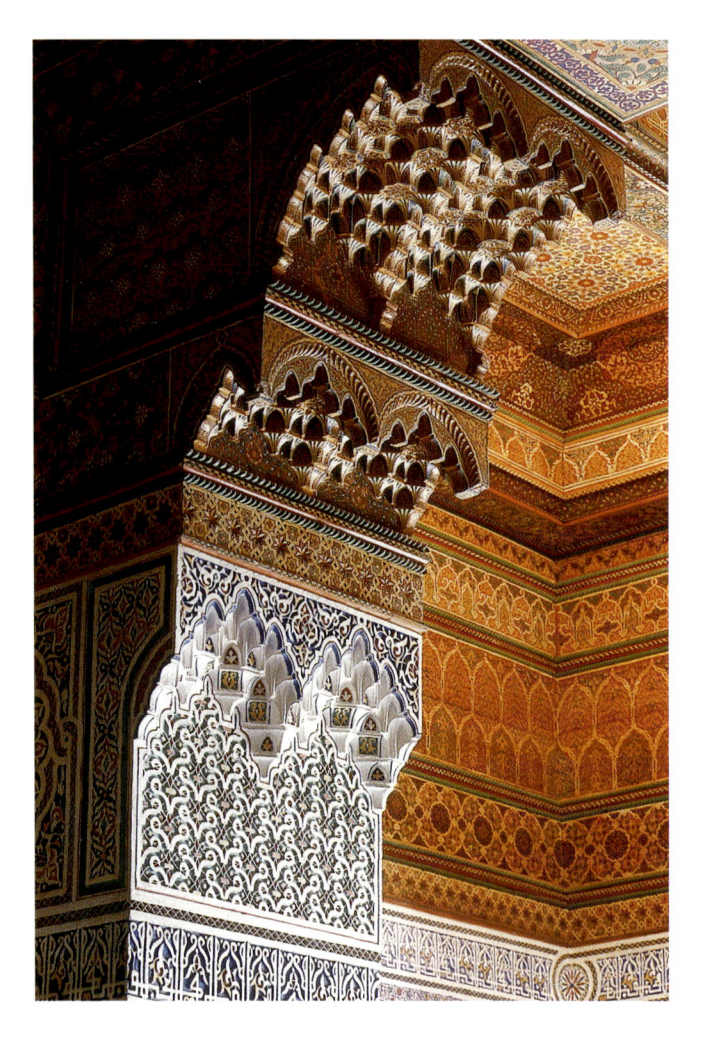

ABOVE:
Sculpted into the cedar, a bees' nest motif decorates the intrados of the arches. Epigraphic friezes praising Allah are inscribed above the columns and arches

OPPOSITE:
The patio at the Madrassah Attarine has been meticulously restored

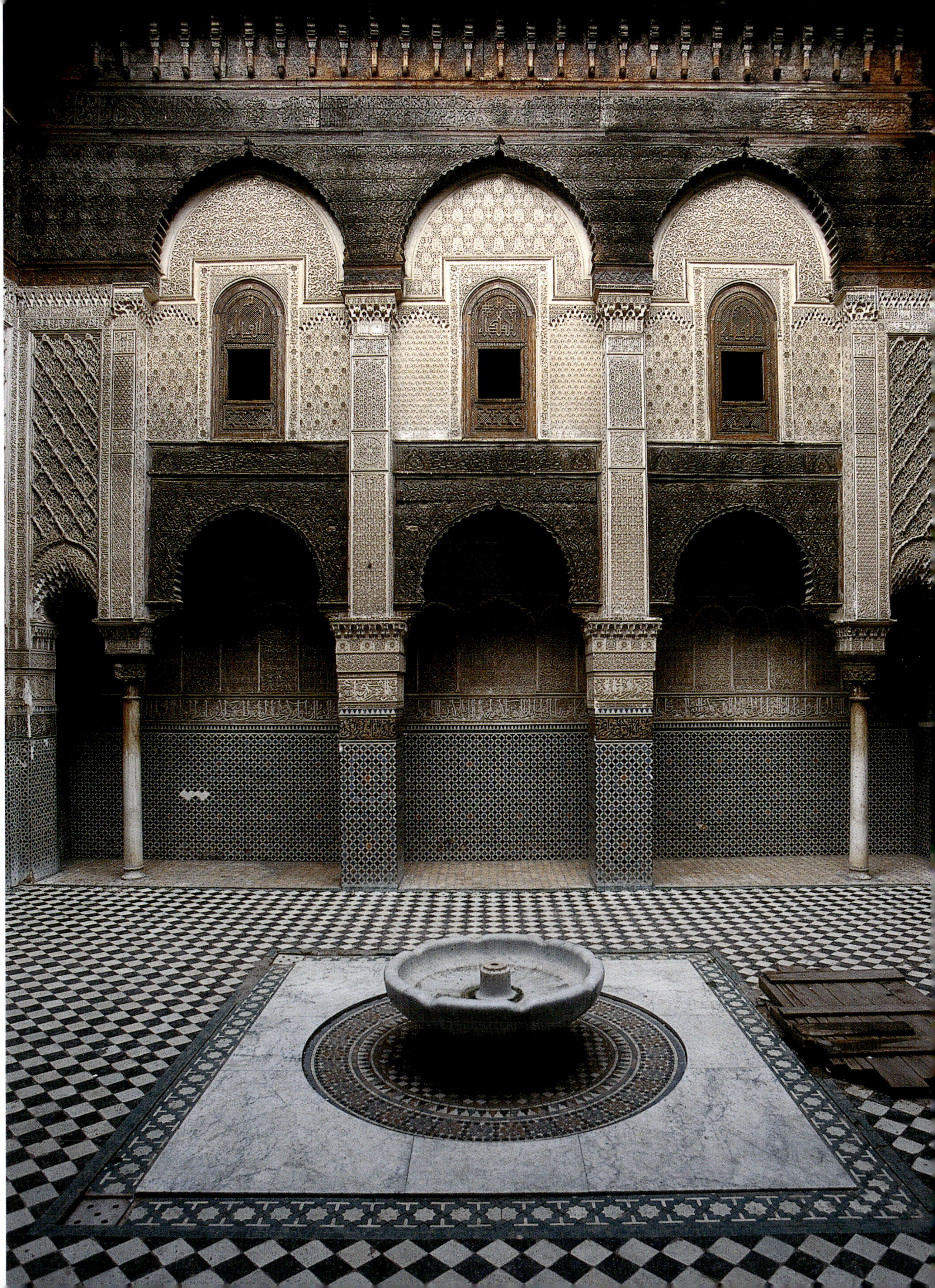

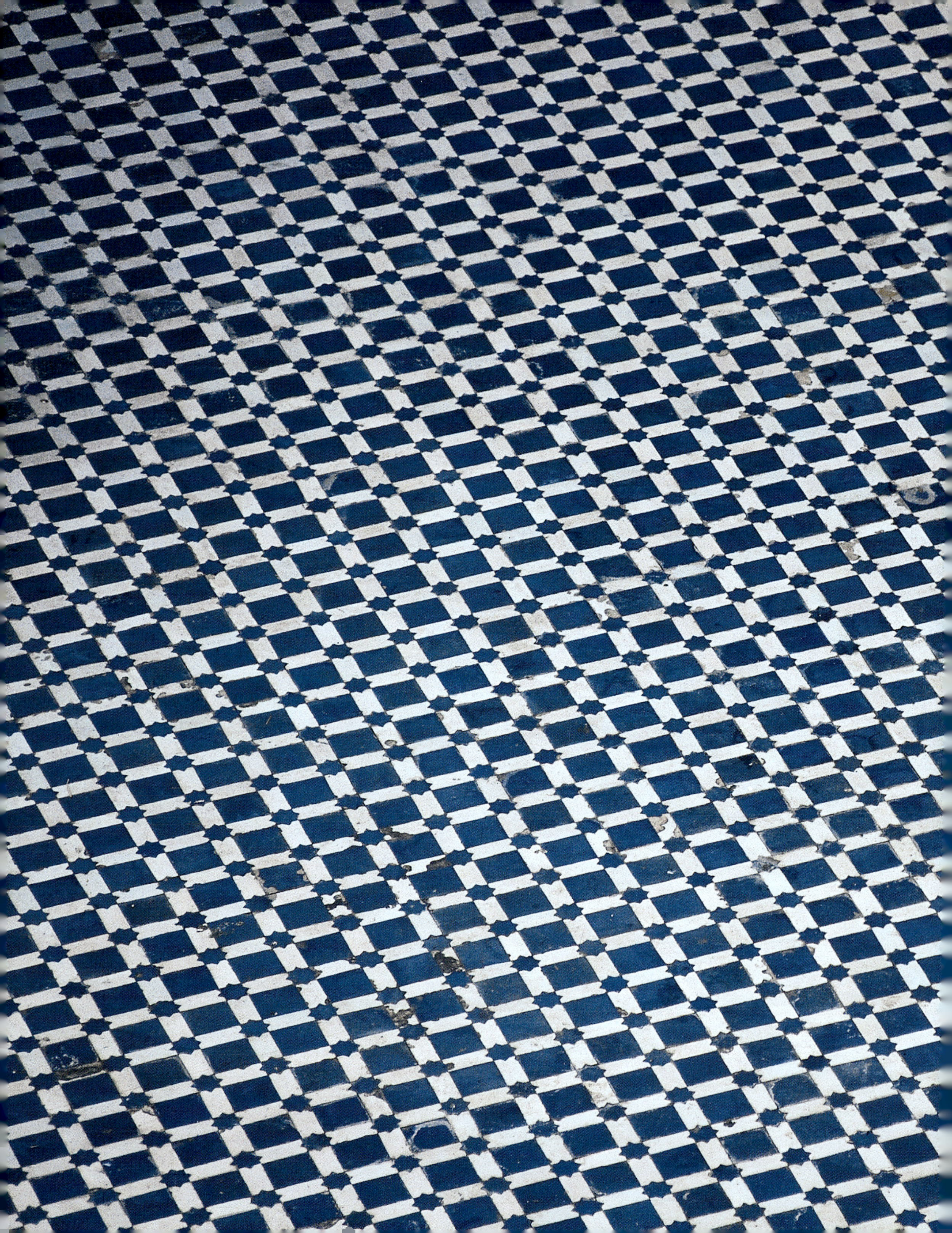

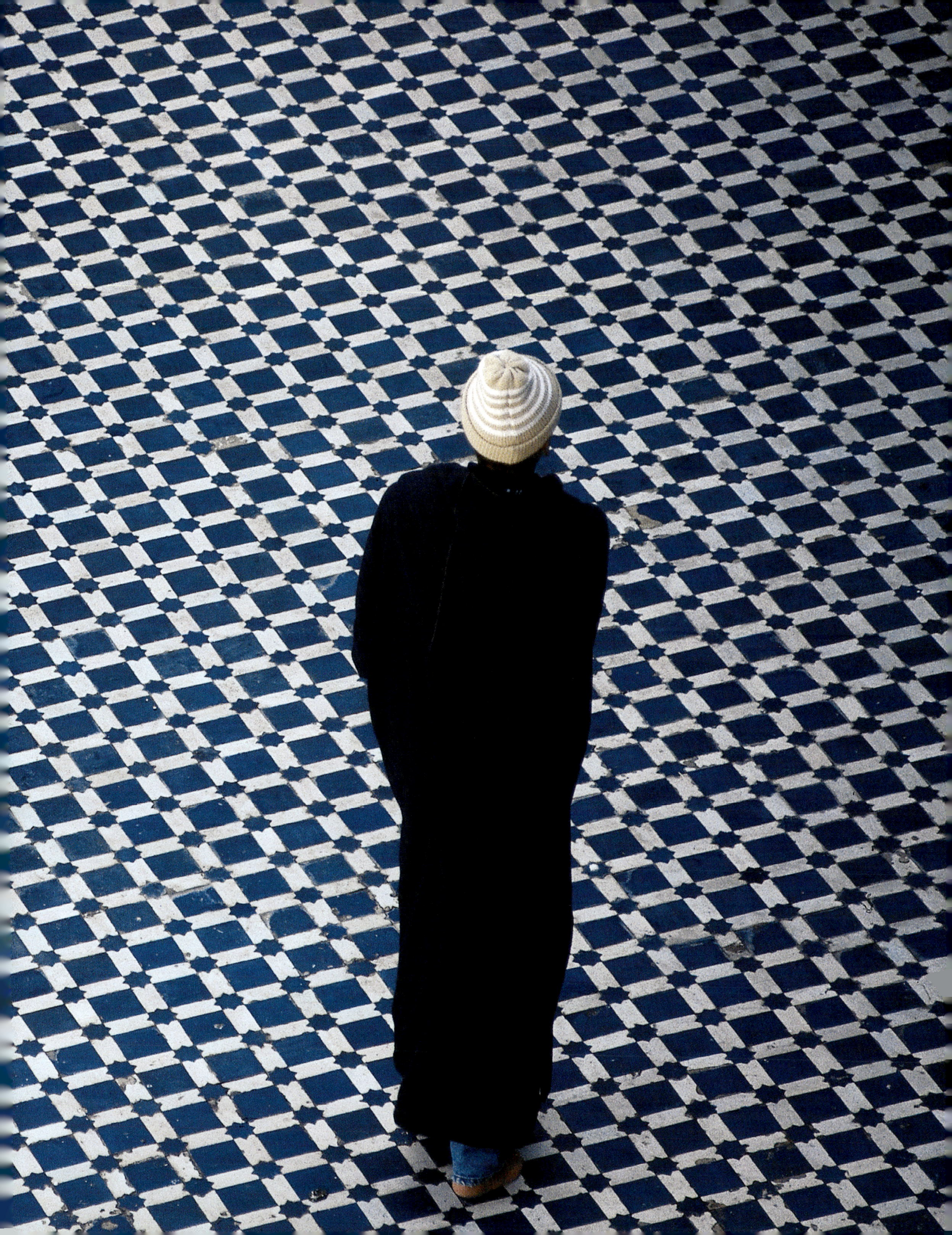

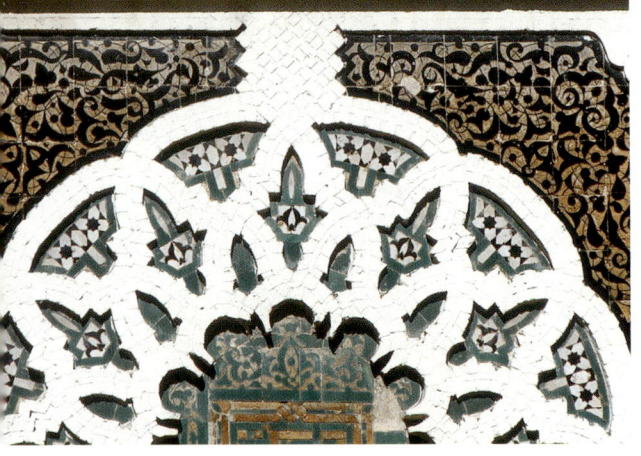

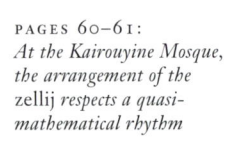

PAGES 60–61:
At the Kairouyine Mosque, the arrangement of the zellij respects a quasi-mathematical rhythm

ABOVE AND OPPOSITE:
The zellij repertory comprises about two hundred pieces that are assembled following a limited number of combinations

PAGES 64–65:
A wall fountain at the Jamai Palace. Fezzi zellij are often covered with blue enamel

62

with floral designs. Generally, *zellij* used for floors are much less intricate than those found on the wall paneling. Laid in a zigzag pattern, they are set alongside *bejmat* (half bricks of terracotta) and, except in the most opulent homes where they are interspersed with marble, the motifs are simple. The most sophisticated designs, however, did not appear until toward the end of the nineteenth century.

Marble, which Morocco has in great quantities, is the prerogative of luxurious residences. There are several indigenous shades: the Marrakech region has veined white marble; in Sefrou it is pink and beige; and in Zagora it is black and fossilized. But the most prized marble is imported from Italy. This is used for fountains, capitals, and pillars. Marble is also used on floors, interposed with *zellij* to prevent it from expanding and contracting from Morocco's extreme changes in temperature. Occasionally marble will be seen on walls, giving the house a natural radiance. Working with marble requires precision and patience since it is both hard and fragile. Blocks are sliced using machines fixed with rudimentary cables. A *maallem* (the designer/craftsman) first traces the motif, then cuts it using cold chisels. This cutting process does not allow for even the slightest error.

Modeled after the Alhambra in Granada, interiors of Fezzi homes often return to the art of chiseled plaster, or *geps* (from the Greek word *gypsum*). Worked as if it were a noble material on a par with stone or marble and sculpted *in situ*—casting is unheard of in Morocco—it is primarily used on the upper parts of the patio, such as the ceilings, cupolas, capitals, and the intrados of arches. Like a braid of lace, it is also used to adorn windows, door frames, and for friezes that run the length of the wall, complementing the *zellij* wainscoting. When placed above doors, *geps* is used to form small ventilation windows in which colored glass panes (*chemmassiat*) are inserted. While a star-like polygon pattern is often seen, motifs depicting bees' nests and intertwined floral designs (*touriq*) are most common. To these must be added epigraphic friezes in praise of Allah that, mixing Arabic script with interlacings, demand of the plaster craftsmen a knowledge of both calligraphy and the scriptures. The décor is primarily white, although some minor variation does exist. The plaster seen in Marrakech, for example, is slightly pinker than what one finds in Safi, and it is not rare to find *geps* that have been dyed or gilded. When decorating a surface, the craftsman prepares just a small amount of plaster. Having first carefully sifted and diluted it, he then presses it, eliminating any lumps. Next, he spreads a coat one-and-a-half to two inches (four to five centimeters) thick, which he smooths using trowels, spatulas, and spreading knives. All work is always done on site with the *maallem*, sometimes even working perched atop a scaffolding. Having softened the plaster with water, he then traces the motif with a knife, using a striker, a compass, or even

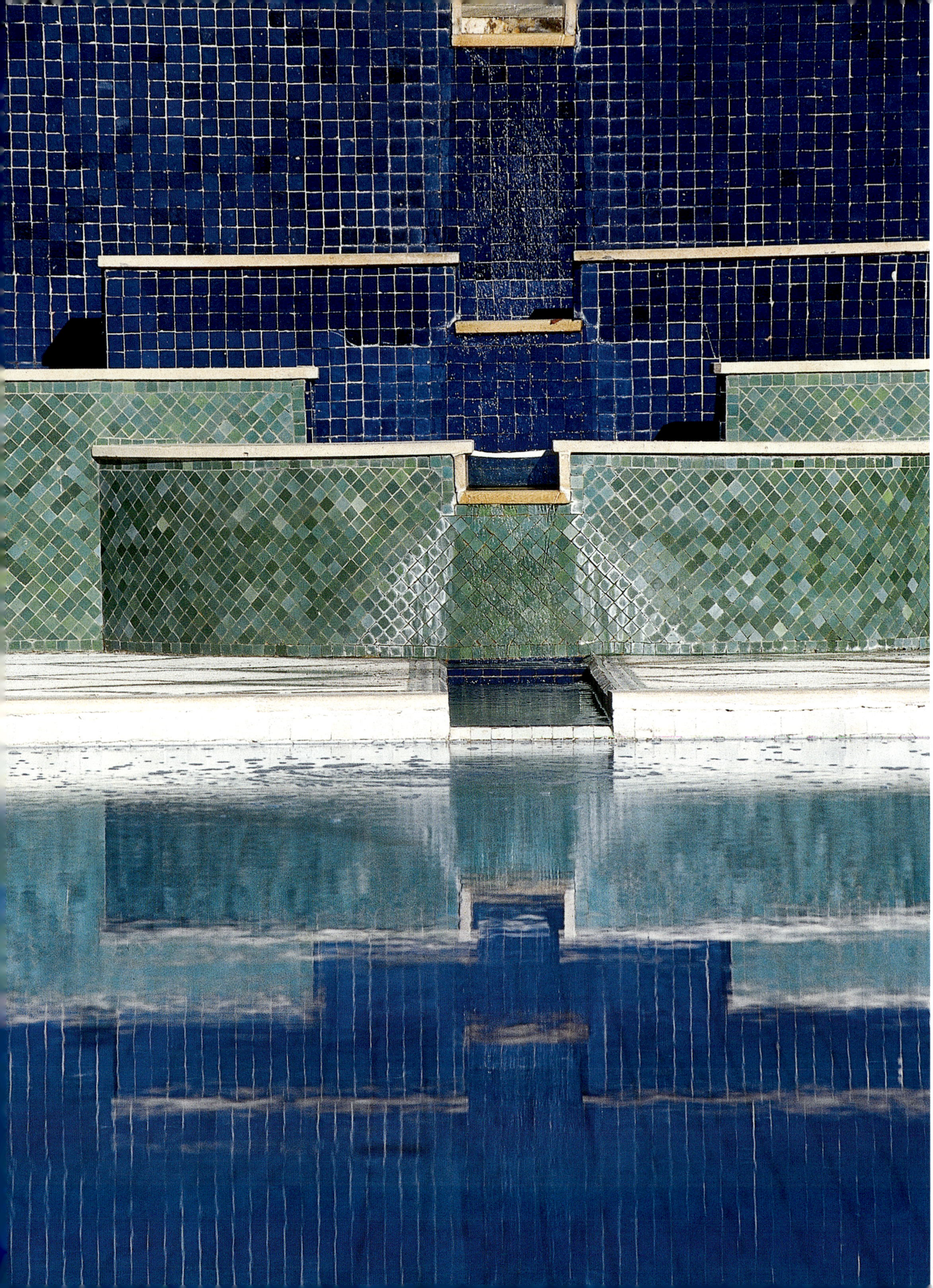

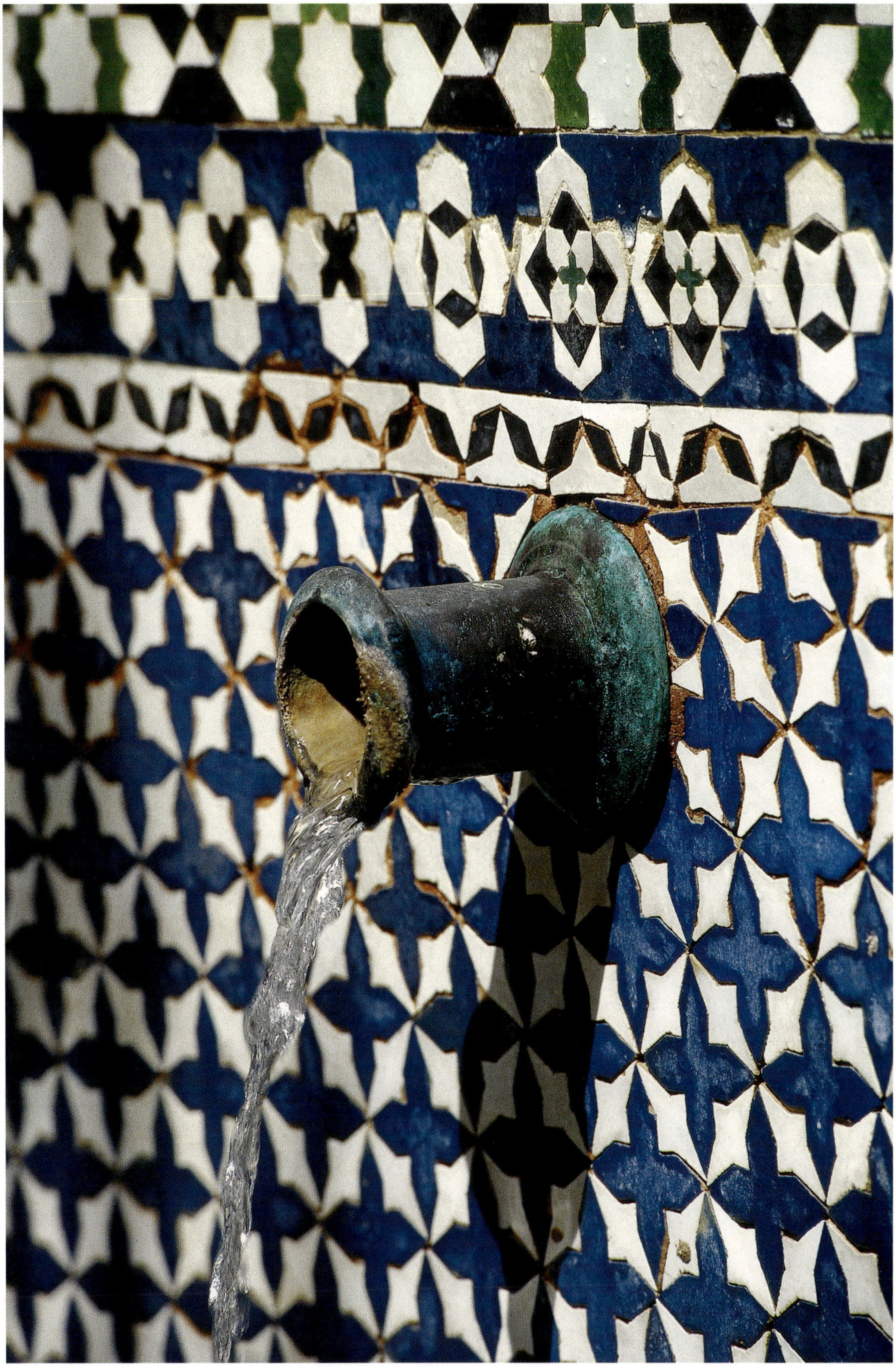

The bourgeois houses of Fès evoke distant images of the East that still hover at the thresholds of our memory.

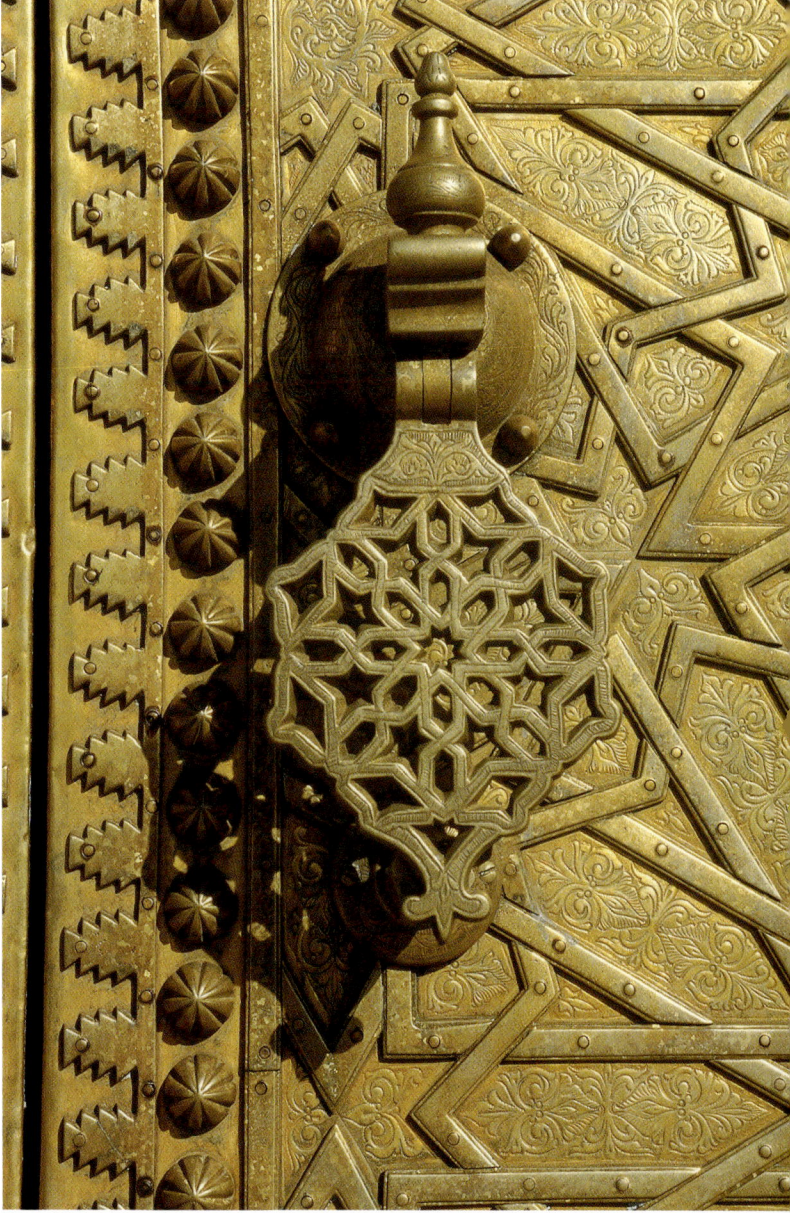

a stencil as an aid. Using a chisel, he then attacks the mass to a depth of three-quarters of an inch to two inches (two to five centimeters), redampening the surface often. Traditionally a *geps* was sculpted on several superposed levels, allowing the interceding space to breathe life into the motif. Thus, while the sculpture is made vertically, ultimately, the impression is oblique, following the cast of one's eye. Although the alveoli in many older *geps* were carved at an angle, the technique of cutting on the bias was only very rarely adhered to. New

ABOVE:
The doors of the palace are armored in bronze and copper and adorned with molded door knockers

OPPOSITE:
The royal palace. Between the zellij and the sculpted plaster there is hardly an empty spot

FÈS 67

methods appeared, including carving on the horizontal, which is easier. Working in plaster, according to some artisans, sounds quite similar to meditation: employing a deep, rhythmic breathing, they achieve a harmony of body and spirit. Mastering this craft requires years of apprenticeship, and today a demand for Moroccan *maallems* exists throughout the Islamic world. Despite its fragile appearance, a *geps* will last for quite a long time, even when exposed to extreme variations of temperature. Some dating from the twelfth century remain in perfect condition.

The roofs of such exalted buildings as mosques, *madrassahs* (Koranic schools), and palaces are covered in curved green enameled tiles and topped with a finial (*jamours*) composed of one or more copper balls set on an axis pointing skyward. The continuum of walls, the canopy roofs, and the doors are also covered in tiles, an ostentatious indication of an elite house that dispensed with richly worked façades that would have been subjected to the substantial rain run-off more frequent in Fès than Marrakech. Palace doorways are sometimes reinforced with bronze plates secured with large, round-headed studs set in a roselike pattern. On the outer doors of bourgeois homes, the molded knockers are an indication of the owner's affluence. Inner doors, on the other hand, may be affixed with large, chiseled copper bolts and even inlaid with silver niello. The houses of the wealthy, as well as mosques, are resplendent in shiny arrays of lattice-worked copper adornments. But the craft of the copper artisan, in earlier times the domain of Jewish coppersmiths and allied with silver- and goldsmithing, is now most often seen in such household objects as platters, vases, goblets, oil lamps, and incense burners.

The furniture itself was exceptional in Fès. In the palaces one found countless divans, along with items from Europe, such as chests of drawers, sofas, and tall-case pendulum clocks. Enormous wooden platters, six feet (two meters) in diameter and made from a single slice of walnut, were used for serving couscous at festive occasions. Sumptuous drapes decorated the beds, walls, and door frames. Embroidered with star-shaped flowers, birds, and trees, these fine pieces took months or years of patient work by master craftswomen, who worked in their own homes. Their renown was the pride of Moroccan artisans through the beginning of the twentieth century. Unfortunately, very little of this work remains. To reconstruct the splendor of the palaces, which no prince has brought back to life, we would have to let our imaginations run free, and recreate images of a distant East—that nonetheless flourishes in the corners of our minds.

FAR LEFT:
A zouaq *door decorated with a polylobed arch*

LEFT AND ABOVE:
A bourgeois and learned city, Fès has always boasted exceptional furnishings transported from Europe or Asia by sea or caravan

PAGES 70–71:
The patio at Dar al Pacha is furnished in both European and Moroccan styles

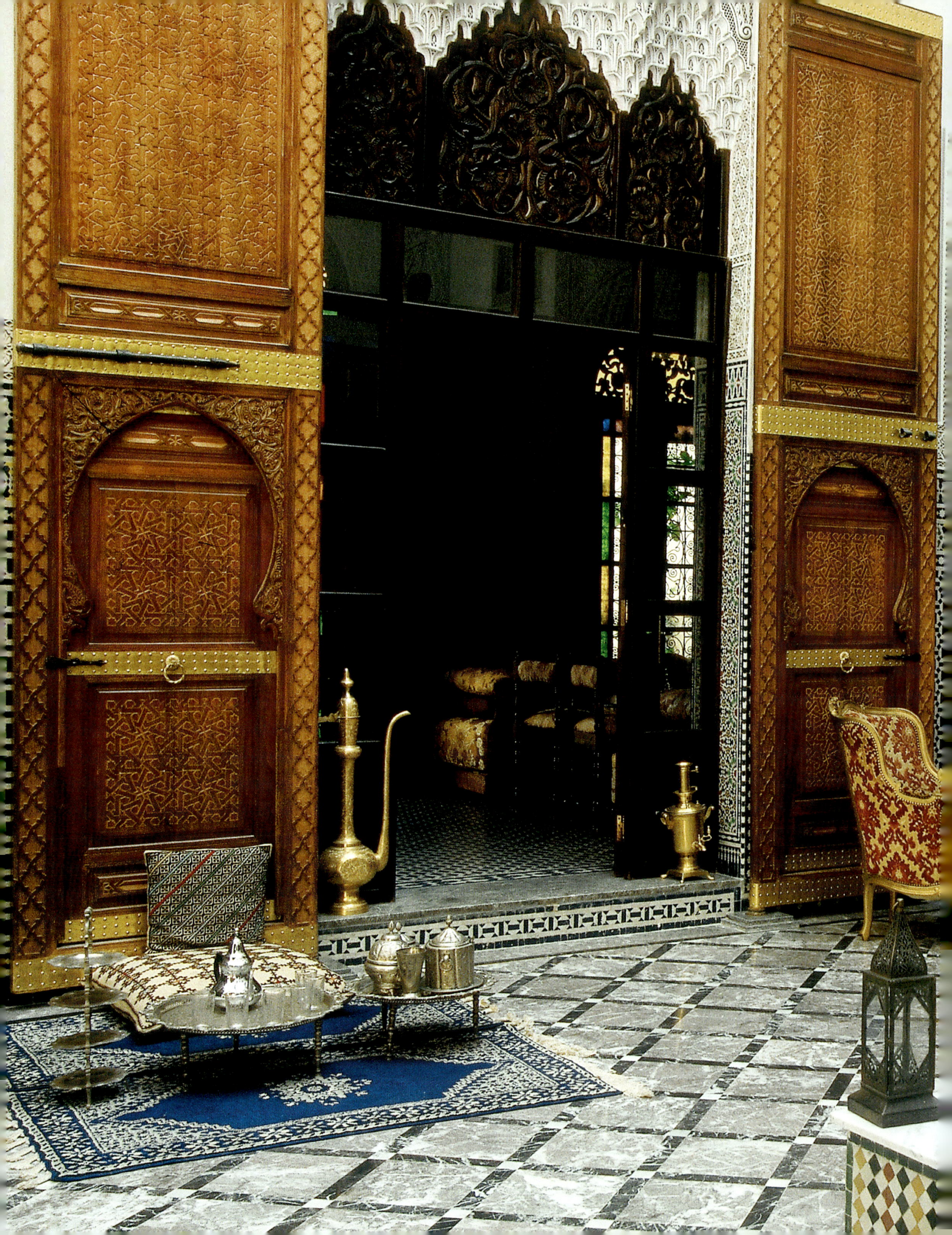

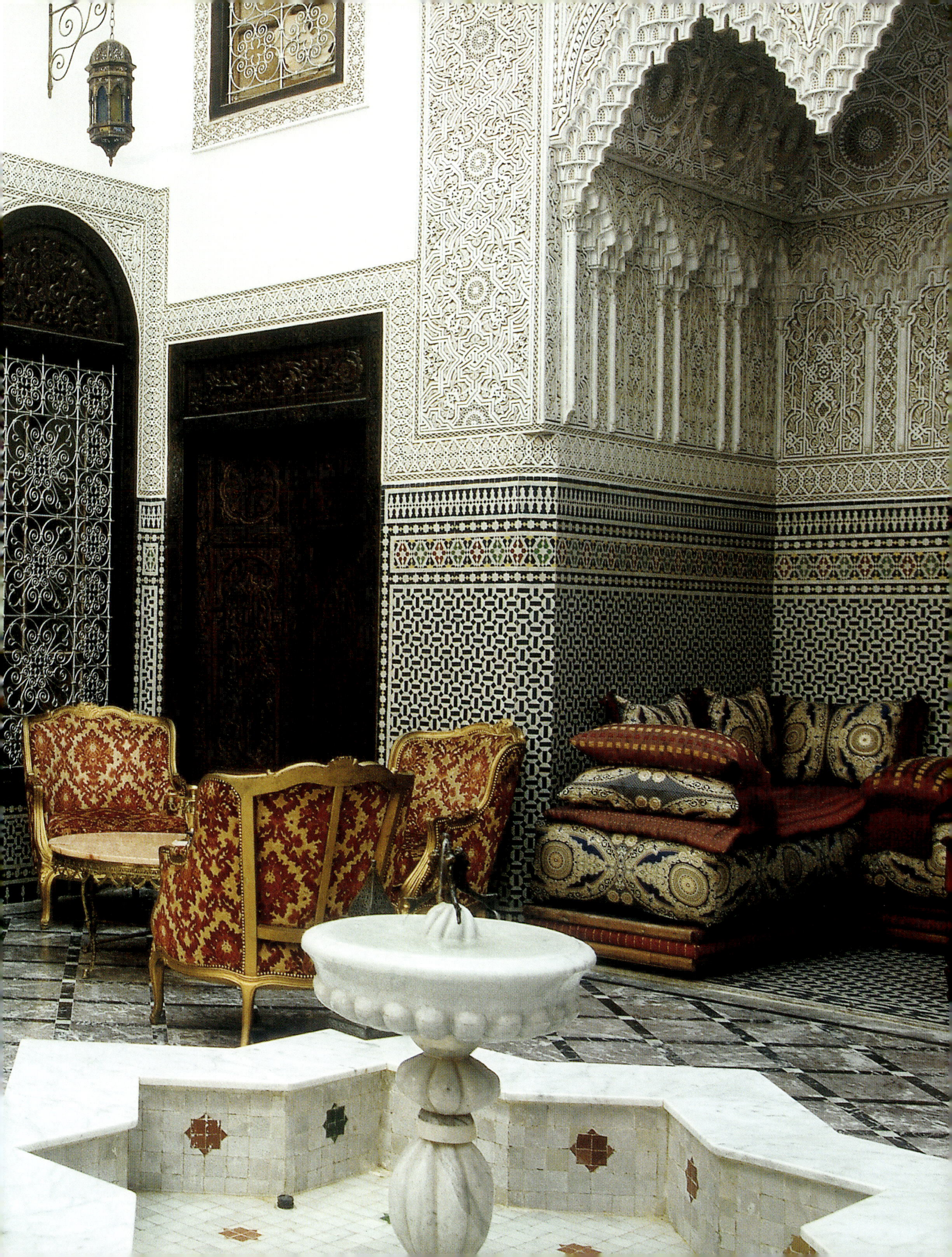

GLAOUI PALACE: A GHOST TOWN

As with so many other villas, the Glaoui Palace is like an abandoned ship slowly sinking into oblivion, rousing not a modicum of compassion. Only its caretaker, the grandson of a past majordomo of a former master of the house, attempts to stave off the effects of time with his paltry means.

At the beginning of the twentieth century the legendary heroes of Morocco's great south won over the Glaoui to the French side. The Marrakech pasha owned a grand pied-à-terre in Fès, where he led a lifestyle set to the rhythms of dazzling parties. The palace was vast. To access it from the street, one had to pass through a series of a dozen or so doors. It comprised no fewer than seventeen sectors that included residences, orchards, stables, a mausoleum, and a Koranic school spread out over an area of three and a half acres (fifteen thousand square meters). Kitchens, where the staff worked day and night with no break, provided entry to all the houses—including the boys', the girls', the parents', the musicians'. A town within a town, the palace had its own mills (for oil and grains) and a cemetery. There were some thirty pools and fountains made from Carrara marble. These have all disappeared, either having been stripped or sold. (Their current value has been estimated at one hundred and fifty thousand dollars, about one million French francs.) Built at the end of the nineteenth century and lived in with great pomp and ceremony for a hundred years, the palace was abandoned at the beginning of 1956 when Glaoui retreated to his

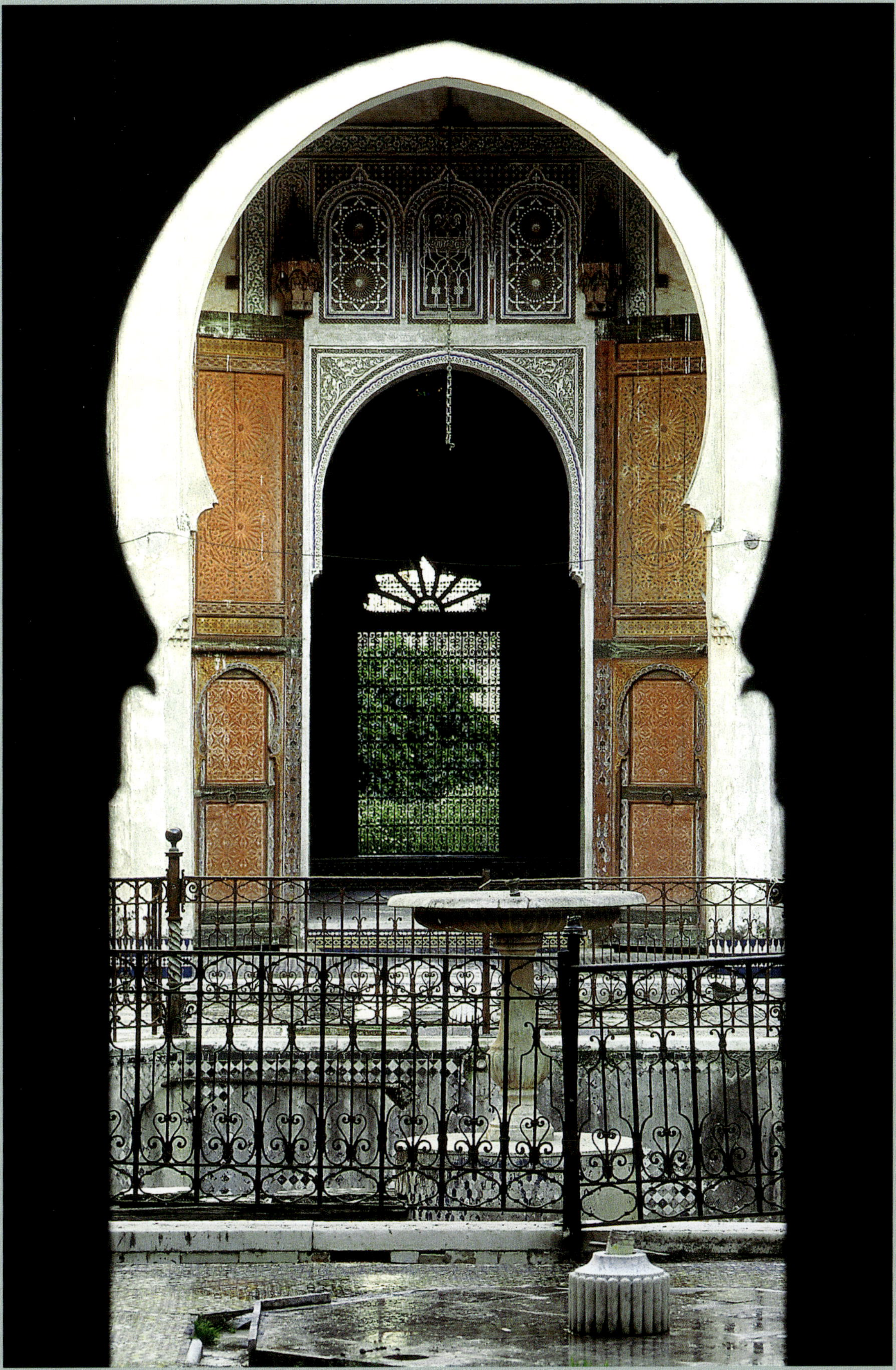

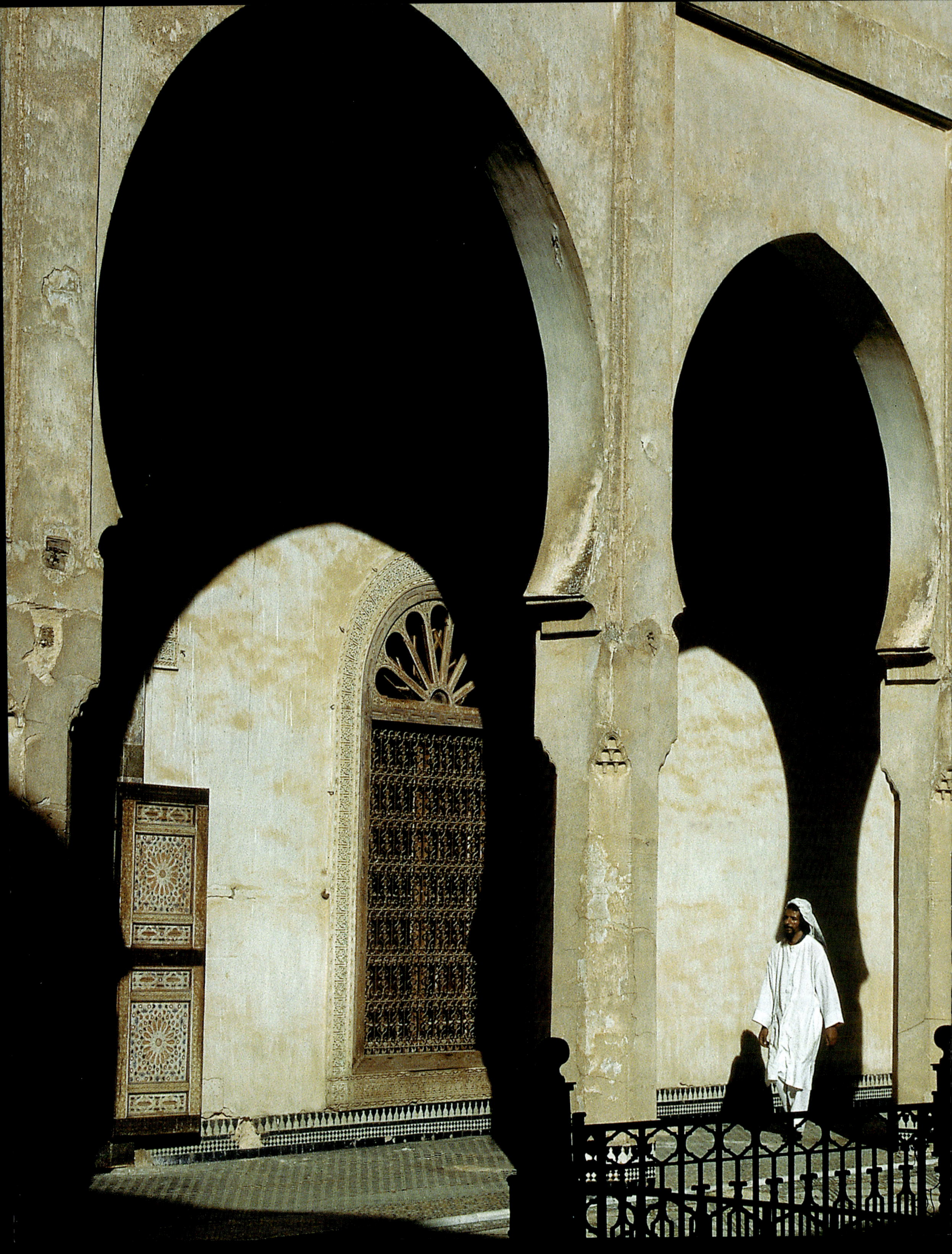

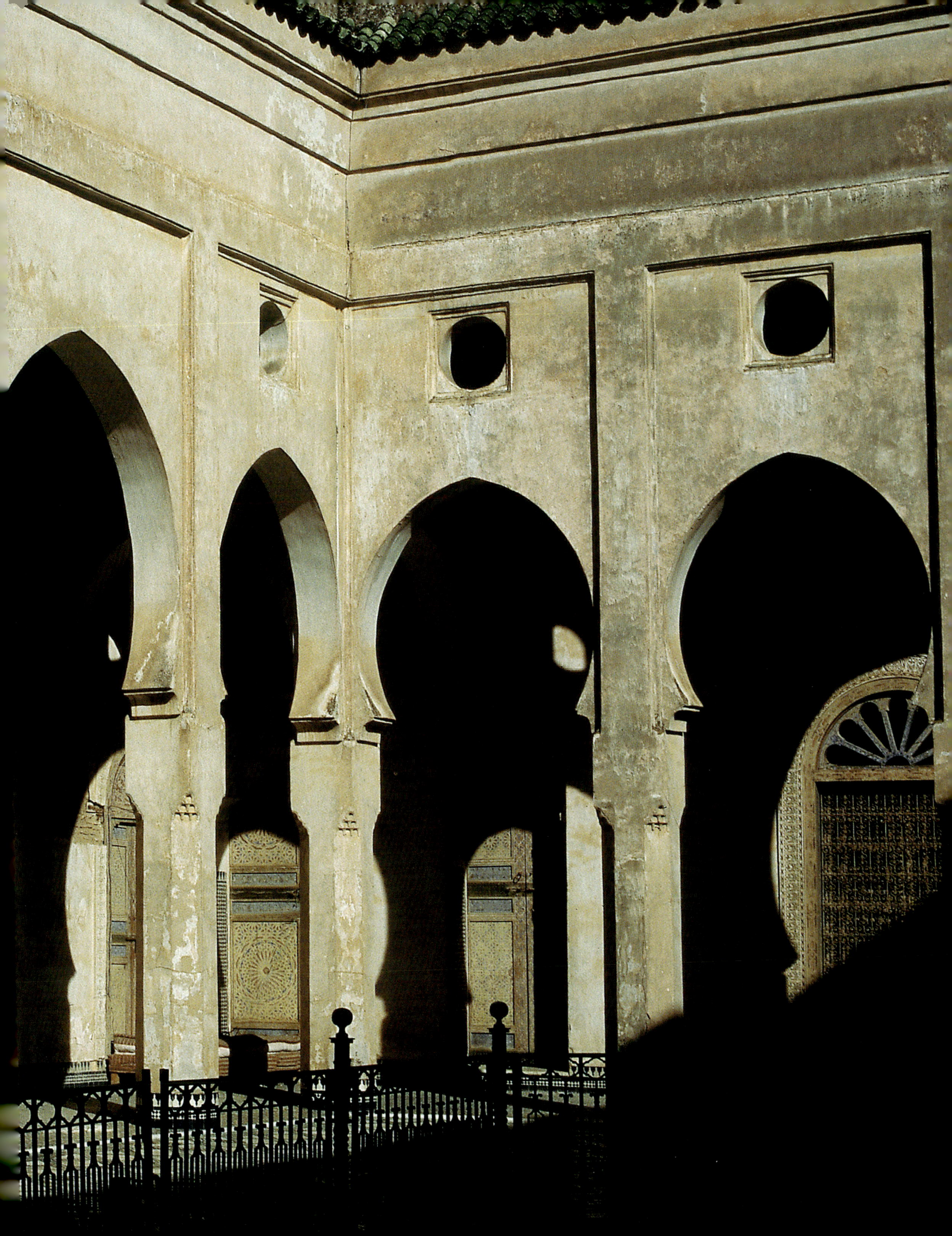

PAGES 74–75:
The galleries of the reception courtyard comprise either five or seven arches, in keeping with the tradition of palatial residences

ABOVE:
Of the seventeen residential sectors in the palace, the harem is one of the largest. The cedar woodwork is slowly disintegrating

OPPOSITE PAGE:
Abou, the caretaker, organizes the guided visits and takes care of the décor the best he can

fiefdom in Telouet, deep in the High Atlas Mountains south of Marrakech, after having been publicly denounced by Sultan (and later King) Muhammad V, whose independence policy he opposed. The slabs of marble have become dull and weeds now sprout up between them. Ceilings are collapsing. The finishing on cedar surfaces is disintegrating. Nevertheless, the palace still presents an image of one of the richest examples of Arabo-Andalusian decorative art. Each salon has its own motifs, and no other home possesses such refined *geps* and *zellij*. In the tradition of art patrons, the Glaoui encouraged artisans, commissioning them to create original decorations (as many as sixty pieces used in an individual *zellij* motif) that would sometimes take as long as eight years to complete. Prefabrication was unknown at the time. Each project was conducted at the palace by a single artisan, whose son would take over his work if the artisan died before it was finished. Differing from the richly decorated bedrooms and salons, the reception courtyard, with its five arcades on one side and seven on the other—the distinct indication of a palatial home—is an example of sobriety. The cedar ceilings of the salons are thirty-three feet (ten meters) tall and are filled with multicolored motifs. The *zouaqs* are finished in a daring purple, which most certainly is not to be found elsewhere. The harem flaunts an enormous wall fountain entirely of *zellij* that may well be the most beautiful in all of Fès.

For its time, the palace was rich in innovations. It was one of the first Moroccan homes to have windows opening onto the garden and a ceiling entirely done in *geps*. It had, prior to the arrival of the French to Morocco, heat and electricity. With advice from Lyautey, the Glaoui even installed a modern bathroom.

Particular care was taken regarding the furnishings. For festive occasions, the palace would be magnificently bedecked in Arabian, Berber, or European style, depending upon the origin of the guests. The dining room, where black slaves served Pantagruelian meals, was ever being divided into two parts—one with European furniture, the other with Moroccan. Large porcelain basins from Europe and Japan covered with multicolored gauze bore pyramids of fruits, walnuts, and almonds, gazelle antlers, jams, dates, and saffron candies. Carafes were heavily gilded. Guests were invited to sit upon fine wool carpets, silk pillows, or European chairs in the Louis XVI or Empire style.

The restoration of the palace, which would cost millions, is of no interest to the heirs. That it has not been thoroughly plundered and remains open to visitors is due solely to the efforts of Abou, the grandson of the majordomo to the Glaoui. Convinced that there exists no palace more beautiful in all of Fès, and determined not to abandon it to ruin, he has fought to safeguard it, taking on not only the role of groundskeeper, but of the keeper of the memory as well. He has moved his family into one of the seventeen houses and in his free time he patches up the ceilings, terraces, and walls with makeshift means. He has only a dozen dogs, intelligent and trilingual by his pronouncement, to help him with this mission he has undertaken.

RIAD AL BARTAL: THE HOUSE OF BIRDS

Near the vast orchards of the Mokri and Glaoui Palaces, the Riad al Bartal presents the image of a typical Fès house. Built with great height around a large patio adorned with cedar, marble, zellij, and carved plaster, it stands as a testament to the refined décors inspired by the Hispano-Moresque style that has been the basis of the city's renown for centuries. Sparrows love to fly through, treating us to the flapping of their wings and their resounding chirps. The residence is named in their honor.

In its present form the Riad al Bartal is in truth merely a *dar*—the structure of the patio, which is square rather than rectangular, has never been divided into four sectors and landscaped with trees and flowers. It does, however, open onto a pleasure garden that, in keeping with Fezzi tradition, includes no residential space.

Built in 1940 in the Ziat quarter of Fès al-Bali, the house was the property of the Belkhiat family, wealthy members of the city's business sector. The date of construction is etched into the façade of the patio—1361 on the Hegira calendar. Bought in 1998 by Mirielle and Christian Laroche, the estate was easily transformed into a guesthouse and the volumes of all spaces were retained. With the exception of the woodwork, which required scraping and

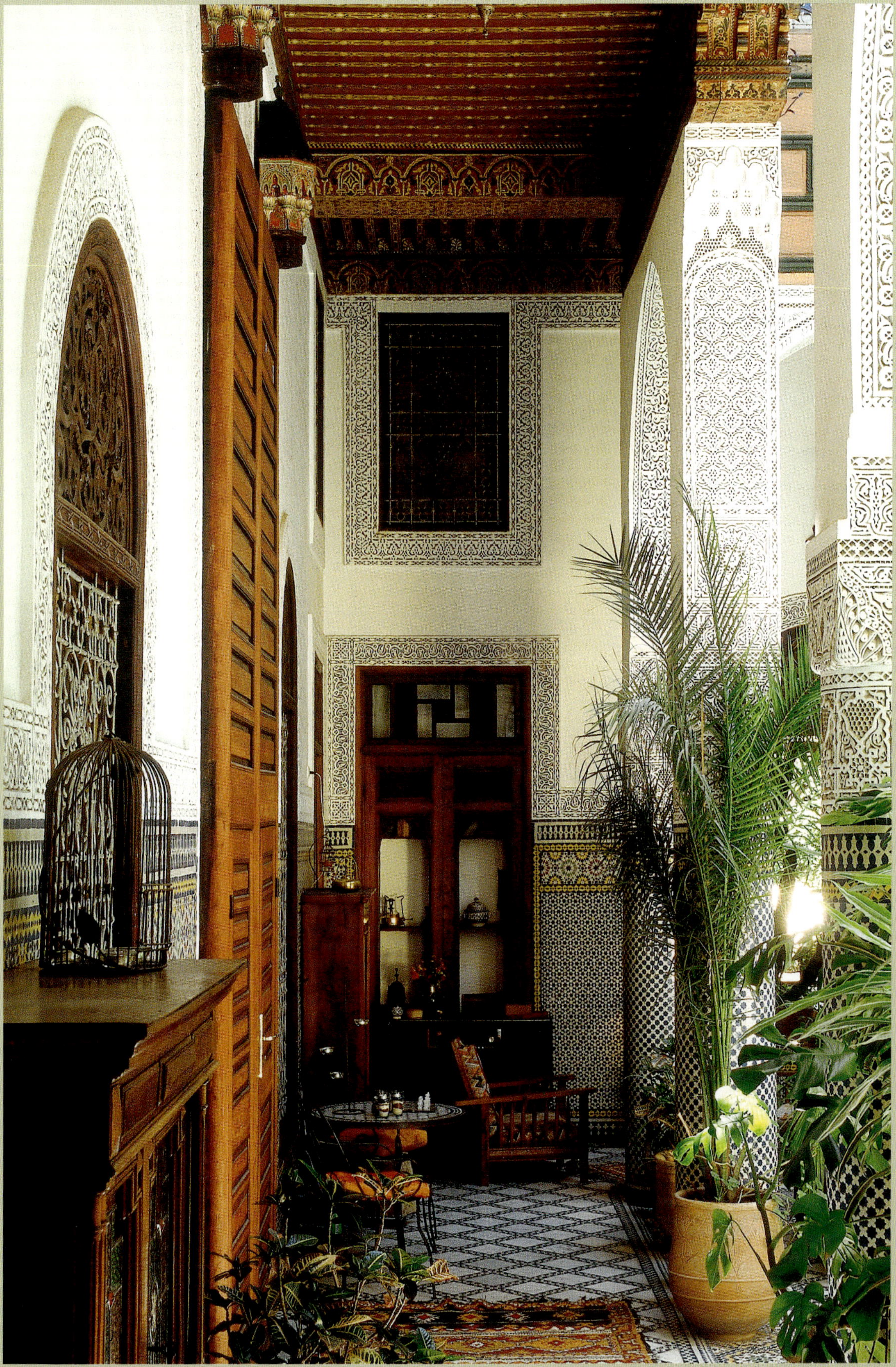

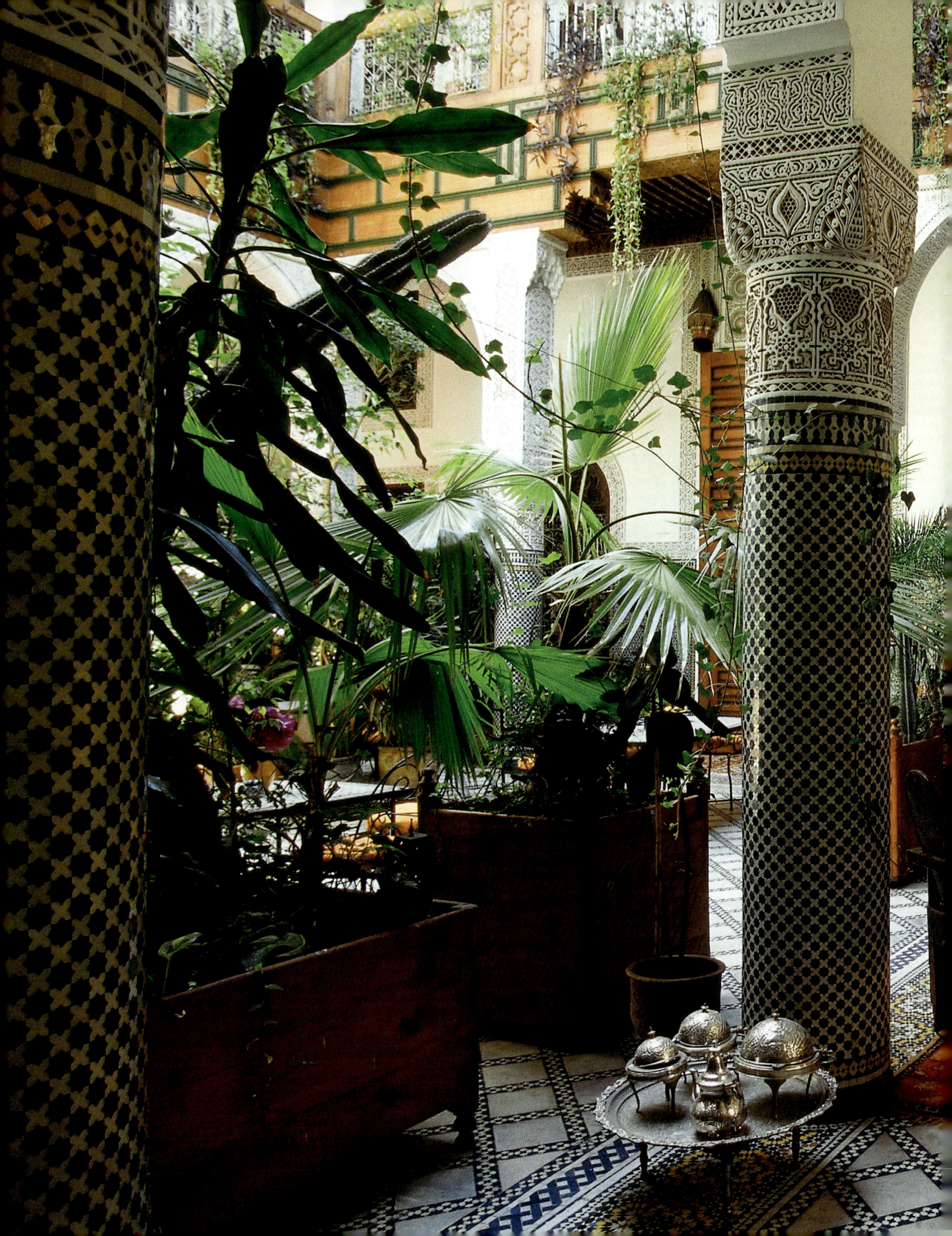

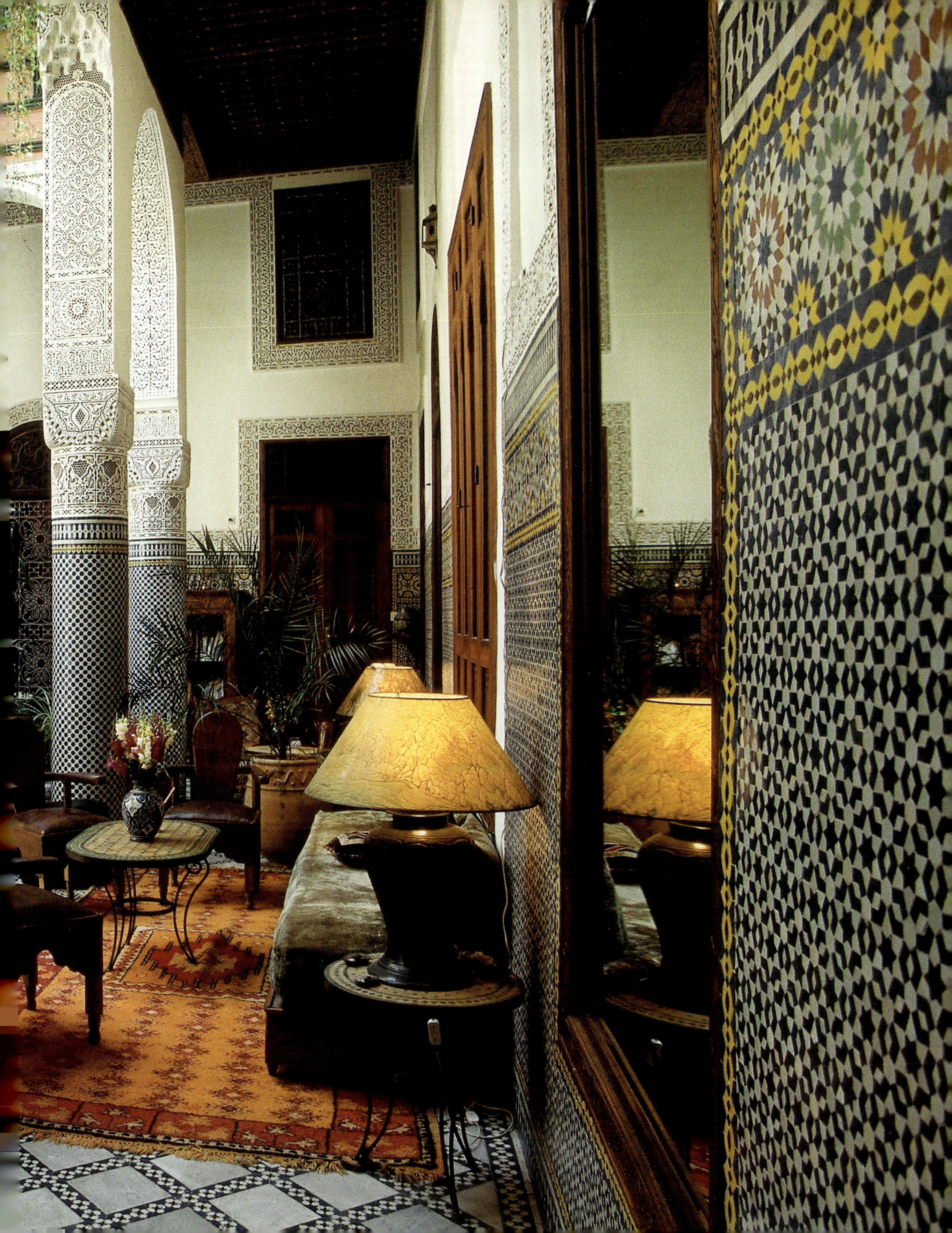

PAGES 82–83:
The patio at the Riad al Bartal is astounding with its bourgeois comforts so typical of a Fezzi home

ABOVE AND RIGHT:
Only the woodwork has been restored. The geps *and* zellij *decorations remained intact*

reinforcement, the decorative work was in good condition. The proportions, materials, motifs, and colors of the home are classic to Fès. The vertical perspectives of the courtyard, for example, are accentuated with façades that reach some forty feet (twelve meters). The countryside surrounding Fès is rich in lumber and joists are longer and thicker than those found in Marrakech. The roofs are made of cedar. The arches are rather vaulted and, characteristic of the sultan's city, are adorned with massive lintels. The interior frames of the doors sport innumerable sculpted motifs and walls are punctuated with lattice works. The ceilings are entirely covered with variegated floral patterns and illuminated with great care. All the wainscoting in the residence, turned in the *moucharabieh* style and carved or painted, are examples of the ancient Moroccan art of woodworking that saw its richest expression during the Merinides dynasty of the thirteenth and fourteenth centuries. The floors are laid with squares of white marble accented by small

blue faience tiles. Commonly found in luxurious homes, Carrara marble was imported from Genoa on ships that then docked in Salé, an Atlantic port city just to the north of the capital Rabat, where it was unladed and transported overland to the imperial cities of Fès and Meknes. The walls, door frames, and columns are paneled with polychromatic *zellij* whose finely crafted compositions produce unnerving optical illusions. Set just up to shoulder level, they prevent residents from dirtying their clothes by coming in contact with plaster or lime. They are also found in bedrooms where divans are placed. The range of available colors increased dramatically with the introduction of artificial pigments at the end of the nineteenth century, when the enamels took on shades of blue, pink, and green, beloved colors in the Islamic world. Added to the usual floral motifs were chevrons, zigzags, merlons, and braids of two sprigs. The upper parts of the walls, the door frames, and the capitals are made of *geps*, which imitates the sculpted marble of the imperial palaces and religious edifices. Through the foliage grilles of the low-ceilinged storage rooms one can contemplate the stunning detail of the carvings. Finally, the doors are furnished with engraved copper knockers in star-shaped polygons.

As was the custom in the homes of middle-class Fès, the Laroches have furnished the house in a heteroclite manner. Works from Moroccan artisans intermingle with furniture from Europe and Asia. In the salon, Murano mirrors reflect Syrian chandeliers. A wood-burning stove lends a note of European comfort. The tabletops covered in blue and white *zellij* evoke the pieces of faience interspersing the white marble floors. Despite a certain baroque excess, the atmosphere of the room remains simple and bright. Potted banana trees and cacti remind one that summers in Fès are as hot as those in Marrakech. Hanging plants cascade from the pale cedar balustrades and small bouquets of wildflowers are set about here and there.

ABOVE:
Houses in Fès are tiled and wainscoted in zellij *up to the bedrooms on the second floor*

From the terrace, which during warm weather is equipped with two tents providing guests respite from the blistering sun, the view plunges down onto the vast orchards of the Mokri Palace and then reaches beyond to the hills of the surrounding countryside. According to Fezzi tradition, a *mesriya* will be located there. This is a small, isolated bedroom where it is said the future bride would stay before and after the wedding. Even though during the winter months a mechanized sliding glass roof encloses the patio, intrepidly, the birds manage to enter as if the Riad al Bartal needed to justify its name year round.

Marrakech

Whereas Fès was influential throughout the entire medieval Islamic world during the eleventh century, Marrakech, in the middle of the country, was still virgin territory. When Yusuf ibn-Tashfin, chief of the conquering Almoravides, arrived from the Sahara, he only had to pitch his tent there for a short time. Nevertheless, as a simple military encampment, Marrakech dethroned Fès and imposed itself as the dynastic capital of an empire that would reach north up to Spain. To build up their new capital, the Berber Almoravides turned to the architects of Spain and then, following the reconquest of Spain (1492 to 1609), also to the Moors, who had been expelled from Andalusia. These Andalusian influences can clearly be seen in the ornamentation of monuments such as the Saadian tombs and the Ben Youssef Madrassa. But Marrakech was never to develop as a cultural center on a par with Fès. An important stop on the caravan route, located near the port of Mogador (present-day Essaouira), its dominance was more as a commercial hub whose residents were primarily of Berber origin.

ANDALUSIAN ART INFUSED WITH RURAL INFLUENCES

Dressed in red and adorned with palm trees, tucked between the hills of the Jbilet Mountains and the snowcapped peaks of the High Atlas Mountains, Marrakech resonates with rural and Saharan influences that bestow upon it an unpretentious charm. Called "the pearl of the south," it hides within the walls of its great gardens, which, like oases, offer cool and relaxing respite.

The houses in Marrakech are striking for the sobriety of their architecture. They are massive and, up until the twentieth century, rarely had a second story. The décor is less refined than houses of the Fès bourgeoisie, as if they were expressing the peasant and pious character of the city's founders. While columns in Fès are adorned with fine, lacelike carvings in Carrara marble, pillars in Marrakech patios are simply covered in a coat of plaster or lime. The local quarries produce only one hard rock that is difficult to sculpt. A scarcity of fuels made it impossible to enamel the earthenware and the region lacked fine woods, such as thuya or cedar. Although the occasional appearance of painted cedar ceilings, carved stucco panels, and polychrome *zellij* floors attests to the sixteenth-century Andalusian immigration, it is the rural spirit that prevails. Ogives are simple and capitals are unadorned. When carved plaster is to be seen above fountains and doors, the work is only sparingly executed.

On the floors, smooth (*tadelact*) or pounded (*dess*) lime replaces mosaics, which are used only to decorate reception salons and fountains or elegant washbasins. The sole traditional cement and additionally, the primary indication of the affluence of the house, lime is omnipresent in Moroccan clay masonry. It strengthened the floors, protected the outer walls from the weather, lightened the dark interior walls, and purified spaces. On the eve of major holidays, women would use brooms made of dwarf palms to whitewash the terraces with it.

Dess is used for covering floors. To make it, the mason moistens the clay and adds a coat of diluted lime.

RIGHT:
Dar al Pacha. Prestigious buildings are recognizable by their rounded green enamel roof tiles. Every city in Morocco has its "house of the Pacha"

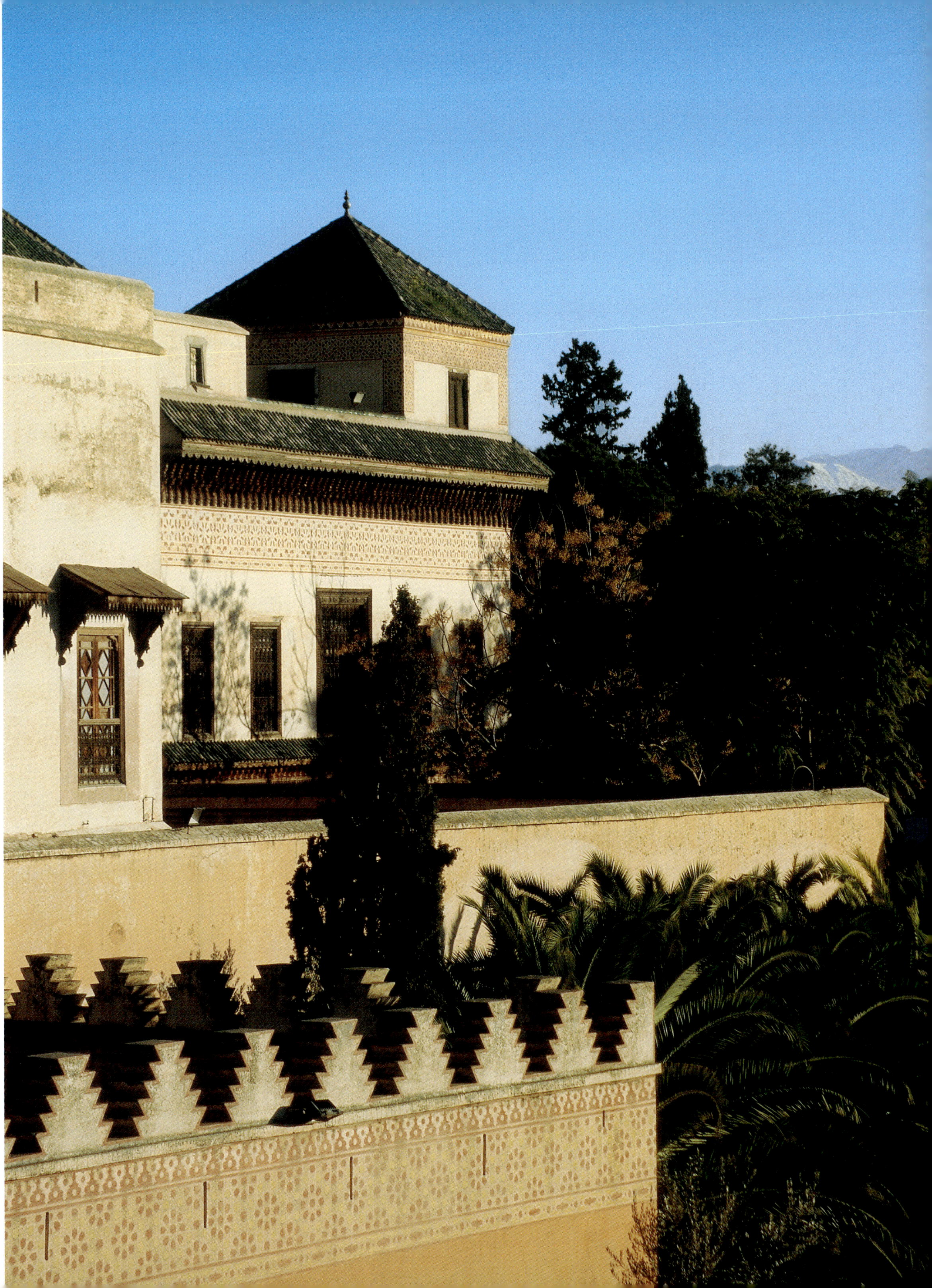

Although deeply influenced by Andalusian art, Marrakech exudes the strict austerity of its pious founders from the Sahara.

He then sprinkles the mixture with sifted clay and with everything and anything—which might include small bits of gravel from the wadi or sand. He packs it down (to the rhythm of the *maallem*), shaping it into a sort of plaque that is left to dry for several hours. Finally, to smooth over the ensemble, he pours one last fine coat of the lime. A *dess* produced in the old-fashioned manner entails considerable work—in older houses, it could be as thick as three inches (eight centimeters).

OPPOSITE PAGE:
Imsala, an open-air prayer site

ABOVE:
The Koutoubia mosque, built in the twelfth century during the Almohades dynasty, is one of the most important sanctuaries in the Maghrib. Its minaret has become emblematic of Marrakech

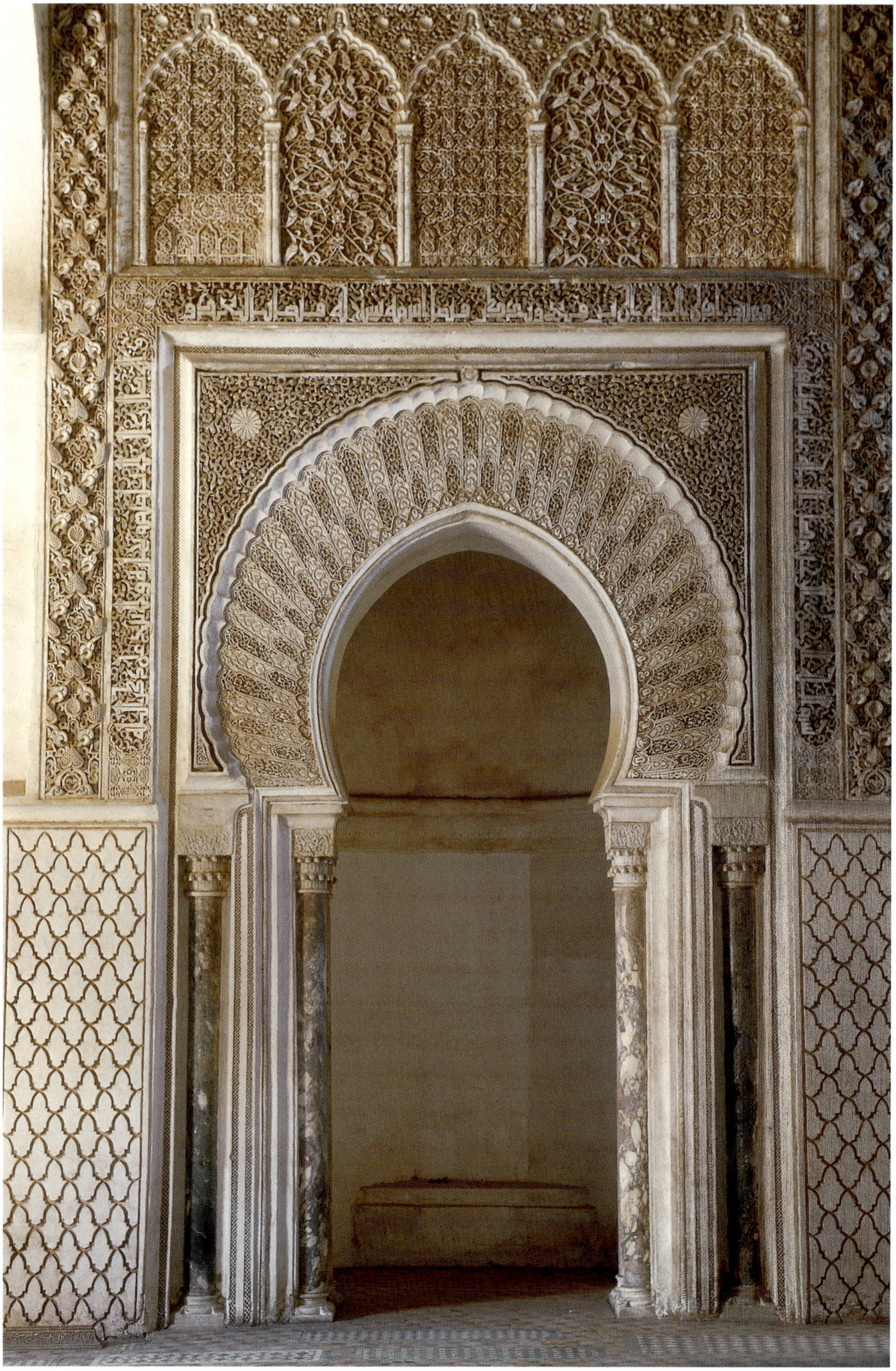

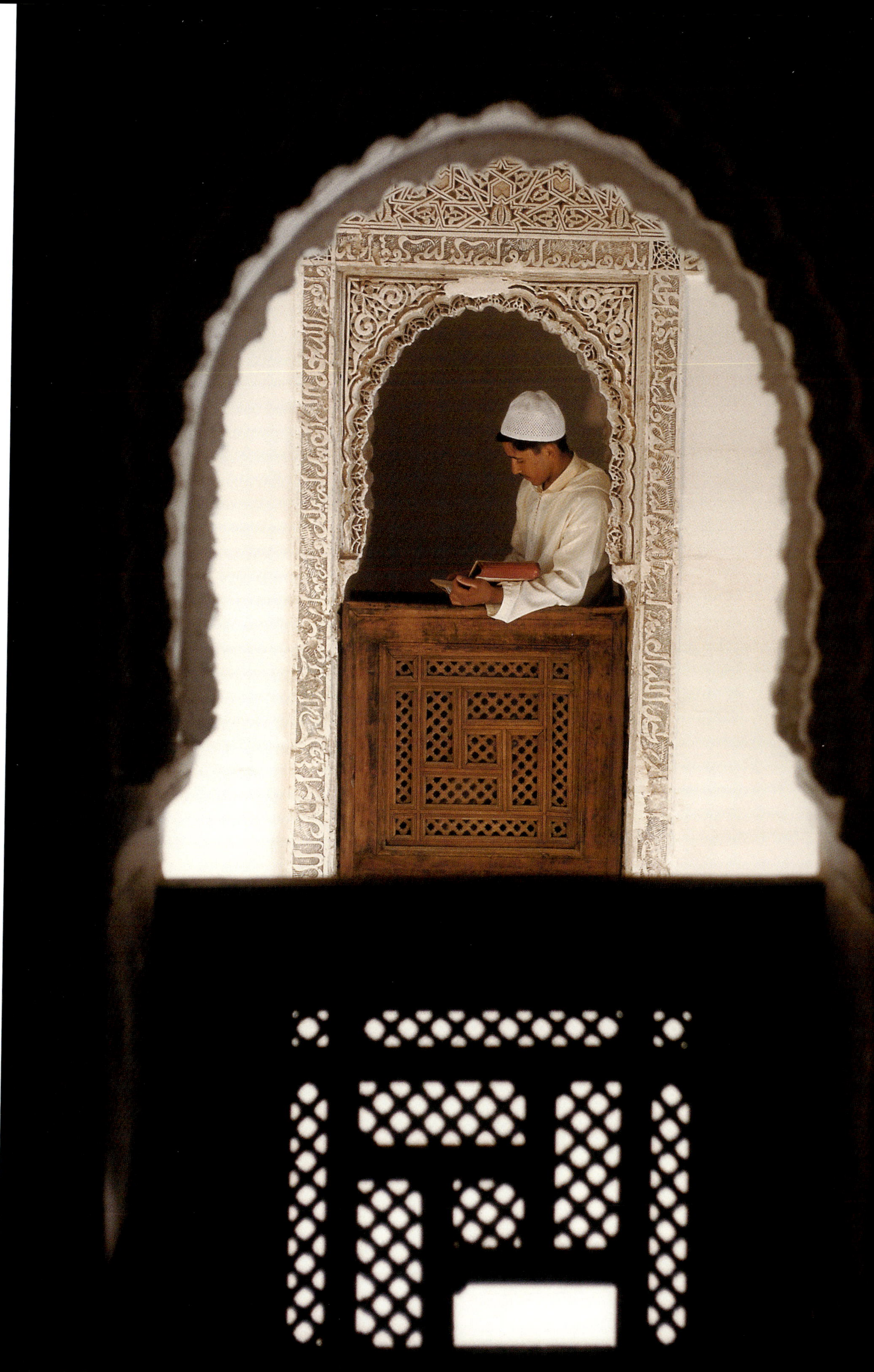

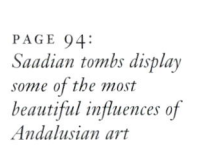

PAGE 94:
Saadian tombs display some of the most beautiful influences of Andalusian art

PAGE 95:
The Saadians, great builders, constructed the Ben Youssef Madrassa in the sixteenth century. The university has some hundred cells and can accommodate up to nine hundred students

OPPOSITE:
Utterly watertight, tadelact *is the preferred covering for hammams, pools, and fountains. Pictured here is Dar Lippini*

Tadelact is the most sophisticated method of finishing. It is applied to walls, to the interior of a pool over a pre-existing solid surface, as well as over *dess*. Limewater is spread thickly over the dampened surface and it is then left to dry thoroughly. Using a circular motion, the artisan then patiently rubs the surface inch by inch with a very hard stone that, through use, becomes polished on one side. To make his stone slide, he will again dampen the surface. In the past, egg white was the chosen material, whereas today, a soft soap solution is used. Little by little, at a rate of approximately one square yard per day, the surface becomes satiny and is transformed into veritable enamel. Completely waterproof, *tadelact* is the preferred finish for hammams, pools, and fountains. It is also found on the walls of reception salons at a level where people might lean, ensuring a clean surface free of the dust so utterly dreaded in homes made of clay battered by wind and sand. The *tadelact* is often dyed. In addition to natural pigments (in Marrakech these are egg yolk, saffron, and ocher clay), synthetic pigments are also used, which although they are more expensive, offer a broader palette of colors. Occasionally stenciled motifs are added.

Tadelact is an active material that requires special maintenance. Every six months or so, it must be polished with natural wax and a soft cloth to return it to its original luster. Over the course of the years, the colors will lighten and the faience-like surface will become harder. It does not withstand abrasive cleansers and solvents and thus is not suggested for the interior of swimming pools that use chlorine. It does, however, age well, as is evidenced by a twelfth-century pool in the Menara gardens. Having long fallen into disuse, *tadelact* has recently experienced a revival in Marrakech. It is not merely being used as a finish on masonry, it has also replaced enamel on pottery, producing softer and deeper shades.

✶ The Particular Charm of House-Gardens

Whereas the enclosed garden, a descendant of the Persian model, spread throughout the Muslim west thanks to the expansion of Islam, it is in Marrakech that one finds the greatest preponderance of *riads*. Presently, it is home to sixty-seven large house-gardens—that is, patios measuring more than 2,150 square feet (200 square meters). In Fès a *riad* may remain a space reserved for the elite few, merely one of life's pleasures, but in Marrakech, it was adopted as a model for living.

While *dars* are located in densely populated neighborhoods, one finds the more spacious *riad* not only in neighborhoods where plots of land are larger, but where they can be accessed by wide, paved roads. A *riad* is, after all, the home of a prominent family—one must be wealthy

MARRAKECH 97

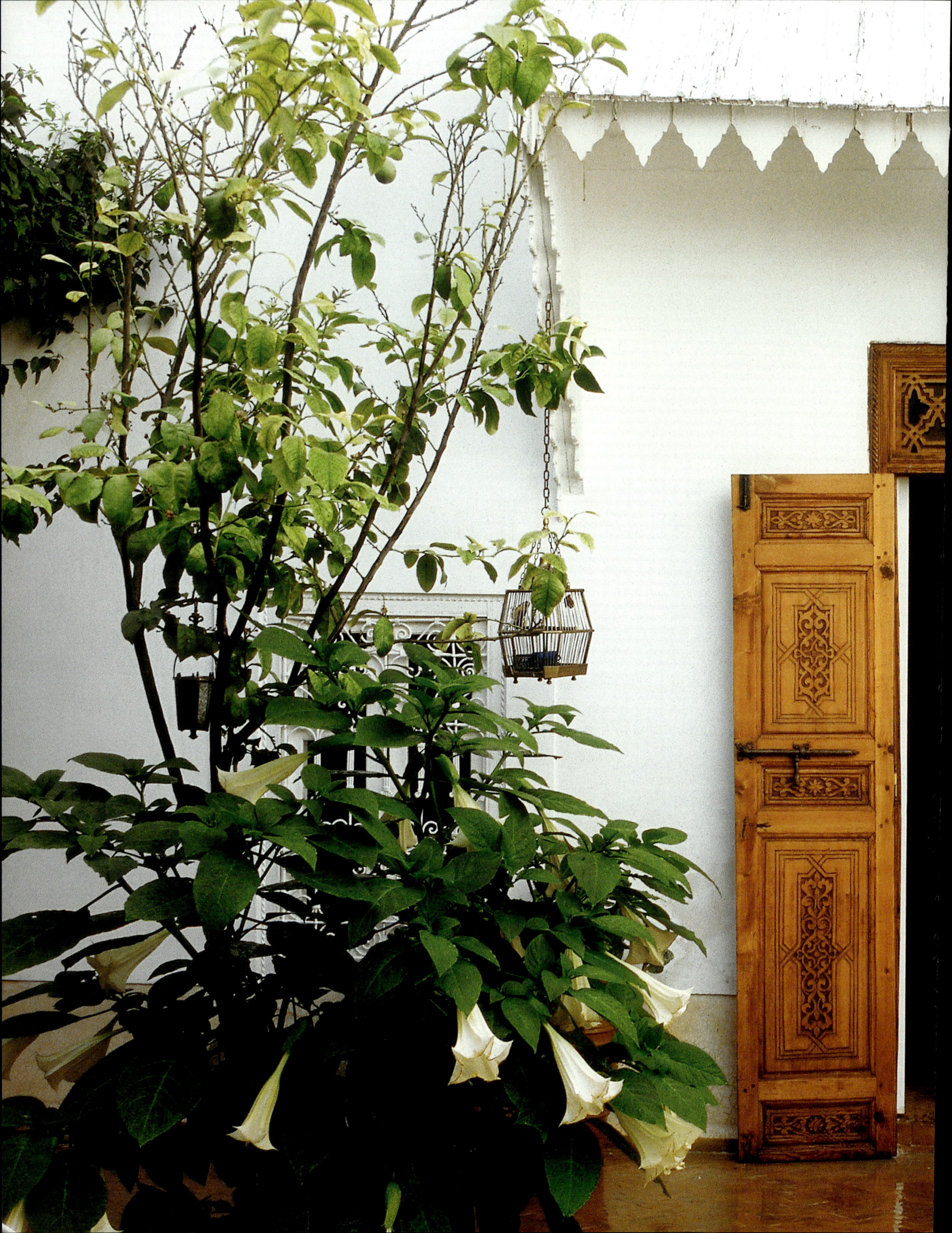

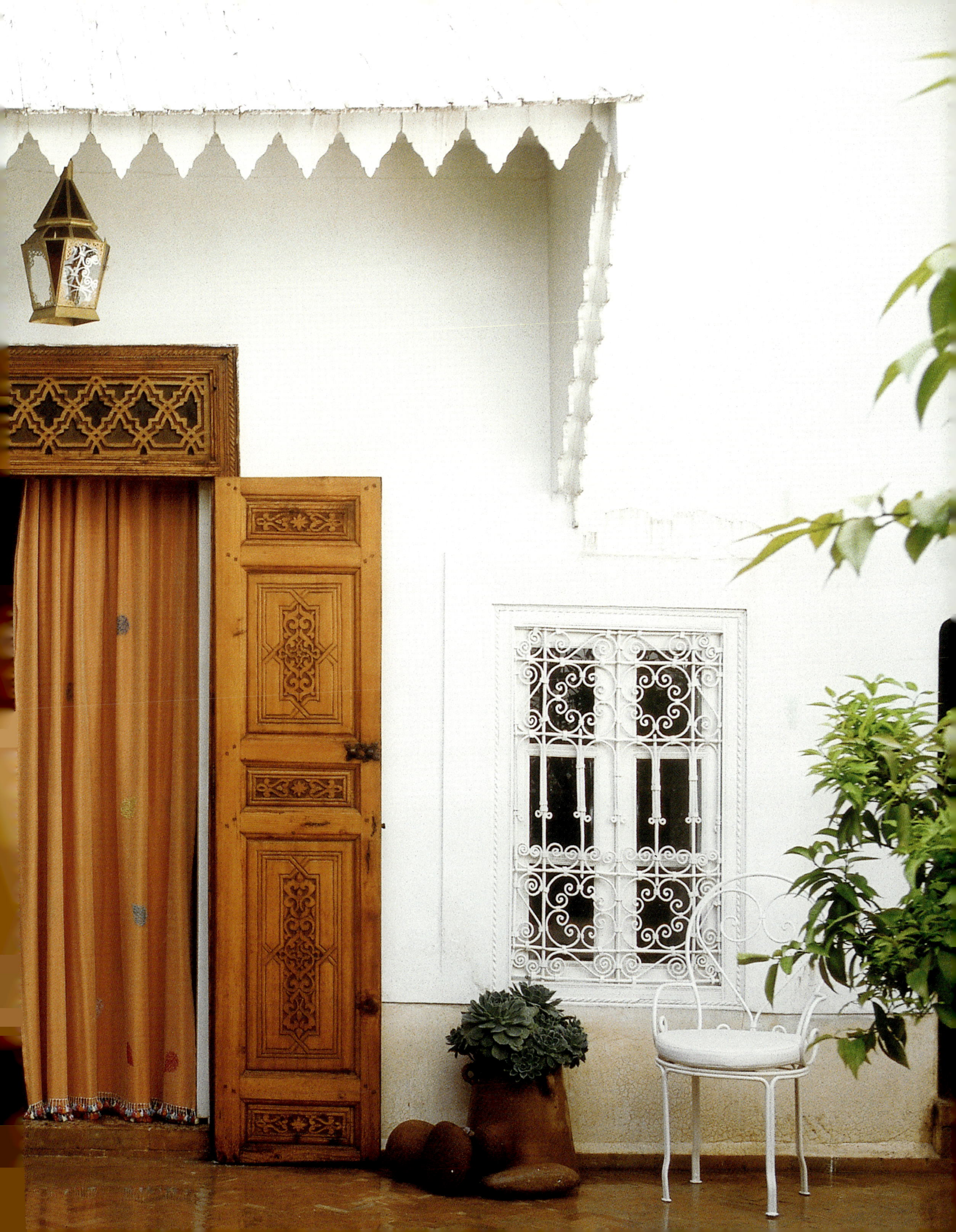

Overwhelmed by the heat of the summer months, Marrakech devised a way of life tailored to its climate—the riad.

to own such a large patio in the medina. Even today, the size of one's garden remains a measure of affluence and prestige for the master of the house.

The majority of *riads* conform to the Andalusian model copied by the Almoravides from medieval Spain. Everything is ordered, delimited, and symmetrical. Two assiduously identical residential quarters branch off from either far side of the rectangular interior courtyard. These are reached by galleries, which are often covered and have their own subsidiary rooms and wall fountains. Although the arrangement may be horizontal, the main perspective is not disproportionate. The patio is divided into four equal rectangles and landscaped with fruit trees, flowers, and aromatic herbs: cypresses, lemon trees, orange trees, pomegranate trees, fig trees, banana trees, jasmine bushes, daturas, mint, coriander, myrtle, and oregano all grow in abundance. But nowhere does the foot touch the earth. A built-up surface landing extends out in front of each room. Two median paths paved in mosaics or *bejmat* (small terracotta bricks) demarcate the borders and accentuate the geometrics of the garden. If the trees were removed, the four-sectored structure of the patio would remain perfectly intact. Nevertheless, in the large *riads*, the garden paths may delineate as many as twelve treed sectors.

The center is clearly indicated: a square, hexagonal, or star-shaped pool finished in *tadelact* and covered with multicolored mosaics is planted at the point where the paths intersect; in it sprouts a marble basin. An endless stream of water emerges from these bowls, imported from Italy, cradling the life of the house. In the homes of the wealthiest, the fountain is in fact a pool (*sahrij*) that reflects the façades surrounding the patio, and its water is used to irrigate the gardens.

The paths are lined with balustrades. Reed trellises tied together with twine from dwarf palms or wrought-iron wires stretch the length, often like arcades, with jasmine, geraniums, and night jessamine. The most sprawling gardens will have gazebos or pavilions with wooden canopies.

PAGES 98–99:
The décor of the Colonel's House, which is much more sedate than the bourgeois houses in Fès, testifies to its rural influences

PAGES 102–103:
Riad Lamrani. In Fès the riad *is merely a pleasure garden; in Marrakech, it is a model for living*

MARRAKECH 101

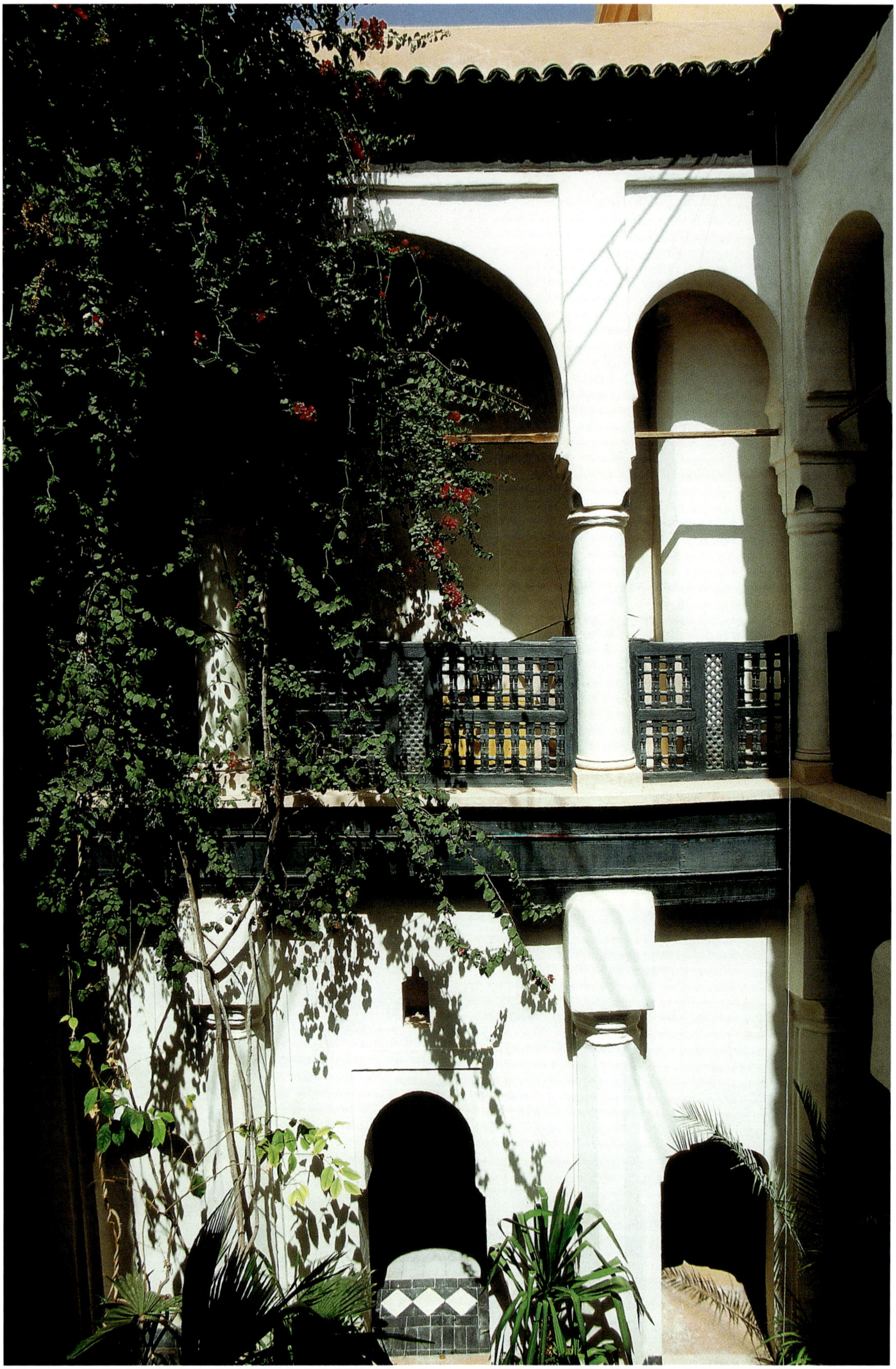

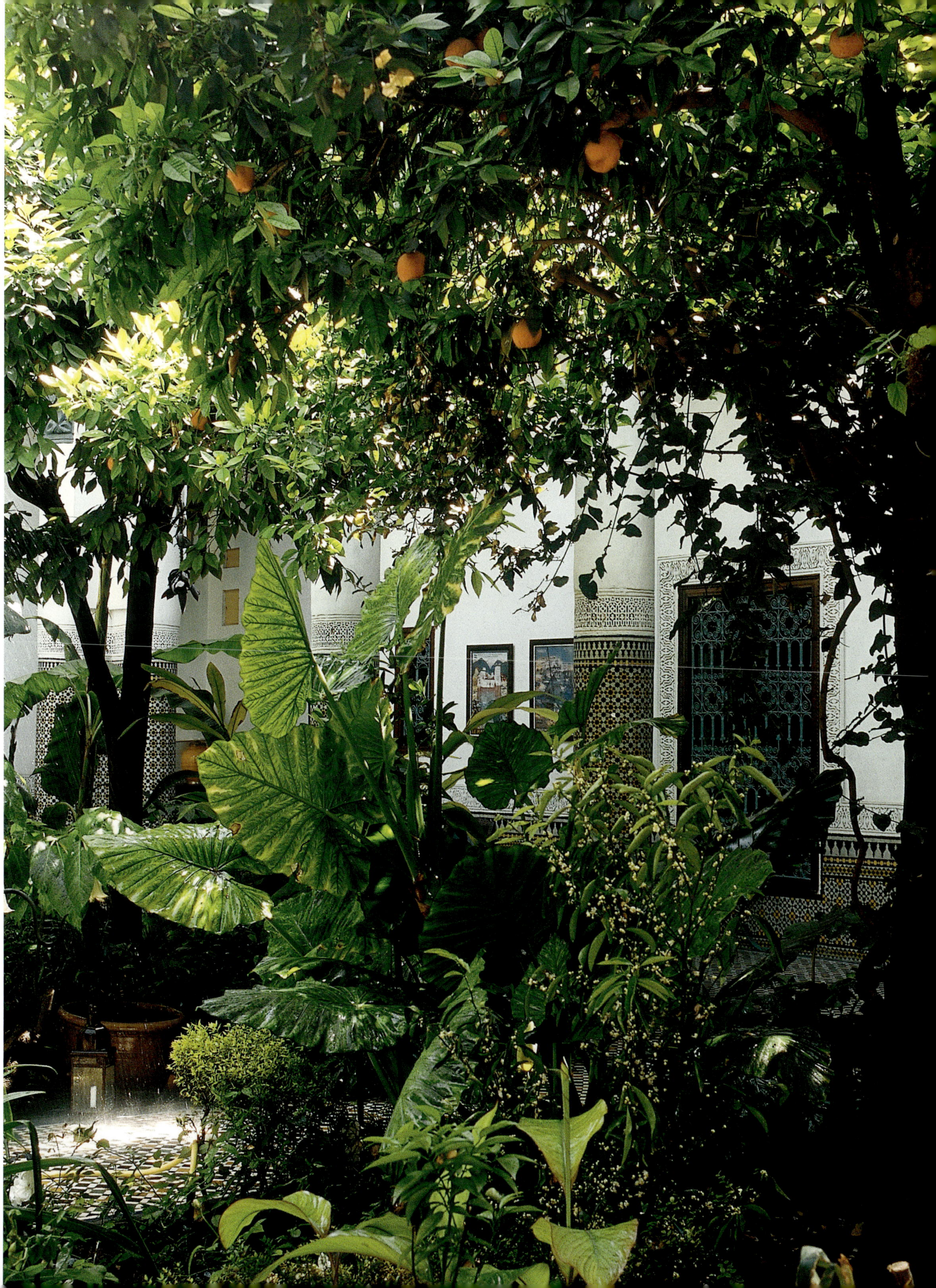

As with the *dars*, a *riad* is entered by following a zigzagging path at an angle to the patio. All the same, the rooms there are more spacious, and often subdivided by arches and a hollowed-out *behous*, a kind of alcove across from the door. Furnished with comfortable banquettes, the *behous* gives a sense of height to the rooms that are necessarily narrow due to the short joists. During the nineteenth century the *behous* were situated outside down the length of the lateral walls of the patio.

In these small garden salons, the master of the house would take his place among his women to sip tea, listen to the musicians, admire the different angles of the garden through the arcades of the portico, and, once night fell, to ponder as the moon passed between the fronds of the palm trees.

A traditional *riad* at best comprises one room on the second story (*douiria*), which is reserved for guests and has a balcony. The staircases, which are no wider than a yard (a meter), are set in the corners so as to remain independent and are sometimes topped with a masonry turret. From the terraces one contemplates that which Marrakech is known for—the unfathomable geometrics of the pink walls, punctuated by minarets and outlined by cypresses and palm trees whose noble foliage are silhouetted upon a backdrop of the snowy Atlas Mountains.

FAR LEFT:
Pomegranate blossoms

ABOVE:
Marble fountains

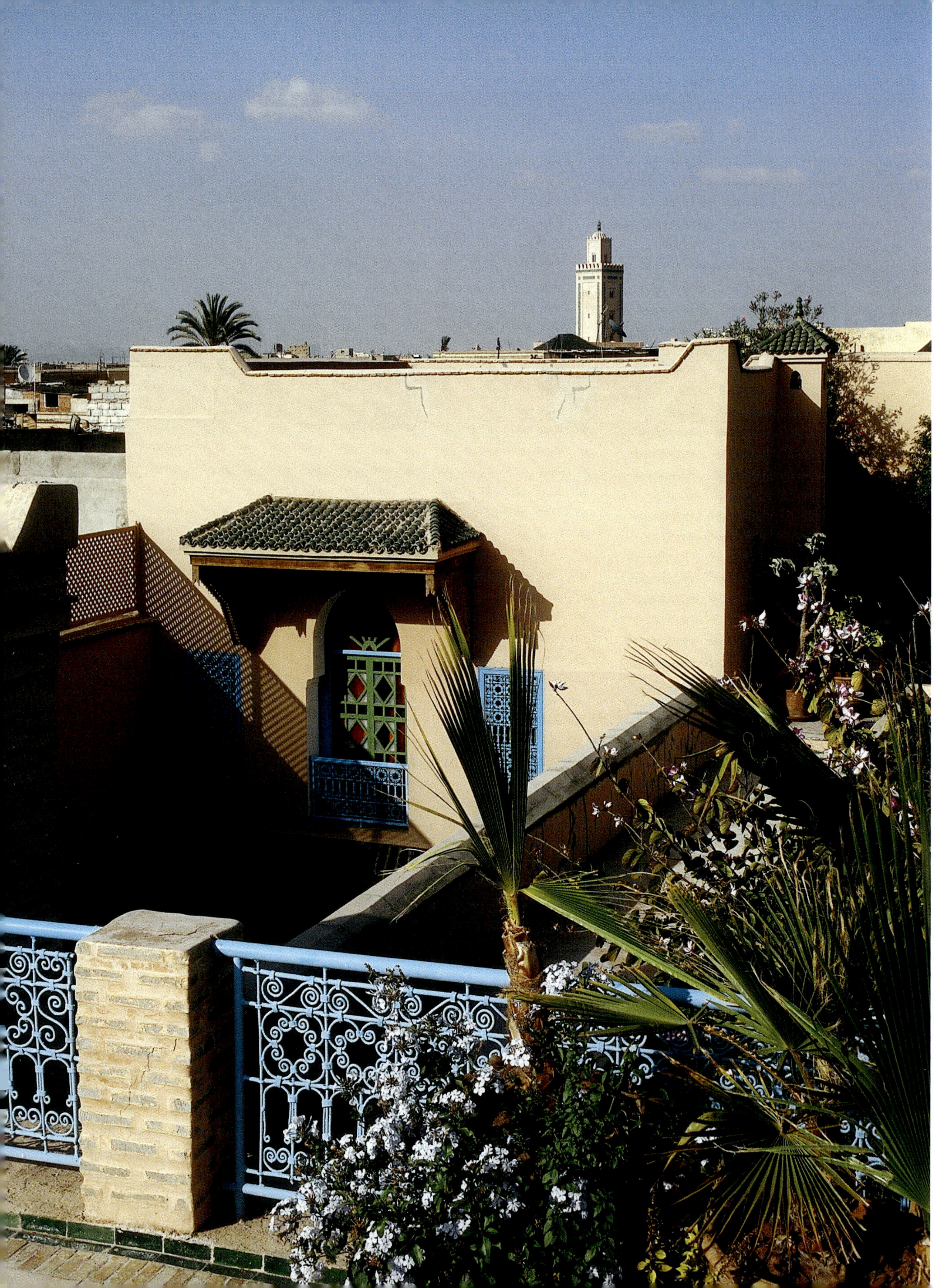

✦ The Garden, a Metaphor for Paradise

The supreme setting for the Moroccan art of living, the garden remains an auspicious place for love. In Arabic poetry, it is forever being celebrated. But still, the image is of a worldly paradise. The Eden depicted in the Koran bears the charm of an eternal garden, rich in flowers, fruit, and shade. The faithful rejoice there in perpetual delight. Cups filled with delicious, clear water from an inexhaustible spring will be passed around. They will be covered in honors, bedecked in gold and pearl bracelets, dressed in green silk, satin, and brocade. Reclining on ceremonial beds, they will find beautiful virgin wives there and not an unnecessary word will be heard, as this garden is for those who will already believe in God and his prophets.

Entirely enclosed and facing inward, the Moroccan garden brings to the fore these images of paradise. It must be a place of serenity and beauty, and favorable for meditation. The floral arrangements express joy and cheerfulness. One must hear the sound of water, savor the tastes of the fruit trees, and breathe in the aromas.

LEFT:
The Riad Lamrani has a single room on the upper floor that is sheltered beneath a tile canopy and has its own small balcony

ABOVE:
For Muslims, fountains and pools evoke their image of paradise

MARRAKECH 107

ABOVE AND OPPOSITE:
Day and night, the patio luxuriates in the scent of jasmine blossoms. The volutes of the ironwork and decorative patterns replicate the floral motifs

PAGES 110–11:
Constructed on a plain, Marrakech has always had large residential plots. The patio at the Riad Lamrani covers an expanse of 4,300 square feet (400 square meters)

The paradise of Islam is often portrayed as a perpetually gushing fountain. Differing from European gardens that are well watered by nature, the Islamic garden has made water the essential principle of its philosophy and aesthetic. In the geometric layout of the patio in the *riad*, there will always be a "fluvial square" that establishes the mythology of water in the Koran—paradise is composed of four rivers, each one oriented on one of the earthly cardinal points. The central fountain returns to the symbol of nourishing water, which since the times of ancient Arabia has served in the collective imagination as an emblem of germination and fecundity, and as an element of purification and prophylaxis. Far from the evils attributed to stagnant waters, the refuge of demons, the flowing water of the fountain is bestowed with divine benediction.

In Marrakech, while *riads* are abundant, large gardens are only found in the vast patrician homes. The Agdal gardens and the Menara pool were created by the Almohads in the twelfth century with a concern for establishing a new style of urban landscaping discrete from the Eastern model—perspectives were unobstructed, the enclosures were multiple and broad, set in a manner to create a sort of cross-border garden. The gardens of the El Badi Palace, planted during the sixteenth century, were inspired by the Persian example of the Alhambra in Granada. On the other hand, during the nineteenth century the El Bahia Palace left room for garden patios. Under the French Protectorate new gardens liberated from Islamic tradition blossomed throughout the new neighborhoods. Species intermingled in abundance and without restraint in the greatest of asymmetries. Numerous kinds of exotic varieties were introduced, including bamboos, papyri, and cacti. All innovations were fair game as the blue paintings of Yves Klein (1928–1962), known as the "Bleu Klein" of the Majorelle Garden planted during the 1920s, attest.

One could marvel at how the gardens escaped the Islamic prohibition of depicting images from the natural world. A recurring motif is the Oriental carpet, divided into four sectors that correspond to the four poles of the Garden of Eden. It is depicted on fabrics, doors, ceilings, etc. A conquered space in an inhospitable nature, the Islamic garden reproduces a world order that is faithful to divine prescriptions.

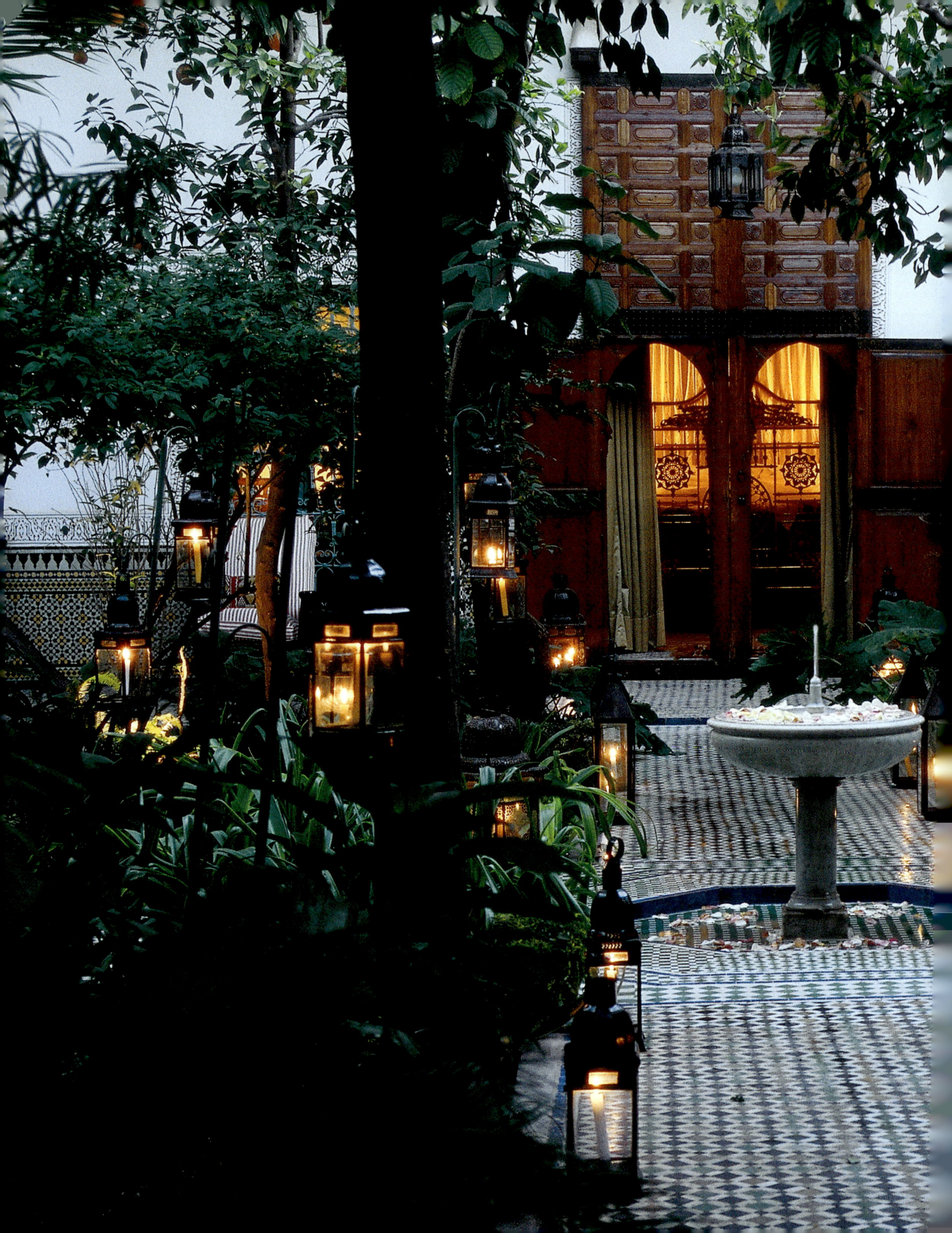

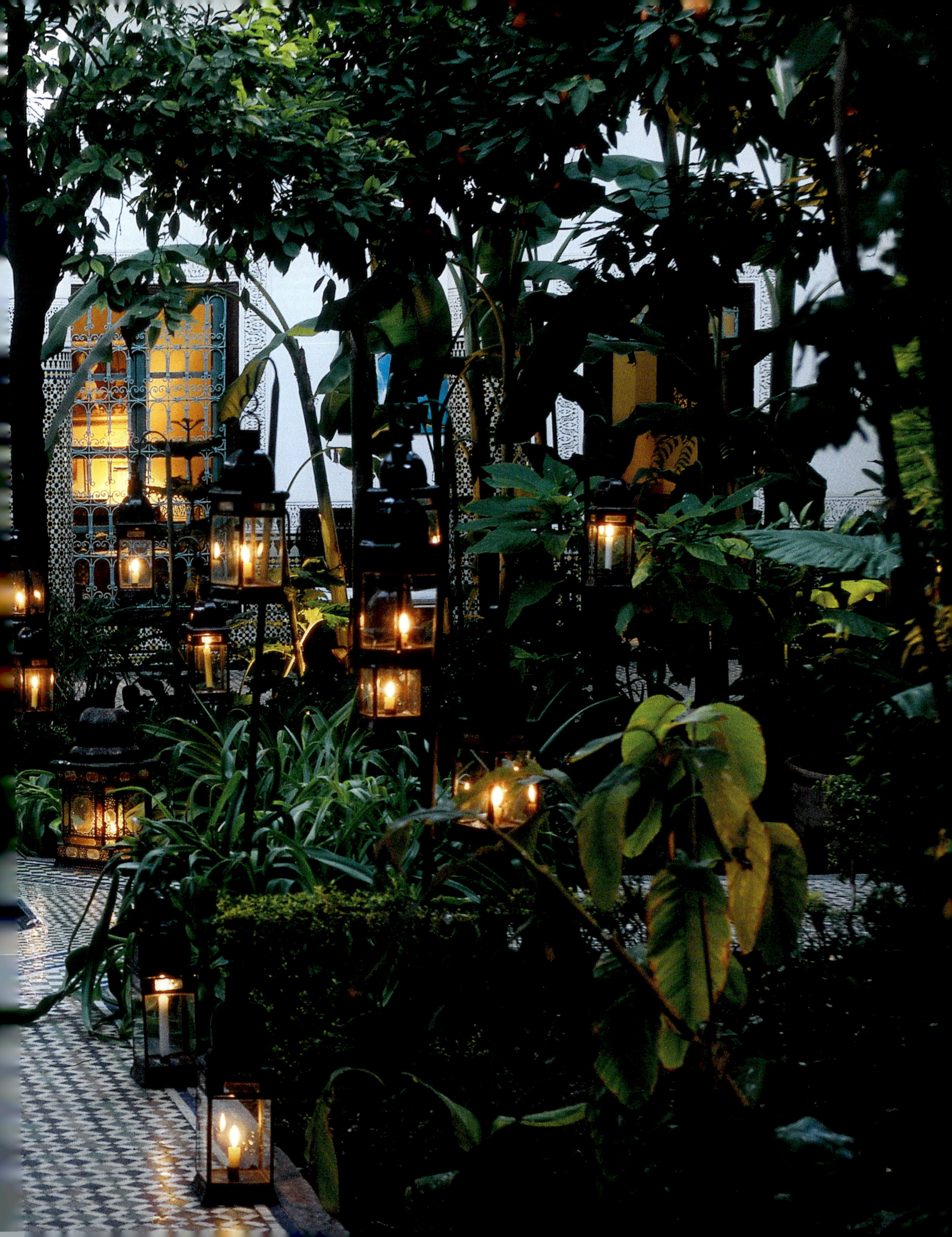

DAR EL QADI: THE HOUSE WITH THE TOWER

Located in one of the oldest quarters of the Marrakech medina (dating from the twelfth and thirteenth centuries), Dar el Qadi, the "House of the Judge," provides a glimpse of what a patrician home during medieval times might have looked like. It is easily spotted with its turret and small observatory, where the first master of the house, a judge and theologian, studied the heavenly bodies.

During the Middle Ages, it was within the domain of a judge to master theological sciences, notably in order to calculate the Muslim lunar calendar. And thus, Dar el Qadi was equipped with an observatory above the height of the terraces. A recess on the right held the scholar's precious manuscripts. The openings on the left and in the center allowed him to observe the city, from the Koutoubia Mosque on the western side, all the way to the Ben Saleh Mosque on the eastern side. The tower would be swept by luscious breezes filled with the aromatic scent of orange blossoms from the neighboring *riads*.

Throughout the centuries Dar el Qadi was always occupied by important people. One of the most illustrious of them, known for the elegance of his fine woolen cloth, was the vizier and theologian at the Ben Youssef mosque. As with the homes of all notables, the residence has its own hammam, as well as numerous low-ceilinged lofts arranged at an angle to the house.

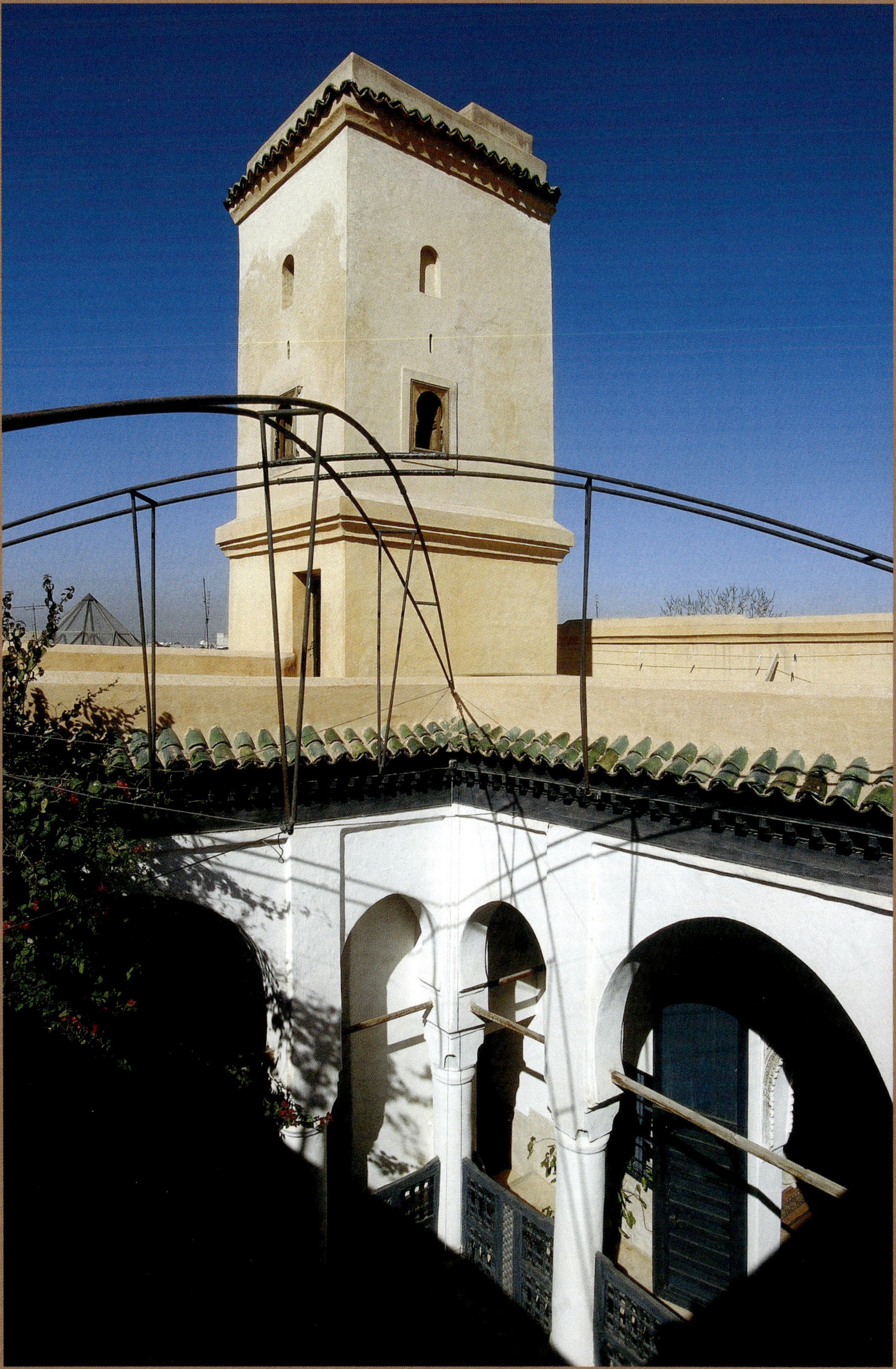

ABOVE:
The solid pillars of the patio are octagonal, probably a legacy from ancient Rome

RIGHT:
Each room has retained its original size

It was in these lofts that wealthy landowners would store the harvests of wheat, barley, olives, and oil from their gardens in the countryside. The customary zigzag entryway is not situated at an angle, but rather gives directly onto the house's interior courtyard. Could a notable defy the archetypes merely because he was called upon to receive many people? Nevertheless, the house did have a *douiria*, the small private apartment reserved for receiving guests. In keeping with the traditional model, this *douiria* is located on the second floor, above outbuildings of the main residence. It is accessed by an independent stairway just inside the entry door, thus guests never penetrate the heart of the house where the women live.

Although it is known that the interior decorations are very old, it is difficult to date them precisely. Probably of the Saadian period, thus pre-eighteenth century, they reflect the most beautiful influences of Arabo-Andalusian art. Although lumber is not at all plentiful in Marrakech, the ceilings are decorated with elaborately worked cedar. Despite its small size (the one room measures only fifty-five by sixty-three inches, or 1.4 by 1.6 meters), the turret, with its painted wood and carved plaster, is a jewel of interior design. The residence also, however, betrays its rural Berber influences. The narrowness of the patio evokes the interior courtyards of the Kasbahs of the south. The walls are thick and whitewashed and the massive pillars are devoid of decoration. Any search for a similar house in Tangiers or in Granada would be in vain. One just does not exist. Through its harmonious blend of Arabo-Andalusian style and Berber, indeed African, influences, the Dar el Qadi illustrates an archaic type of Marrakechi residence.

The current owner, Quentin Wilbaux, an architect by training, has restored the *dar* to perfection. The UNESCO program charged with the preservation of Marrakech's medina appointed him to head the renovation.

ABOVE:
The douiria, *a guest apartment on the upper level, is the room with the most ornate décor. Its central shaft of light recreates the structure of the patio*

RIGHT:
The walls of the salon are covered in antique drapes from kaid tents (haitis)

He then embarked upon an archeological expedition with the goal of returning the el Qadi to its original state. At the time of its acquisition in 1993, the house was divided into seven residences. The turret was partially destroyed and the doors had been heavily repainted. He undertook the tedious task of scraping the doors and revealing once again their original design. While providing modern comforts and conveniences, he did not alter the structure of the building. Old storage rooms have been converted into bathrooms, the sprawling kitchens remain as spacious as ever, and the hammam's furnace has been restored to working order. So as not to create a contrived décor, the floors have neither been redone in the customary Marrakech rustic lime finish (*dess*) nor the renowned Fezzi *zellij* that is so adored by tourists. And even some of the irretrievably lost carved plaster has been left unfinished. In his effort to safeguard every vestige of the past, Wilbaux has undertaken the preservation to the extent that he retained some

ABOVE RIGHT:
The doors were carefully scraped, revealing zouaqs that date from the Saadian period

PAGES 118–19:
From his tower, the judge observed the stars and calculated the Muslim lunar calendar

graffiti scratched by a *maallem* (master artisan) into a piece of centuries-old *tadelact*; this is just one example of how every aspect of the décor remains authentic. Nothing has been removed, nothing added. The furnishings are simple, rustic, and not at all ostentatious. With the strength of its structure and the power of its original décor, the Dar el Qadi possesses the beauty of a woman, ever so gently made up, in the prime of life.

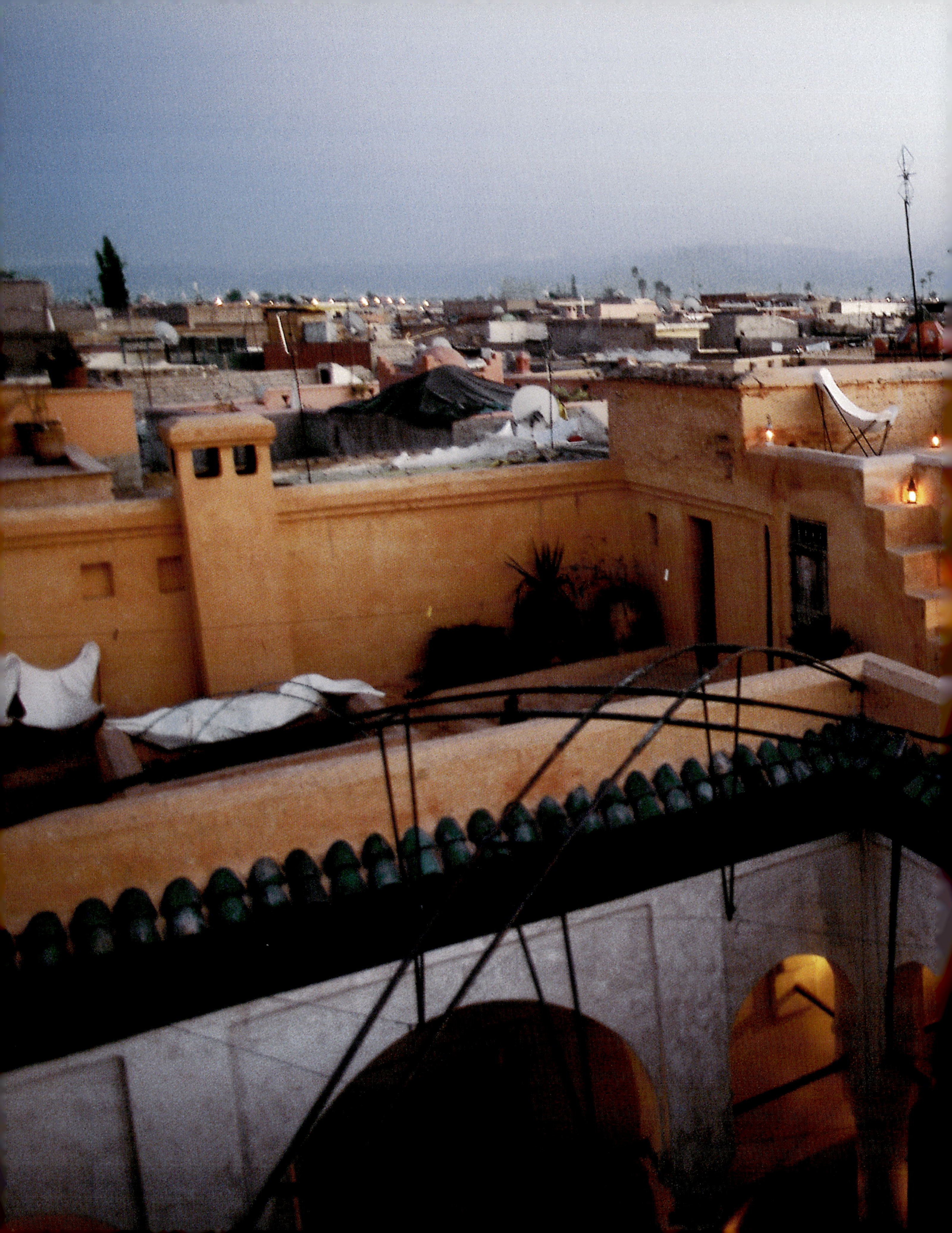

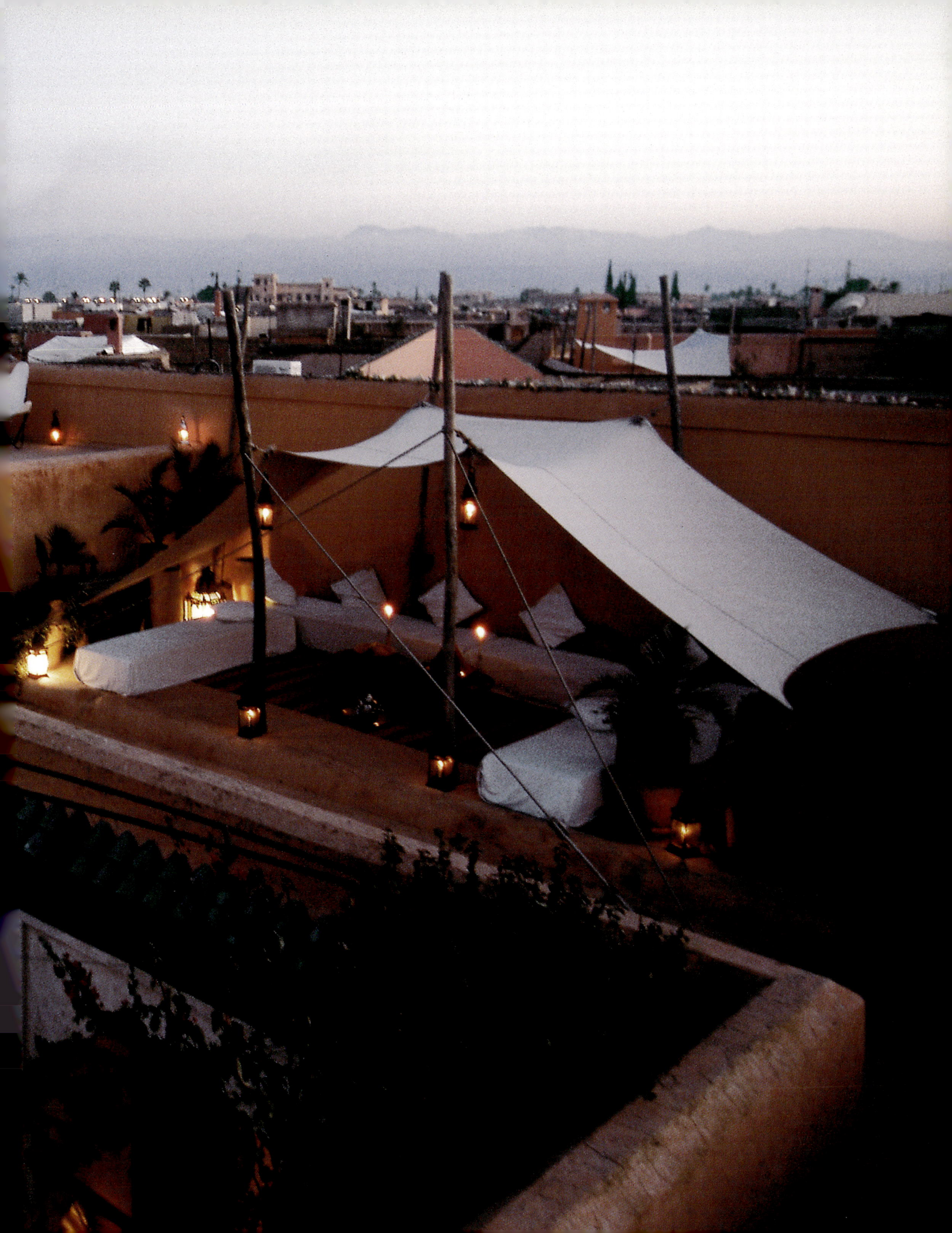

RIAD LAMRANI: THE MAGNIFICENT GARDEN

Located in the heart of the Mouassin quarter in the Marrakech medina, the Riad Lamrani is a paradigm of the Islamic garden. A verdant carpet split by two straight paths with a fountain at their intersection, the structure is a perfect homage to the pure classicism of the Persian tradition. The exuberant nature whose shadows stand out, violent, against the polychrome of the décor, here arouses the senses to the holy sensual delights.

Built in 1900, the *riad* was the home of the Lamrani, a family of high-ranking officials. The patio is vast—4,300 square feet (400 square meters)—and is covered with a canopy of foliage through which light plays as though cast through delicate prisms. Out from under the shade of palm trees extends an orchard that, in season, produces an abundance of sweet and bitter oranges, olives, bananas, figs, and even papayas. Below the polychromatic interlacing *zellij*, plots sprawl with plants and flowers such as papyri, bamboos, orchids, daturas, and roses. The scent of jasmine vines wafts through the arbor. Rose petals float in the marble fountain where the paths cross. Turtledoves coo with joy, having such a beautiful garden for their nest.

The décor of the house resonates in balance with the patio. The walls and pillars of the arcades are covered with *zellij* that state the theme of the

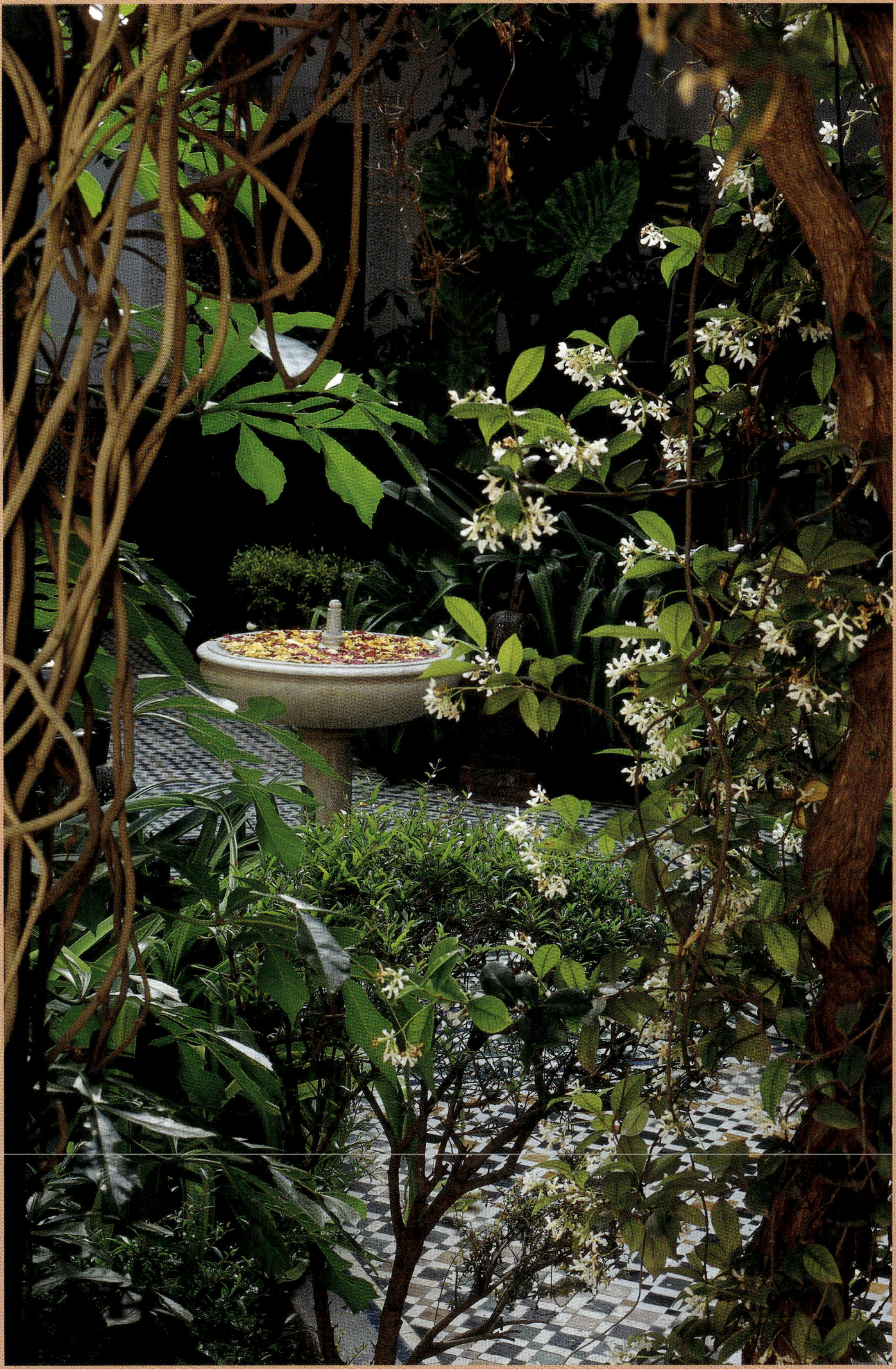

ABOVE AND OPPOSITE: Zellij *is a décor reserved for luxurious homes. The tiles climbing up to shoulder level keep clothes from getting soiled from the plaster or lime whitewash*

garden through rosettes and arabesques. This enamel pointillism is bordered with plaster friezes in which complicated plantlike compositions have been carved. On the windows, wrought-iron grilles with an Iberian influence repeat the flower motif in spirals and scrolls. At the threshold of the *riad*, a wall fountain springs forth in a multicolor mosaic.

It is likely that in 1900 the residence was even vaster. The Lamrani had set up a hitching courtyard, as was *de rigueur* for the homes of important people. In keeping with the upper classes of the time, the family had a decided preference for European and Eastern furnishings. Persian carpets covered the floors of the salons. Brought on the backs of camels by pilgrims returning from Mecca, these carpets were so much in vogue during the nineteenth century in Morocco and Europe that they were copied in Rabat, giving rise to the now-famous carpets of the Moroccan capital. Still a rarity, the tea, which was served in Saint-Louis crystal glasses, was brewed in Charles Wright silver-plated metal teapots imprinted with a double seal—

English and Arab. This manufacturer experienced a flourishing business in Morocco thanks to several families from Fès who were then living in Manchester. The clocks—rather prized possessions—would sound their chimes in the salons. Imported on European cargo ships and unloaded in Mogador (present-day Essaouira), mirrors in gilded frames, crystal hanging chandeliers, and simple glass Bohemian-style jewelry would then be carefully transported along the chaotic roadways of Morocco. Of all this furniture once owned by the Riad Lamrani, today there remain two exquisite copper canopy beds, which bear a stamp indicating their English provenance. As a sign of respect, the master of the house would invite his honored guests to sit on them. Martine Sageot, the present owner of the *riad*, preserves them, as if they held some of the soul of the house. At the bottom of an old well, she also found some old teapots and a Carrara marble sink basin. Conforming to the taste of the period, Sageot has furnished the *riad* with Victorian and Syrian pieces that she hunted down in London.

ABOVE AND OPPOSITE: *Just as was found in bourgeois homes, the furnishings of Riad Lamrani are a mix of Victorian, Syrian, and Moroccan styles*

Heaps of small antiques sit nestled in corners. A wealth of antique porcelain is laid out on the tables, its translucence enlivened by the soft light from the copper chandeliers. Old photographs and road maps dating from the 1930s adorn the walls, evoking that bygone era.

It has been sixteen years since Martine Sageot restored and embellished the Lamrani estate. It was a love for the Marrakech medina—where she had lived since 1969, even before the arrival of Yves Saint-Laurent and Pierre Bergé—that led her to the purchase. The *riad* is now as it had been at its birth; the cedar ceilings and the *behous* have been preserved intact. The *zouaqs* and *geps*, deemed in a sufficiently good state, were left untouched. Without having altered the basic structure, the secondary *douirias* that had previously been lofts have been converted into small bedrooms. The somewhat disproportionate roof over the kitchen has been retained, as has been the metal exhaust hood, which no doubt holds memories of the banquets of yesteryear. It is here that Martine Sageot makes her bitter orange marmalade from the fruit of her garden. Upon leaving, each of her guests receives a small jar as a gift, a provision for the journey bearing a nostalgia for the house-gardens of Marrakech. Over the years, the house has once again become what it was a century ago—a family house, lived in year-round and filled with the laughter of children.

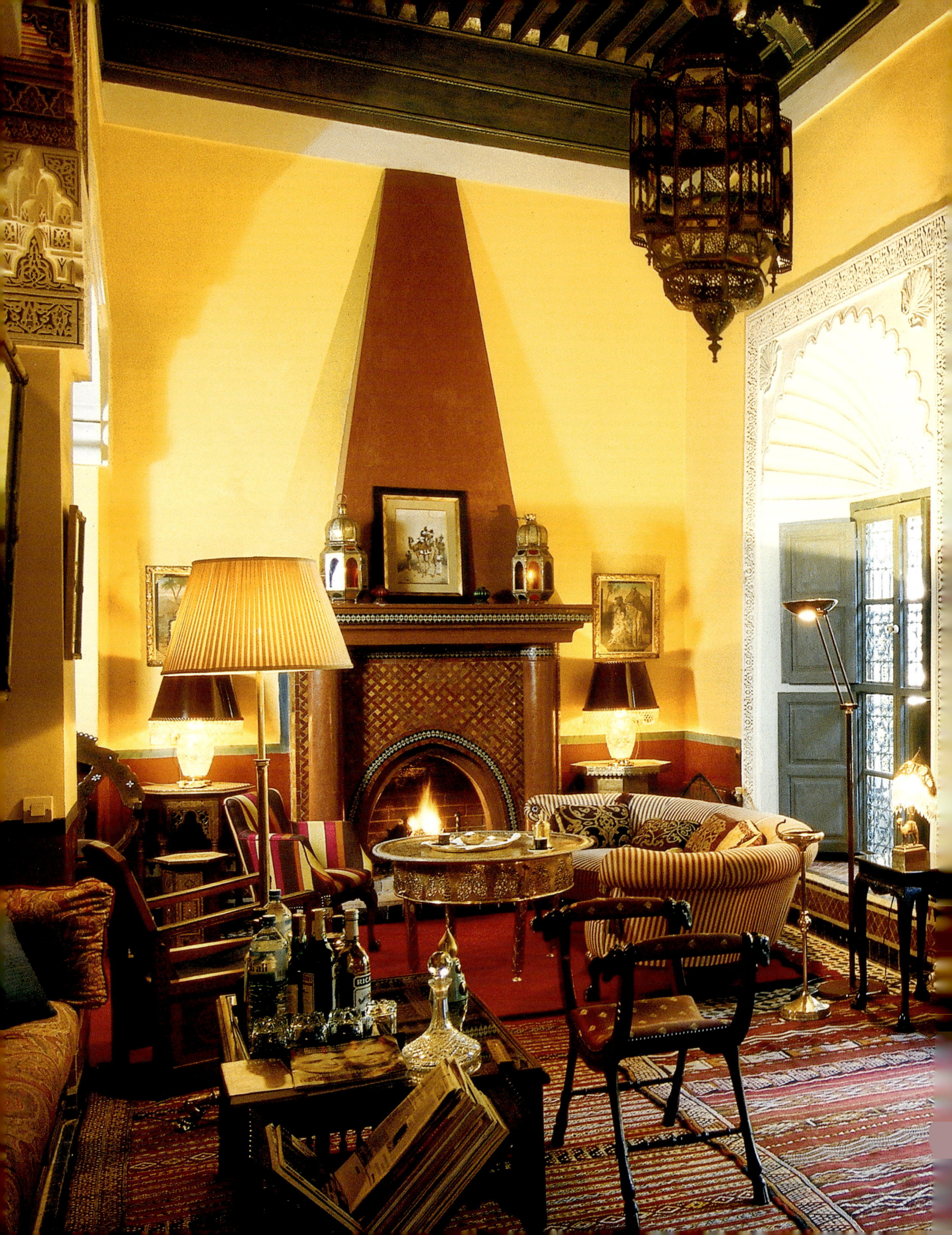

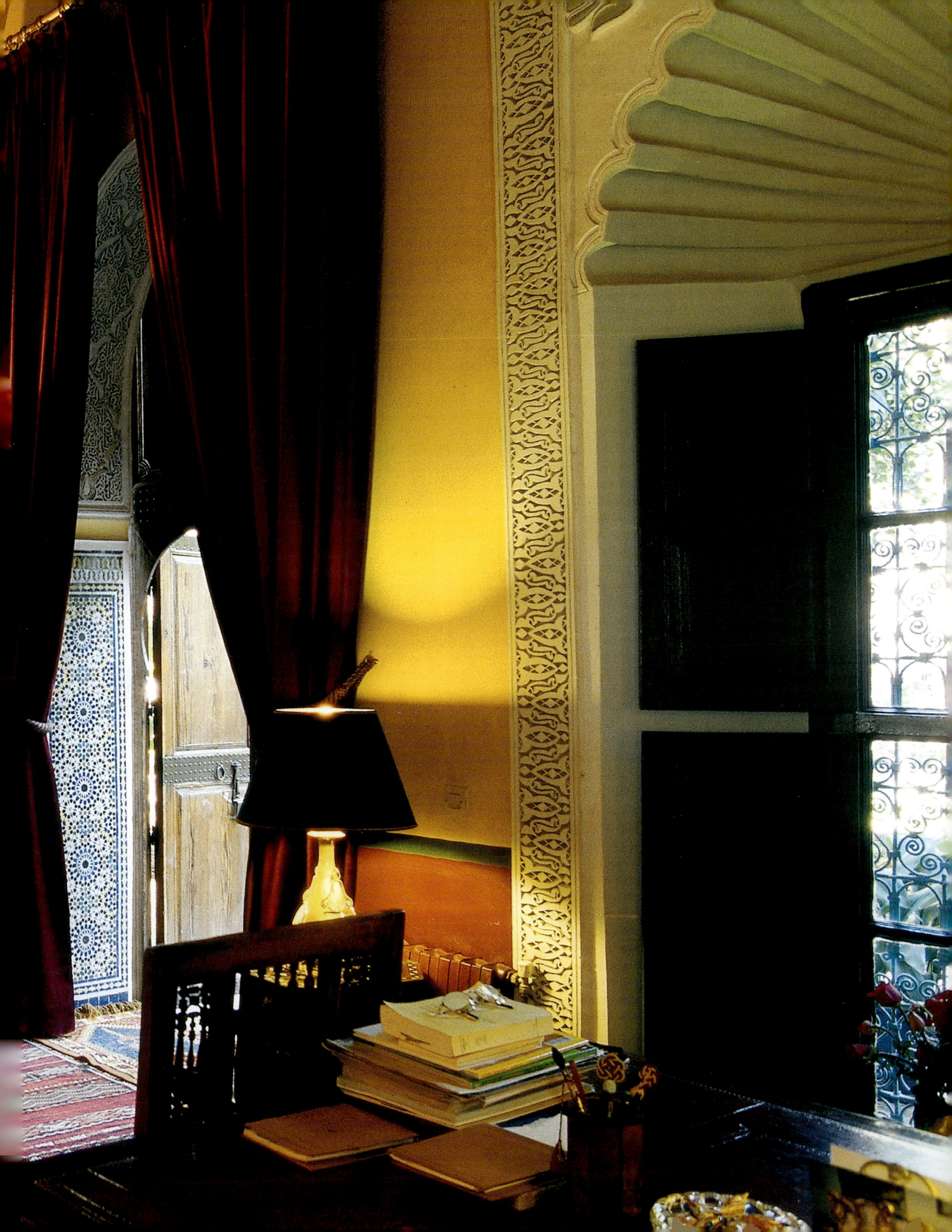

Essaouira

Built at the end of the eighteenth century on a site that had been baptized Mogador two centuries earlier by the resident Portuguese, Essaouira may well be one of the most picturesque medinas on the Atlantic coast. With exteriors of glistening white or saffron yellow with blue trim, the architecture is distinctive. Almost a rocky island jutting up against the waves, besieged by seagulls, it offers up its sturdy fortifications to the elements. Enclosed within the rocks and encircled by defensive walls armed with bronze cannons pointed seaward, Essaouira is well deserving of its Arabic name, "Little Rampart." The configuration of the walled town can easily be seen from the terrace of any house. The town is, after all, only an expanse of seventeen acres (seven hectares). Known for its climate, exceptionally temperate for the region, with summer and winter temperatures in the 70s Fahrenheit (20s Celsius), the town is battered by violent summer winds that locals have ironically named Wled el-Bled: "Child of the Country." As protection against the winds, the alleyways are really covered arcades, men wear the *burnous* (a heavy, full-length cloak with a tasseled hood), and women still wrap themselves in the old-fashioned manner in white woolen *haiks* that completely conceal them. The region is rich in sedimentary rocks and houses built of stone in a style that is true to the character of the city.

A COSMOPOLITAN TRADING POST

Essaouira—Is it Berber, African, Portuguese, or Arabo-Andalusian? Rubber plants harmoniously grow side by side with araucarias. And with its blue and white striped awnings and Vauban-style ramparts, the city even boasts a subtle Brittany influence. It is, in fact, the sister-port of Saint-Malo.

✦ A New and Eccentric Medina

History has bestowed upon this medina a distinctive charm that sets it apart from all others in Morocco. Created *ex nihilo* by the Alaouite sultan Sidi Muhammad ben Abdallah in 1760 at the intersection of the maritime and inland Saharan routes, Essaouira was built on a completely original design. He entrusted the project to the French urban architect Théodore Cornut, who preferred broader, octagonal medinas to the conventional labyrinthine form. There would be no risk of getting lost, even in the knot of less rectilinear streets that ran adjacent and so often, as in all medinas, led to dead-ends. A pioneer city conceived as an international trading post where caravans would come to relieve the cargo ships of their goods, the sultan populated it by recruiting people from all corners of the country. As some commercial transactions were taboo for Muslims, these were delegated to Jews or Christians, or even to the Sudanese slaves of French military conscripts. In time, these slaves infused their Saharan culture—with its rituals, music, and dance of the Gnaoua brotherhood—into the city's life. The Jewish legacy to the city has been the art of jewelrymaking, while the Europeans, primarily businessmen and consuls, proudly built houses in the affluent districts that addressed the needs of storage and commerce. Eighteen syndicates represented different European nations, among them England, Germany, Italy, Switzerland, France, Denmark, and, above all, Spain, whose nationals accounted for a third of the foreign population.

RIGHT:
Constructed in the eighteenth century on a peninsula, Essaouira rises up in front of the Atlantic Ocean

PAGES 132–33:
The exteriors of houses in Essaouira are endowed with windows and the doors display polychrome pediments

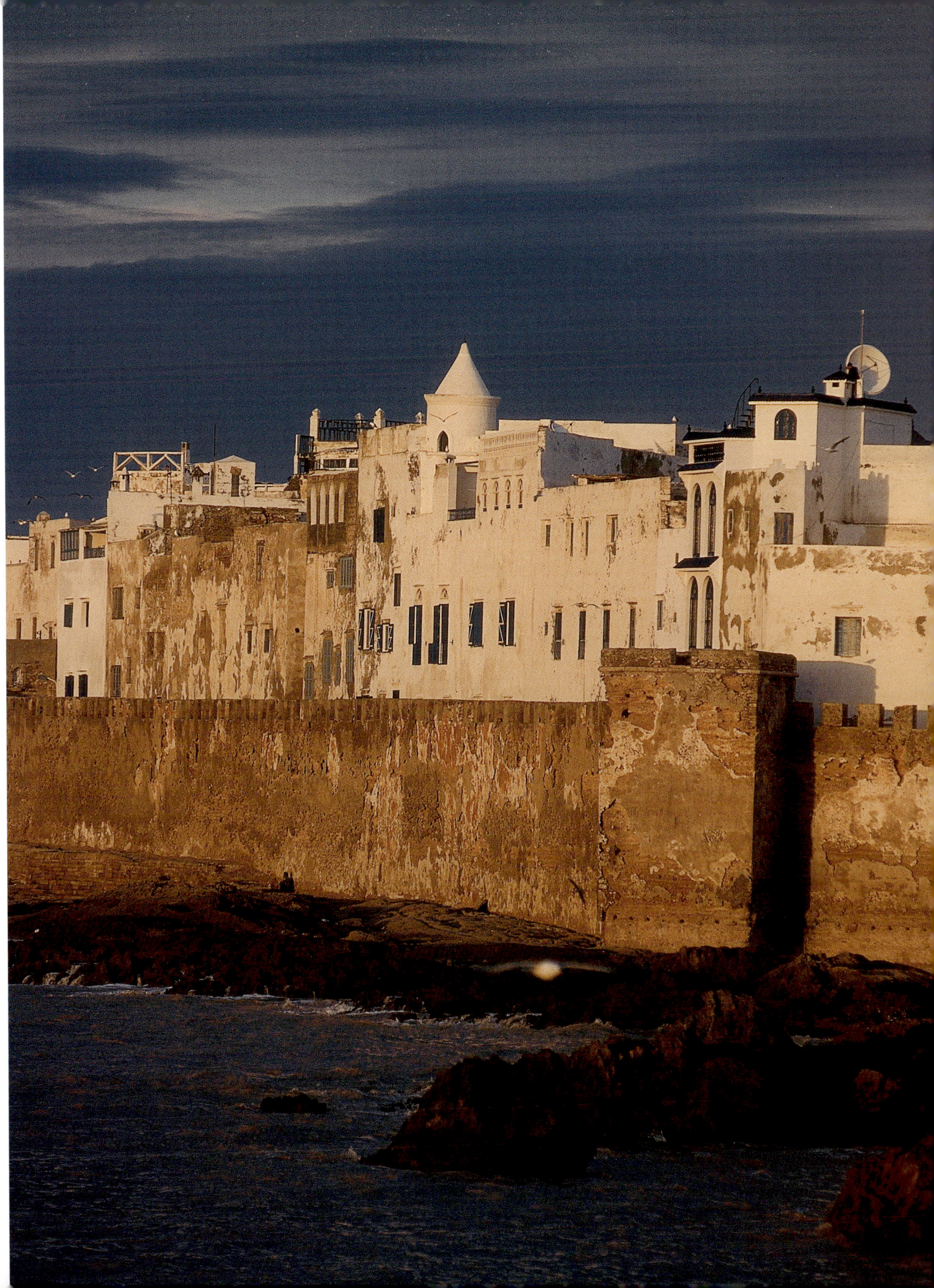

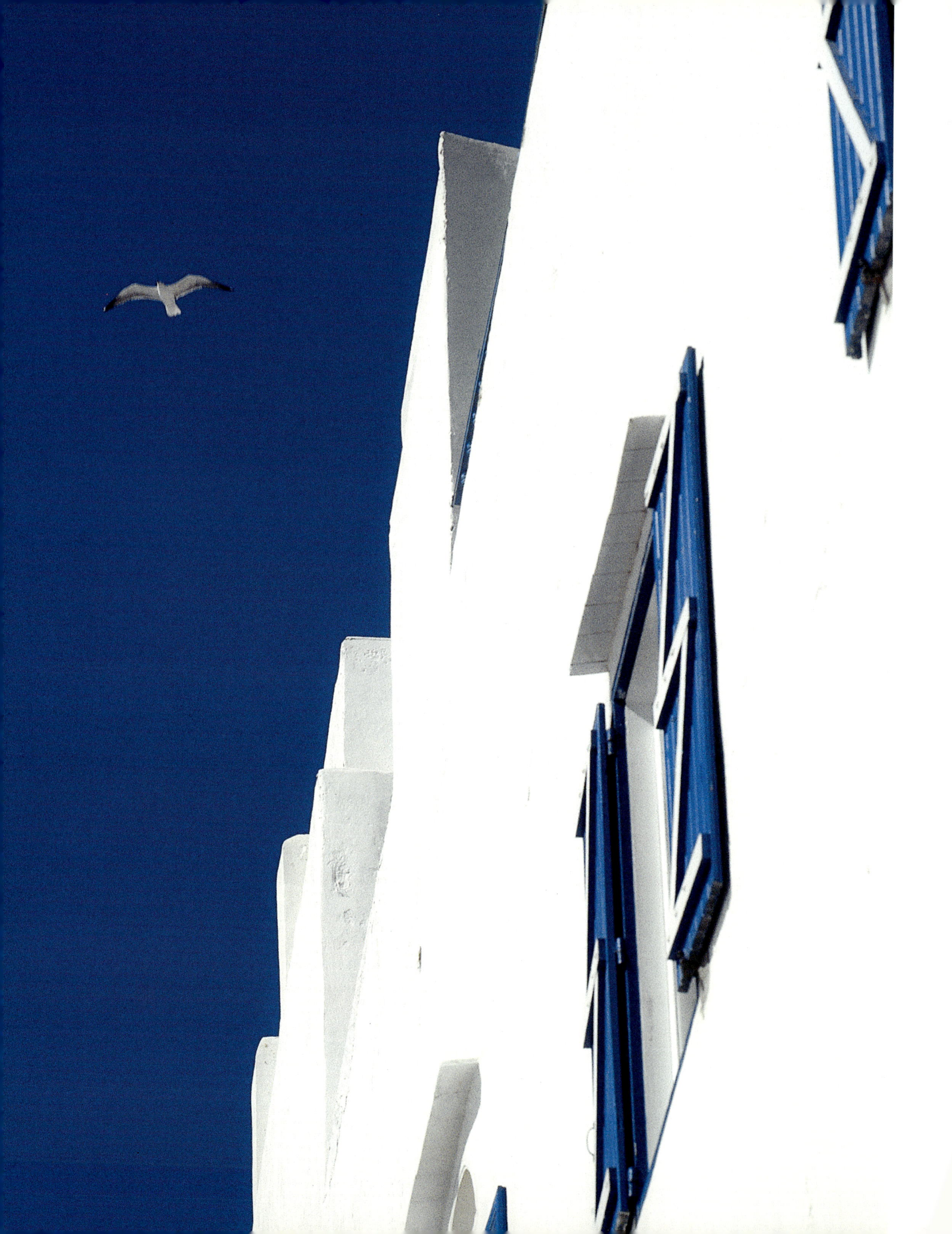

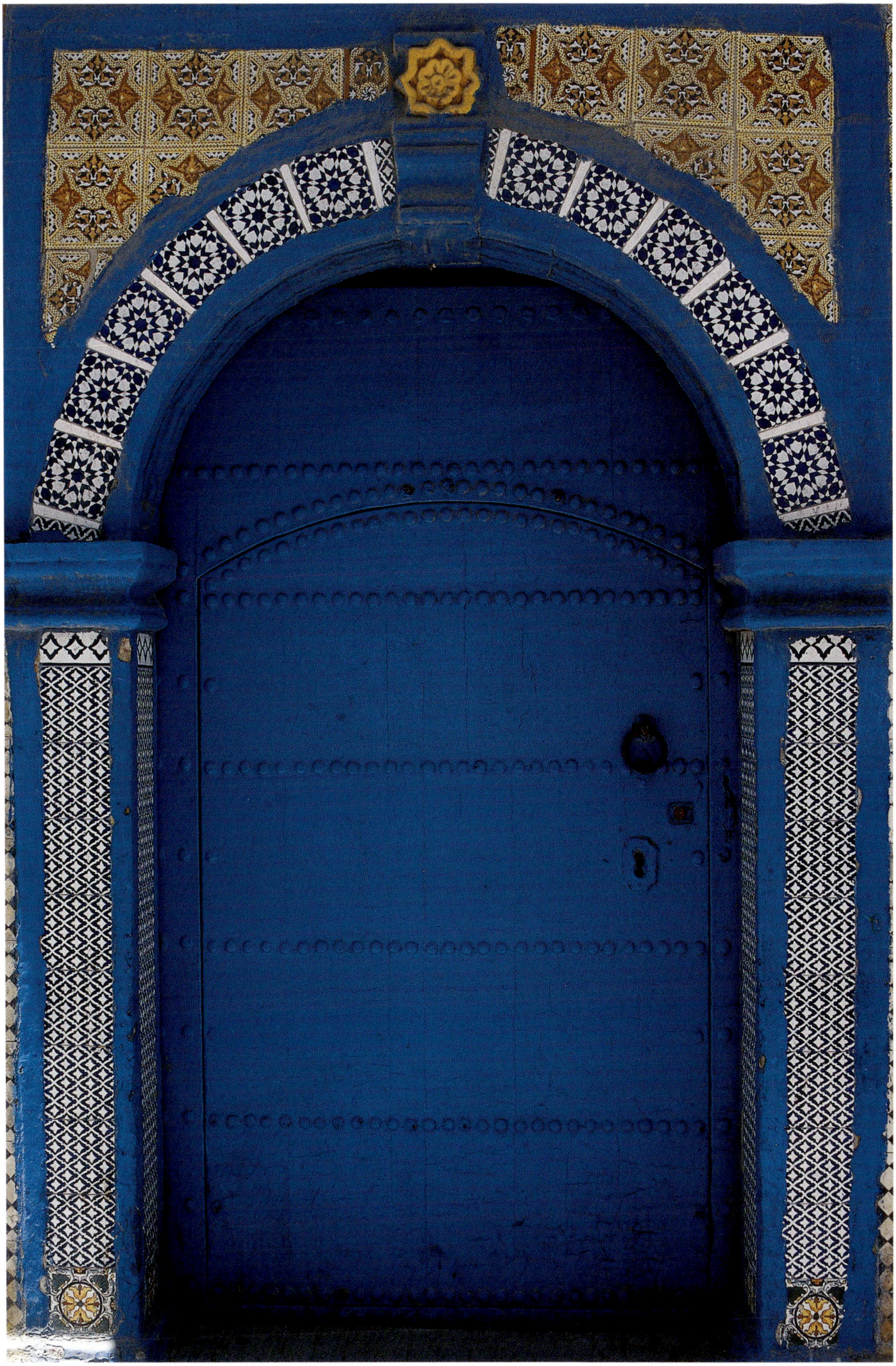

Essaouira confronts the violence of the trade winds with a solid stone architecture that keeps alive its vocation as a port.

While today Essaouira may merely be a small fishing port, it holds in its walls its cosmopolitan past. Following the Andalusian tradition, houses are always bright white, their walls and terraces regularly whitewashed. Façades are punctuated with windows, all with blue painted shutters. The yellow-washed stone pediments seem to evoke the color of the beach that stretches down the coast, far beyond the city walls.

OPPOSITE AND ABOVE: *The patios of the old trading posts are spacious and open directly onto the streets, for easy access to transport*

PAGES 136–37: *The stone columns and arcades at Dar Zorzor are typical of houses in Essaouira*

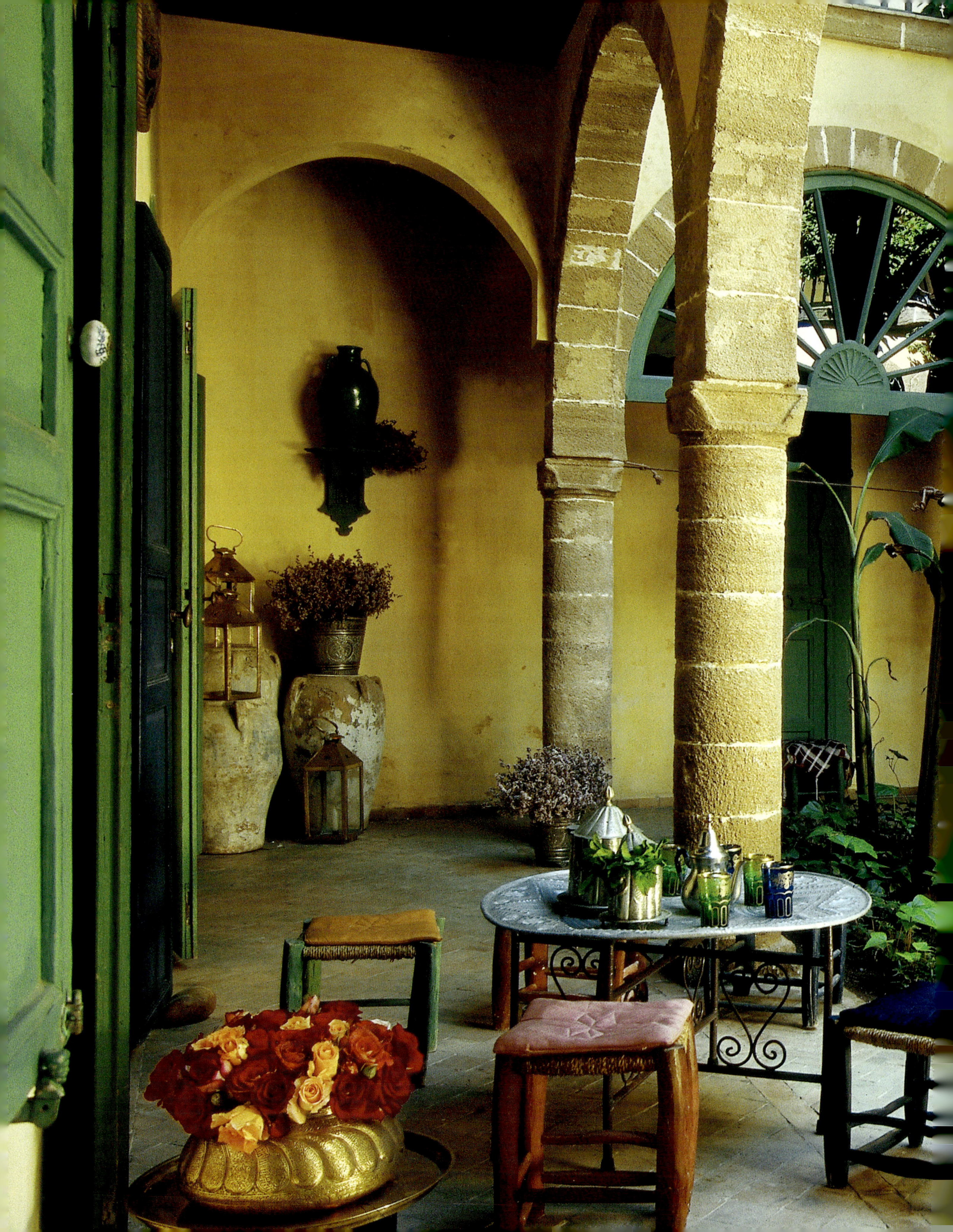

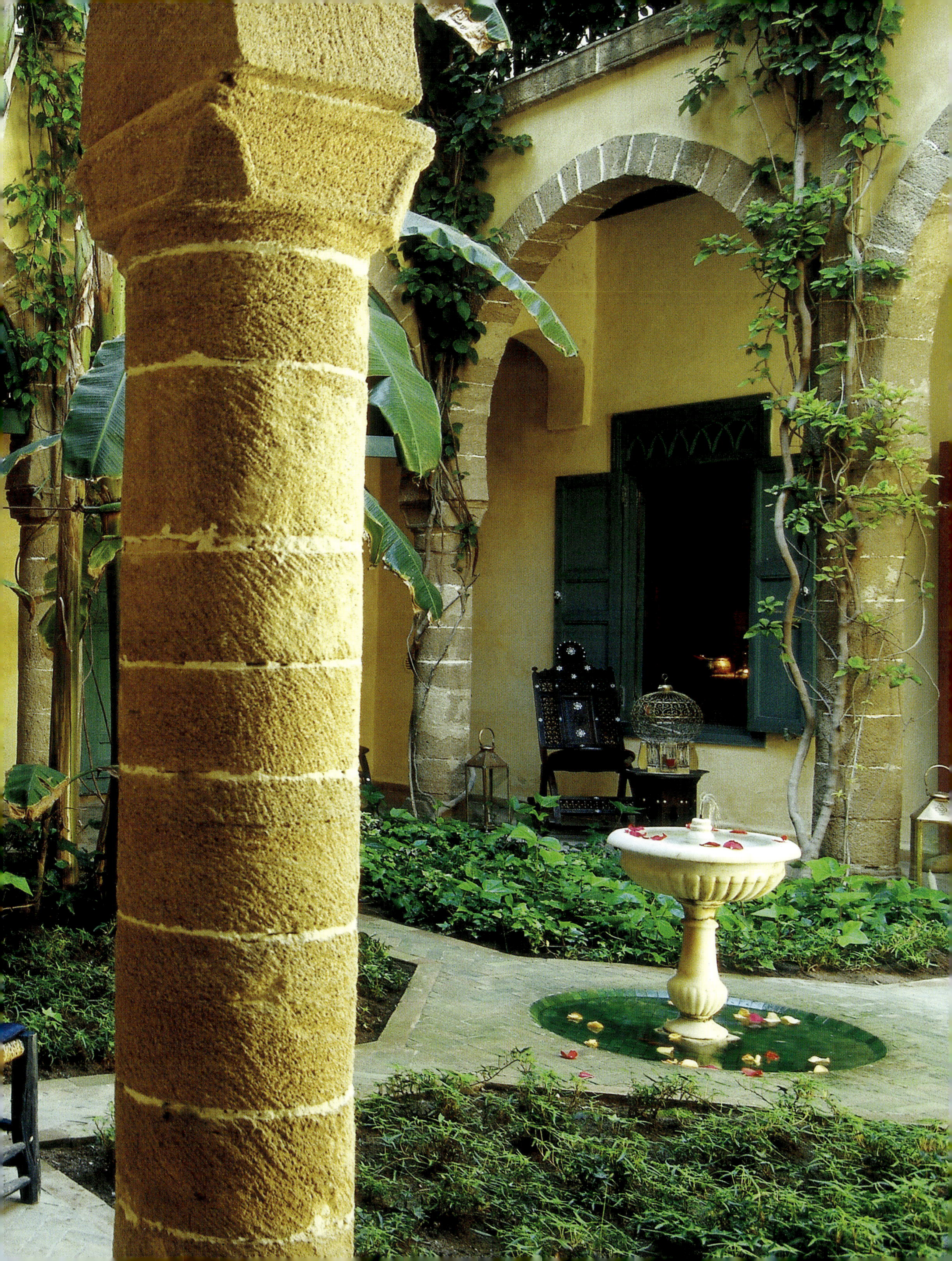

✦ Patios Made of Stone and Wood

Essaouira has confronted the violence of the ocean with solid stone architecture. But the stone is also an element used in the décor. Upon entering a patio of a bourgeois house, one is immediately struck by the elegance of the tall and slender columns that support the galleries. The yellow stone said to be from Salé is used alongside pink sandstone from Essaouira. Capitals are adorned with carved motifs that often include the famous six-petaled rose called "the rose of Mogador." In addition to the arcades, stone is used on window frames and façades, as well as carved into basins for the central fountains in patios.

The buildings of the former European businessmen not only were used as warehouses, but also had to provide quarters for visiting merchants and were endowed with some of the most beautiful stone patios in the city. Their architecture evokes a *fondouk* (caravanserai), with its vast central courtyard surrounded by a circular gallery, whose second story was furnished with eight to ten residential rooms, as the ground floor was reserved for business dealings. The zigzag entryway had been eliminated, thus the courtyard opens directly onto the street to facilitate the movement of the goods. Terraces were equipped with European-style watchtowers, making it possible to oversee

ABOVE:
Riad Damgaard is furnished in the regional style with thuya wood and Zemmour woven blankets

RIGHT:
Casa Lila

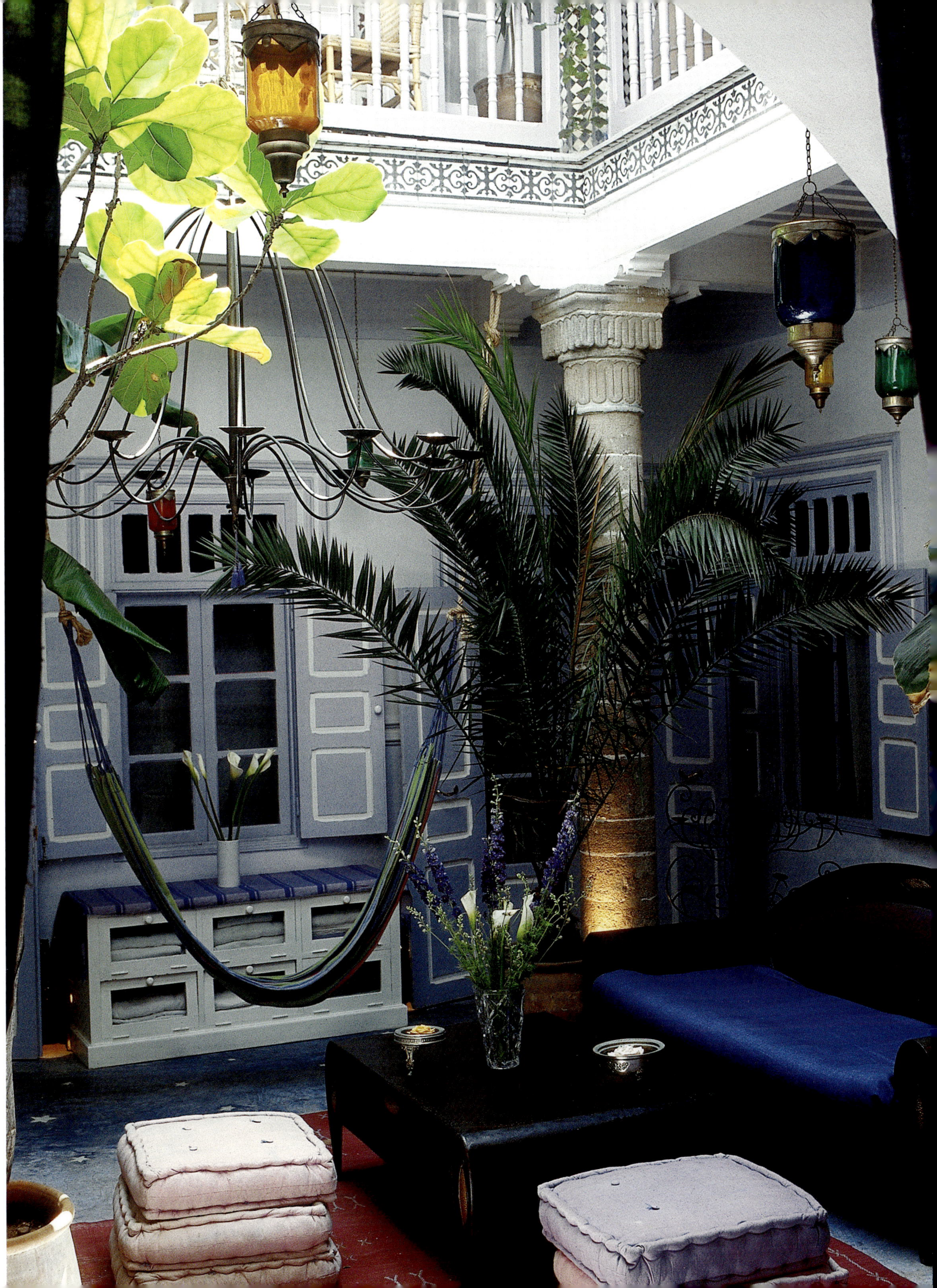

the dealings. Exterior façades are punctuated with windows that sport grilles with decorative leaf-like arabesques.

Until the nineteenth century, ironwork was essentially reserved for farming implements and was something for the servant classes. With the European influence, its usage expanded to include architectural décor, in particular, window grilles that were as much ornamental as they were protective. Hispano-Moresque in origin, these grilles were first used in the Spanish-influenced cities along the Atlantic coast of El-Jadida and Mogador. They were then adopted throughout the kingdom. Some are works of great beauty, veiling the countryside in a fine black, white, or golden-colored lace, which, on occasion, is even copper-plated. The foliage designs that twist in spirals and scrolls are affixed with links to an iron grid.

Houses in Essaouira are also distinctive because of their expansive use of tamarisk and thuya (*arar* in Arabic), two woods that grow in abundance in the region. Thuya has a delicate reddish-brown color and like cedar, it is fragrant and does not rot. But it is less submissive to the sculptor's chisel and is far too resinous for painted decorations. This is why decorated ceilings are nowhere to be found in Essaouira. On the other hand, thuya was often used for furniture. Inlaid in the Syrian style of marquetry with mother-of-pearl, ebony, lemonwood, ivory, and even camel bone, which the caravans supplied in great quantities, the wood was used for tables, chairs, stools, and other everyday objects. Ever since the 1920s, more and more artisans have returned to the burred grain of the thuya tree, so highly treasured by foreigners. To this day, houses in Essaouira overflow with European, African, and even Asian relics, and the local antique shops are still filled with Jewish liturgical objects. This is a testament to the unusual destiny of this city born solely of the desires of one prince who caressed the dream of opening the Cherifian Empire to foreign nations.

OPPOSITE AND ABOVE:
As thuya wood is highly resinous, it cannot be painted. It is, however, often used in marquetry

PAGES 142–43:
Patio of the Villa Baghdad

ESSAOUIRA 141

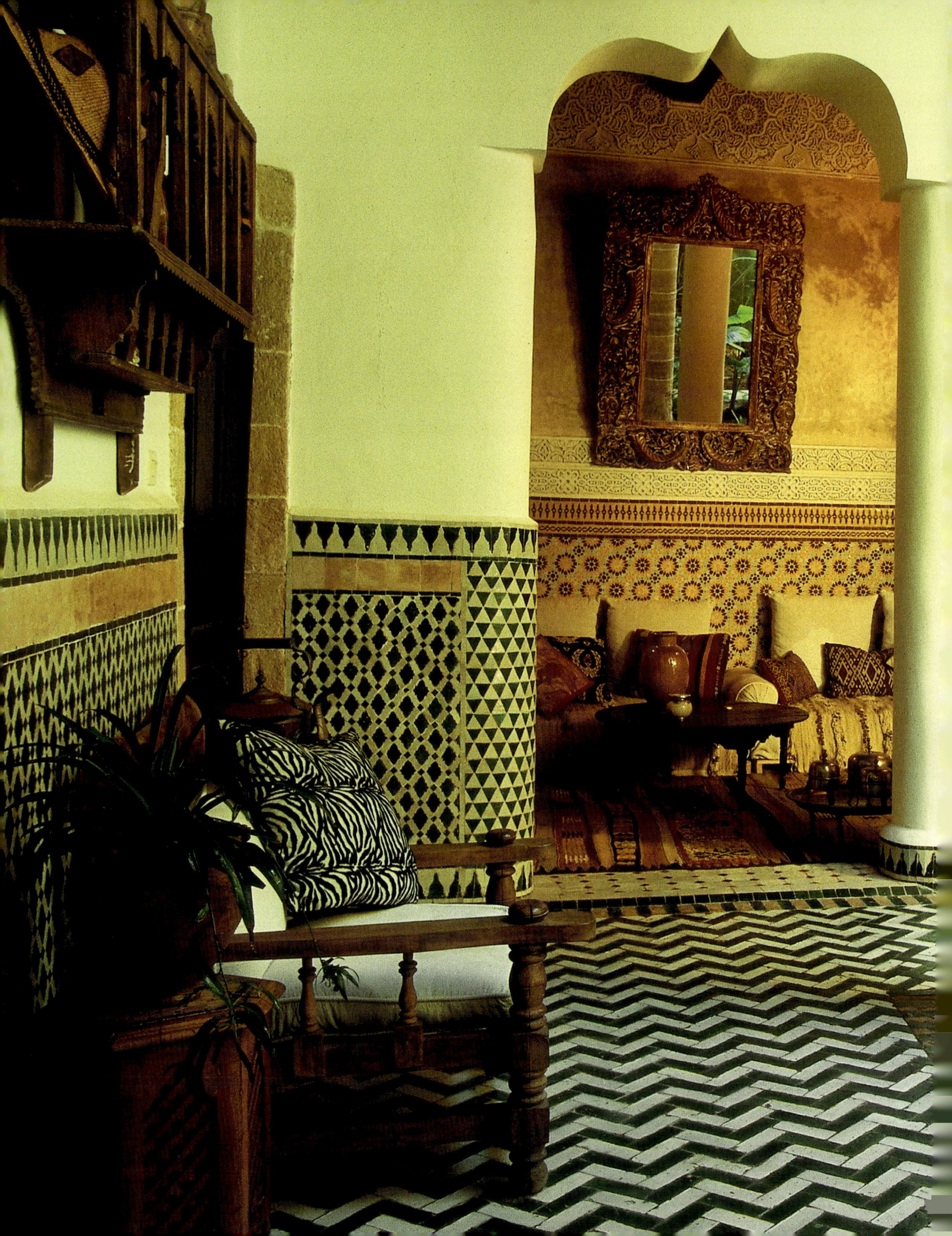

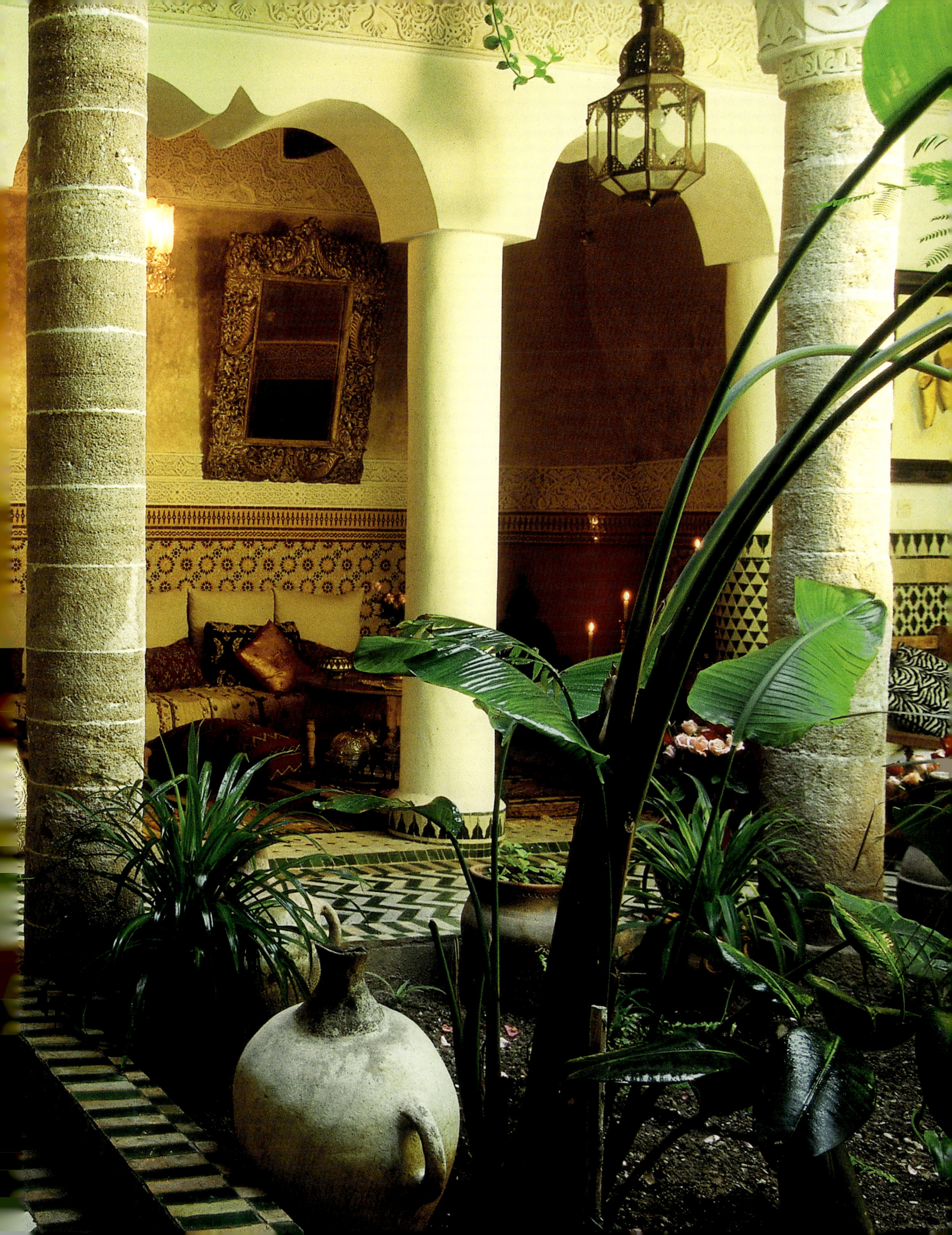

VILLA BAGHDAD: AN ALCHEMY OF AFRICA AND THE EAST

In the amalgam that is the city of Essaouira, Villa Baghdad aptly offers its guests a décor and ambience that will transport them back into a colonial adventure. Built in the nineteenth century of stone from Salé and thuya wood, and carefully renovated, the villa exemplifies the characteristic principles of Essaouiran residential architecture.

The former estate of wealthy Berber kaids, landowners of the Smimou region, Villa Baghdad, like all homes of prominent people, is at the end of a cul-de-sac. Near the medina gate Bab Doukkala in the working-class Chbanat district, access is through a *derb* filled with the yeasty aromas of a bread oven. The constant comings and goings of pedestrians, bicycles, donkeys, motorbikes, and *carrossa* (pushcarts hauled by men in threadbare *burnous*) bring life to the quarter. The atmosphere here is particularly feverish at the end of the day, when crowds of people make their way. But pass into the home and onto the porch and the clamor recedes, yielding to the calm, sweet song of the birds.

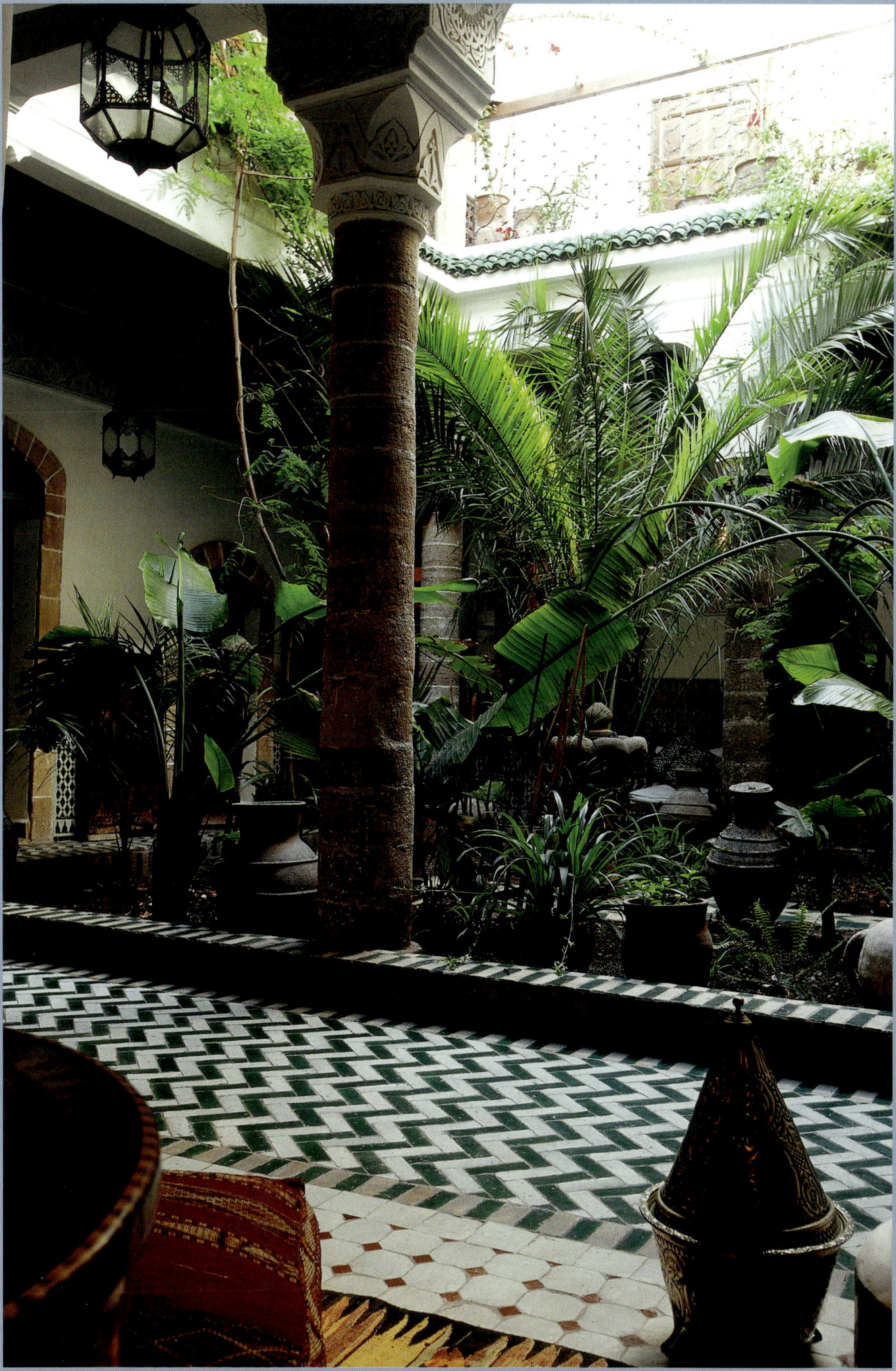

ABOVE AND
FOLLOWING PAGES:
*The owners are collectors
"without borders"*

    The patio is home to a dense garden filled with banana trees, palm trees, and Nile papyri that reflect in their delicate leaves the soft hue of the six stone columns supporting the galleries. These slender columns, with their carved plaster capitals, are characteristic of bourgeois houses on the Atlantic coast. The floors are completely devoid of ostentation—merely terracotta interposed with an emerald green *zellij* set in a chevron pattern. In keeping with the rural tradition, ceilings are a simple construction of thuya and acacia branches grown shiny with the passage of time. They serve as reminders that Essaouira—different from Fès, Marrakech, and Meknes—was never an imperial city.
    The old structure of the house is there to be seen almost perfectly intact. The original front door and the zigzagging entryway remain, as do the original wells, storage rooms, and the independent guesthouse

(*douiria*). Although today the *douiria* has an opening directly onto the patio, the original street access still exists and the residence is constructed around a column of light from the ceiling. The bathrooms have been placed in the corners and tiled with *zellij*. In a gentle bow to the East, dressing areas have been set off behind wooden screens turned in the *moucharabieh* style.

When Michel and Caroline Daheb bought the villa in 1995 they had already spent much time in Morocco. Like many residences in the medina, the house had been divided into separate apartments and marred by modern refacings that had completely covered over the original ornamentation. The present owners patiently restored the building over a three-year period and then transformed it into a guesthouse. Passionate about Africa and the East, they furnished the eight rooms in an original

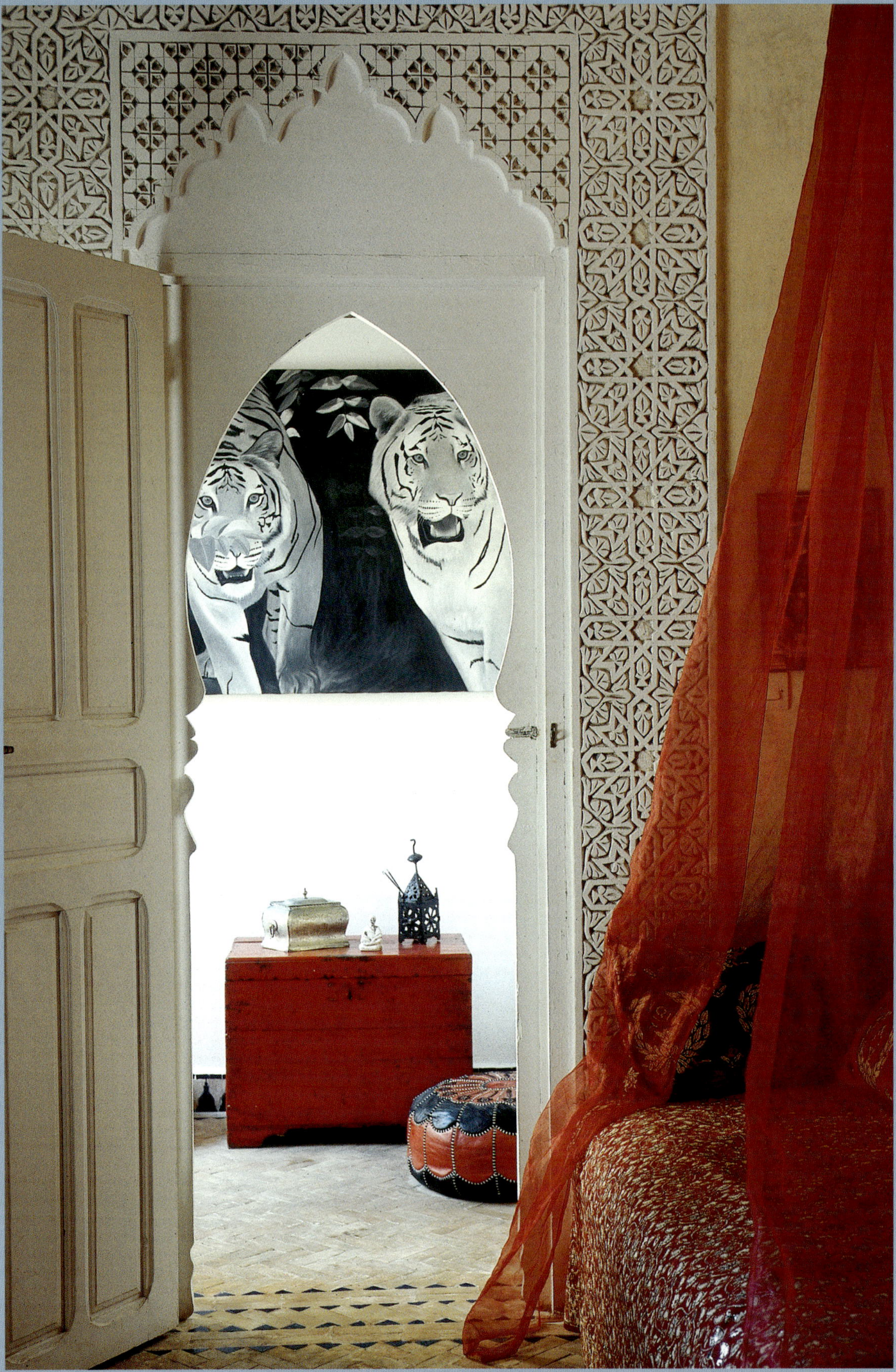

style with the flair of collectors. The Berber room has an array of traditional dress belts and henna-dyed fabrics, while the Fezzi room displays pottery and wedding caftans. The African room is decorated with ceremonial masks, pillows adorned with cowry shells, and fabrics the color of the savannah. The Indian room glistens with shimmering fabrics and the Moresque room is ablaze in shades of purple. The Touareg, Mauritanian, and Saharan rooms, located on the enormous two-story roof terrace, are decorated with leather handicrafts.

    The salons, each with a *tadelact* fireplace for keeping warm on those evenings of the great winds, present a graceful blend of Moroccan, African, and Asian styles. The *bejmat* floors are covered with *Zemmour* woven blankets and the sofas have been reupholstered either in white cloths adorned with sequins from the Middle Atlas region or with *haiks* woven in the workshops in the medina. Some of them that had been woven in a blend of black and white threads have naturally taken on the somber and elegant ecru color of linen. The pillow covers have gold and silver threads incorporated into the magenta velvet—that is, those that are not imitation panther. The mirrors from India rival those from Murano and are so prized in Morocco that many reproductions are now manufactured in Fès. The tables are examples of the old marquetry typical of Essaouira. Antiques, such as a bride's chair and *fantasia* saddles, are scattered about. The masters of the house are avid collectors "without borders." Paintings in the Orientalist style hang comfortably side by side with tapestries from Lyons.

But the soul of the house—a good reason for a long stay—abides in the collection of old posters, postcards, and black-and-white photographs.

ABOVE:
A collection of old photographs designed to evoke the colonial period

PAGES 152–53:
The roof terrace has three bedrooms decorated in Saharan style

These images are found in each room, evoking the "scenes and faces" of the colonial empire. The observant visitor wandering upstairs will even discover a series of shots of Farid El Atrach, perhaps one of the most popular singers in the Arab world, posing for a film with the titillating title *The Sheik in His Harem*.

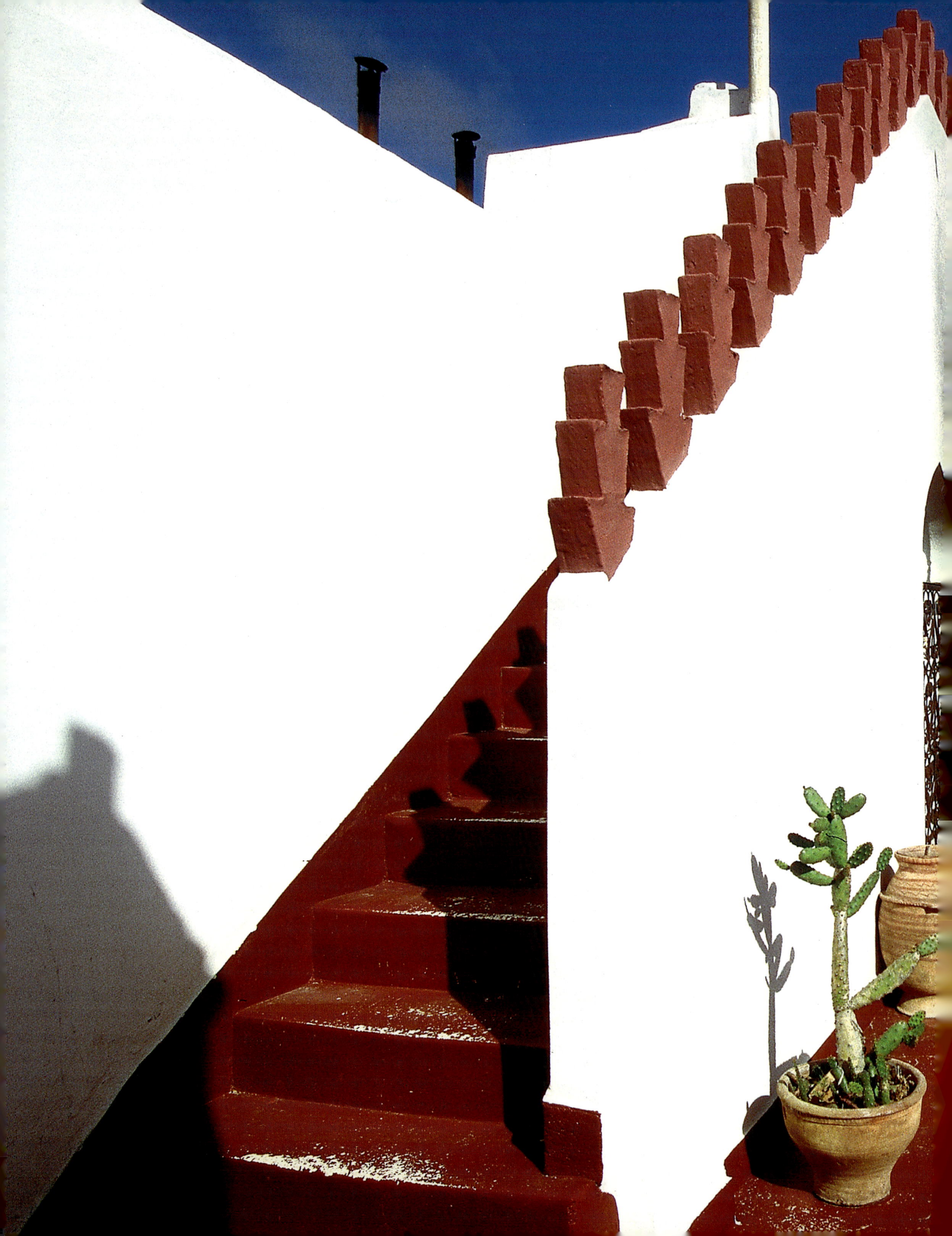

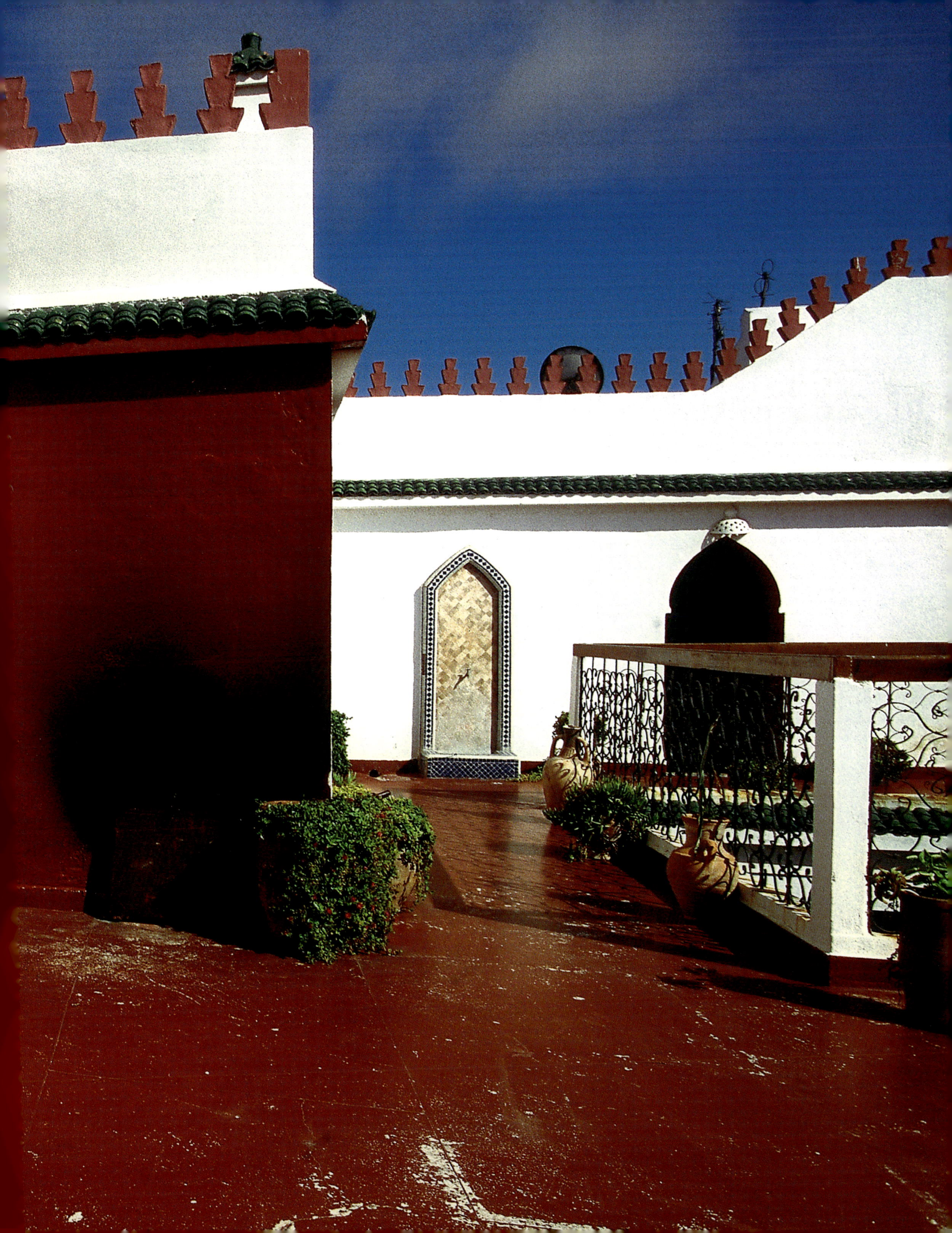

Kasbahs of the Oases

The architectural wonders of Morocco are not solely concentrated in the cities; nor is the art of living. While man's mark on the face of that earth may be rare and humble, the countryside throughout the kingdom is filled with unexpected delights. Stone and clay hamlets, bordered with hedges of aloes and Barbary figs, are to be found across the plains. In the High Atlas Mountains, villages perched on the hillsides overlook small, meticulously cultivated fields as if they were garret-citadels sitting atop rocky spurs. Beyond the mountains, at the edge of the desert, majestic kasbahs punctuate the Dra, Drades, and Tafilalt Valleys. Whether somewhat in the distance or merely set apart behind a rampart, an established agricultural center flourishes at the feet of these kasbahs, reliant upon an ingenious network of canals, *khettaras* (underground irrigation systems), and *seguias* (irrigation canals) to irrigate even the smallest of plots. In those parts of Morocco where rainfall is scarce, water is life. Along the vast wadis on the south side of the Atlas, kasbahs sprout up in the middle of groves palm, date, and olive trees in whose shadows barley, small amounts of wheat, vegetables, henna, and roses are cultivated. Beyond the oases, in the sprawling arid and barren steppes with their soaring birds of prey, nomadic shepherds live in black woolen tents.

AN ARCHITECTURE UNIQUE TO NORTH AFRICA

Kasbahs constitute one of Morocco's richest heritages. They are nowhere to be found in the north or the west of the country. Unique to oases, these residences are concentrated in the southern extents of the eastern High Atlas Mountains and they disappear just where the wadis become lost in the sands of the Sahara. There are some, however, that have been constructed in the region surrounding Marrakech.

Thanks to the early twentieth-century paintings of Jacques Majorelle, European travelers were familiar with the kasbah's proud silhouette so in harmony with its landscape. Their architectural archetype is unique to the Maghrib. Likely born of the desert civilizations that had settled alongside the Ziz wadi in the ancient city of Sijilmassa during the first centuries of Islamic history, the architecture admired today rarely dates from earlier than the first quarter of the nineteenth century. Built with slits that resemble loopholes in a fortified wall, spiked with corner turrets topped with merlons that have been worn away by erosion, they could be taken for something out of the European Middle Ages.

Constructed from indigenous mud or clay, kasbahs are of the same color that dominates the valley. Ranging from simple and refined lines to the sophisticated contours of the decorations on the upper portions of the building, they present a striking exoticism that is both austere and fragile. Might they have been feudal fortresses where a tyrant exerted his power, or perhaps, fairy-like castles that materialized from *Tales from A Thousand and One Nights*?

The thick kasbah walls that rise up skyward as high as sixty-five feet (twenty meters) are reminders of the turbulent past of these oases, fraught with tribal wars. The structures, invariably quadrangular and massive, were flanked by towers at each corner for keeping a watch over the valley.

RIGHT:
The Ksar Ait Ben Haddou has been classified as a World Heritage Site by UNESCO. It was constructed completely of earth, using no lime for binding

PAGES 158–59:
The Kasbah Taourirt was the Ouarzazate residence of the Glaoui

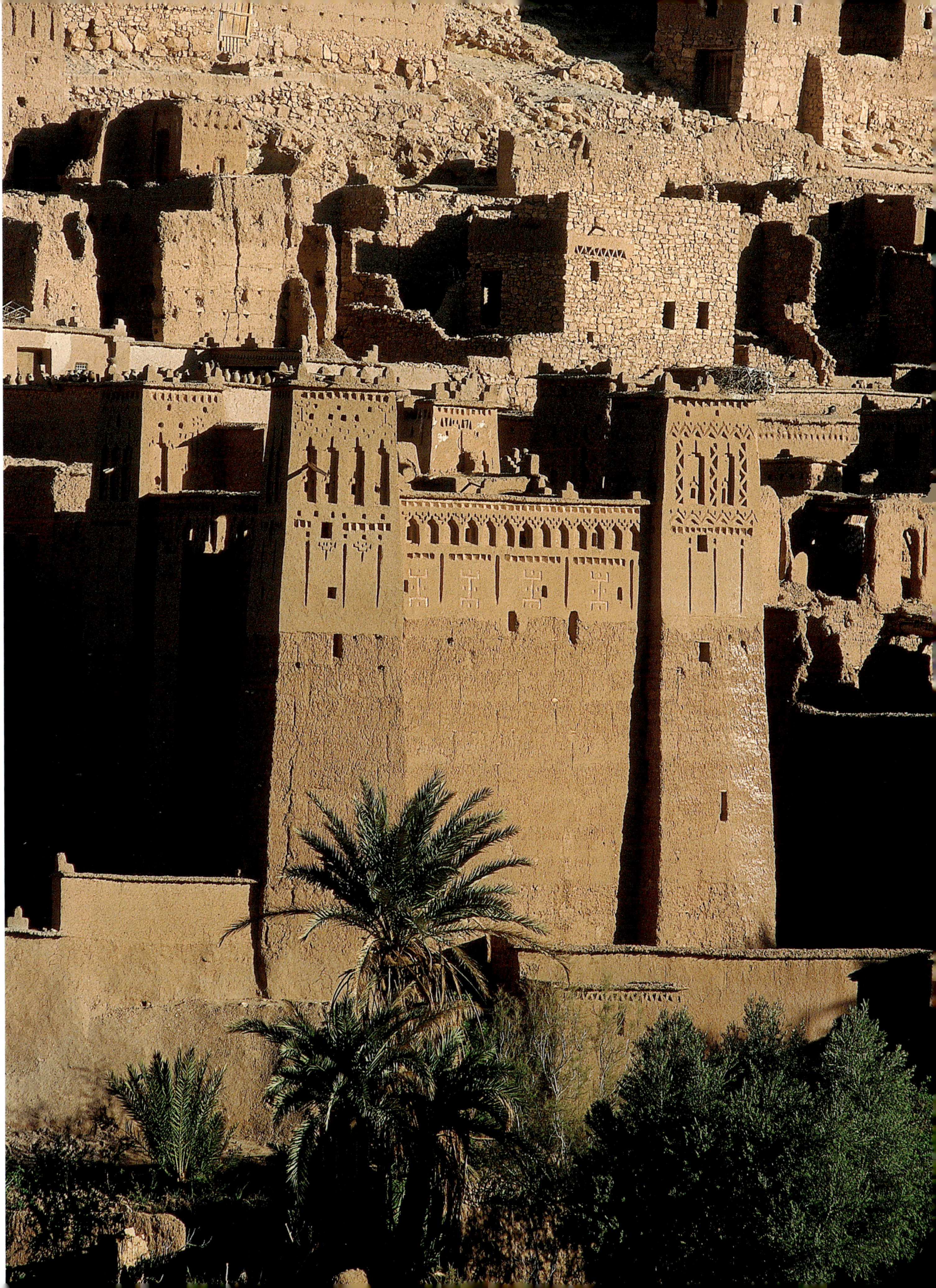

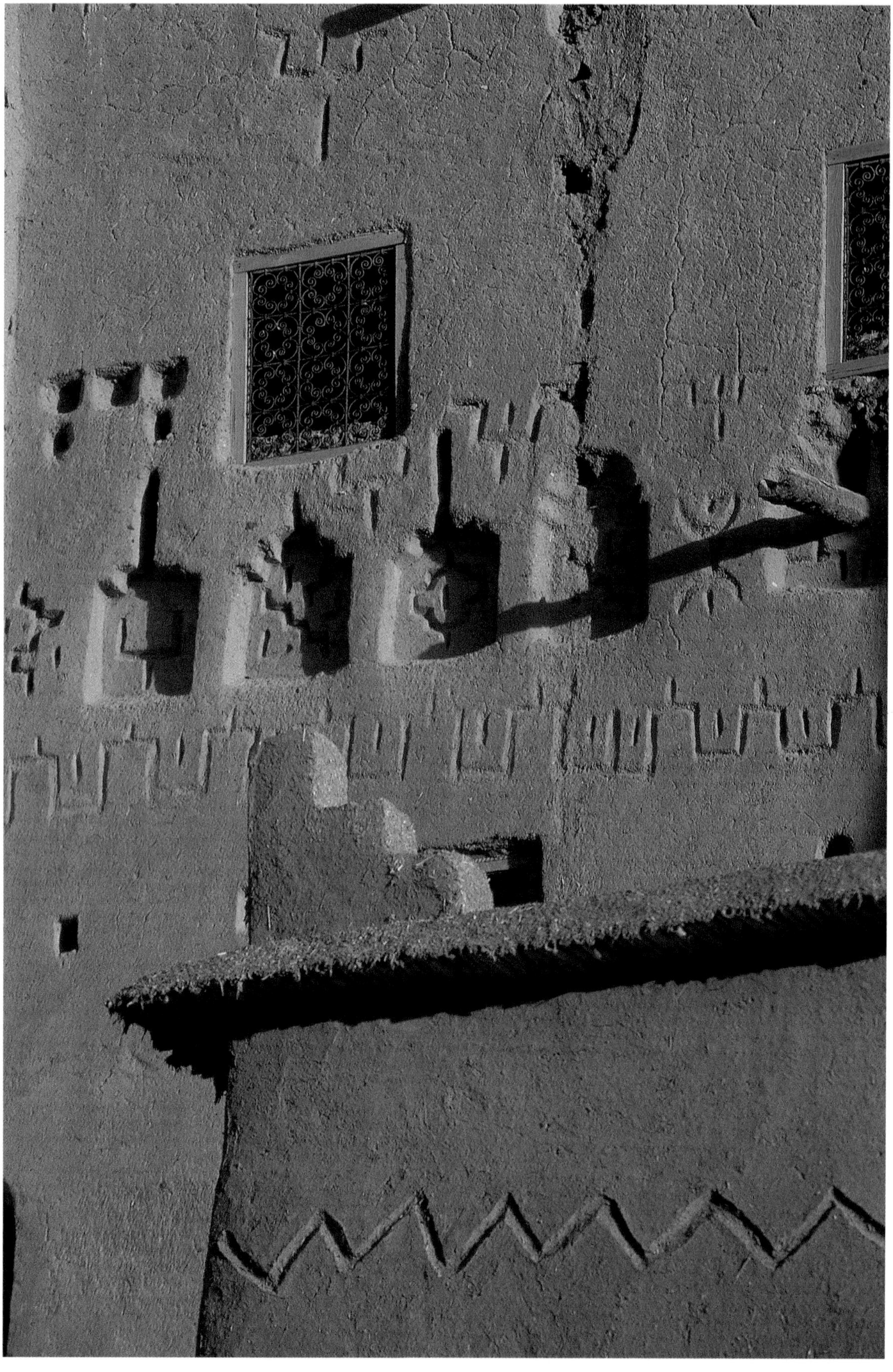

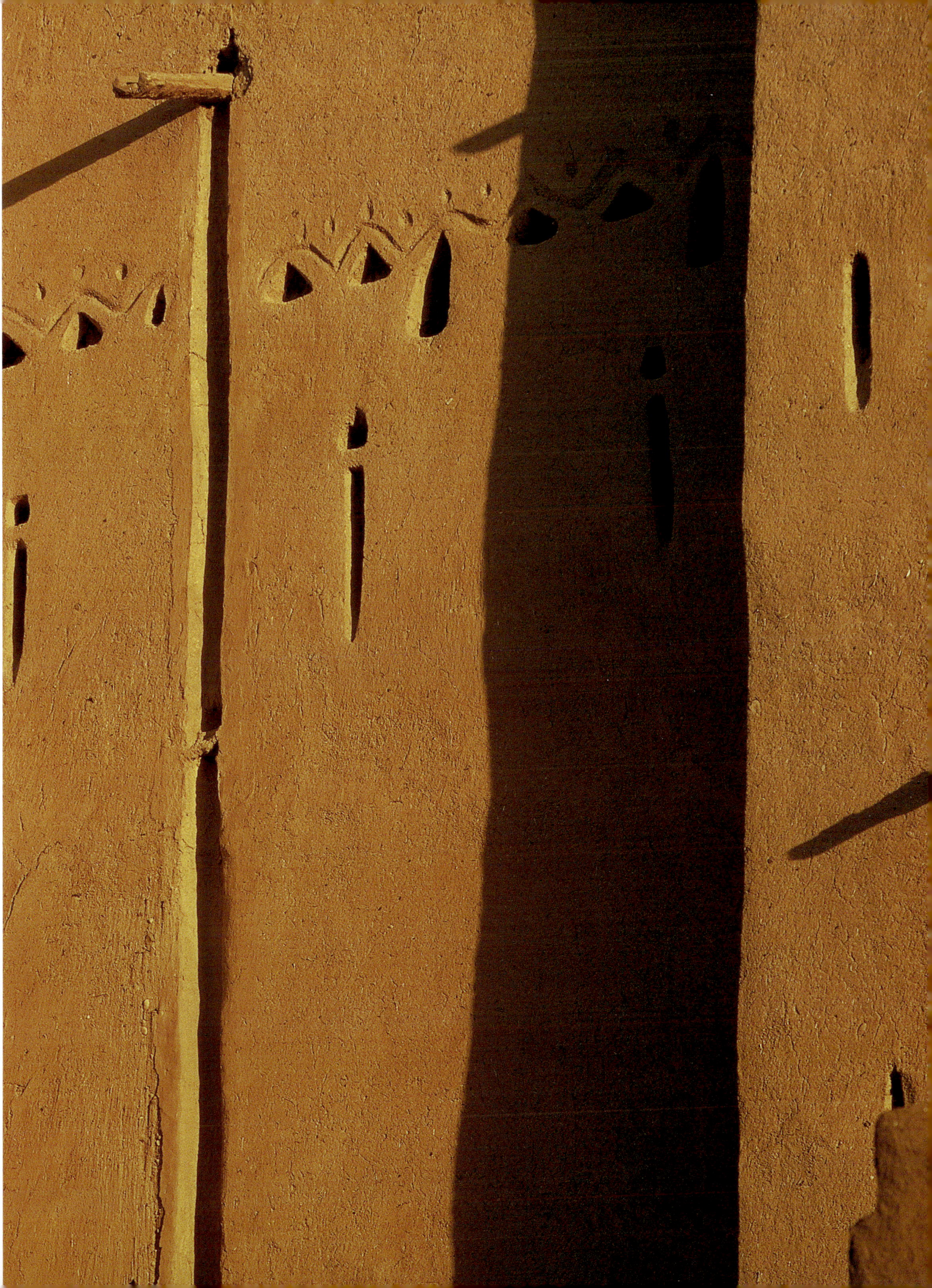

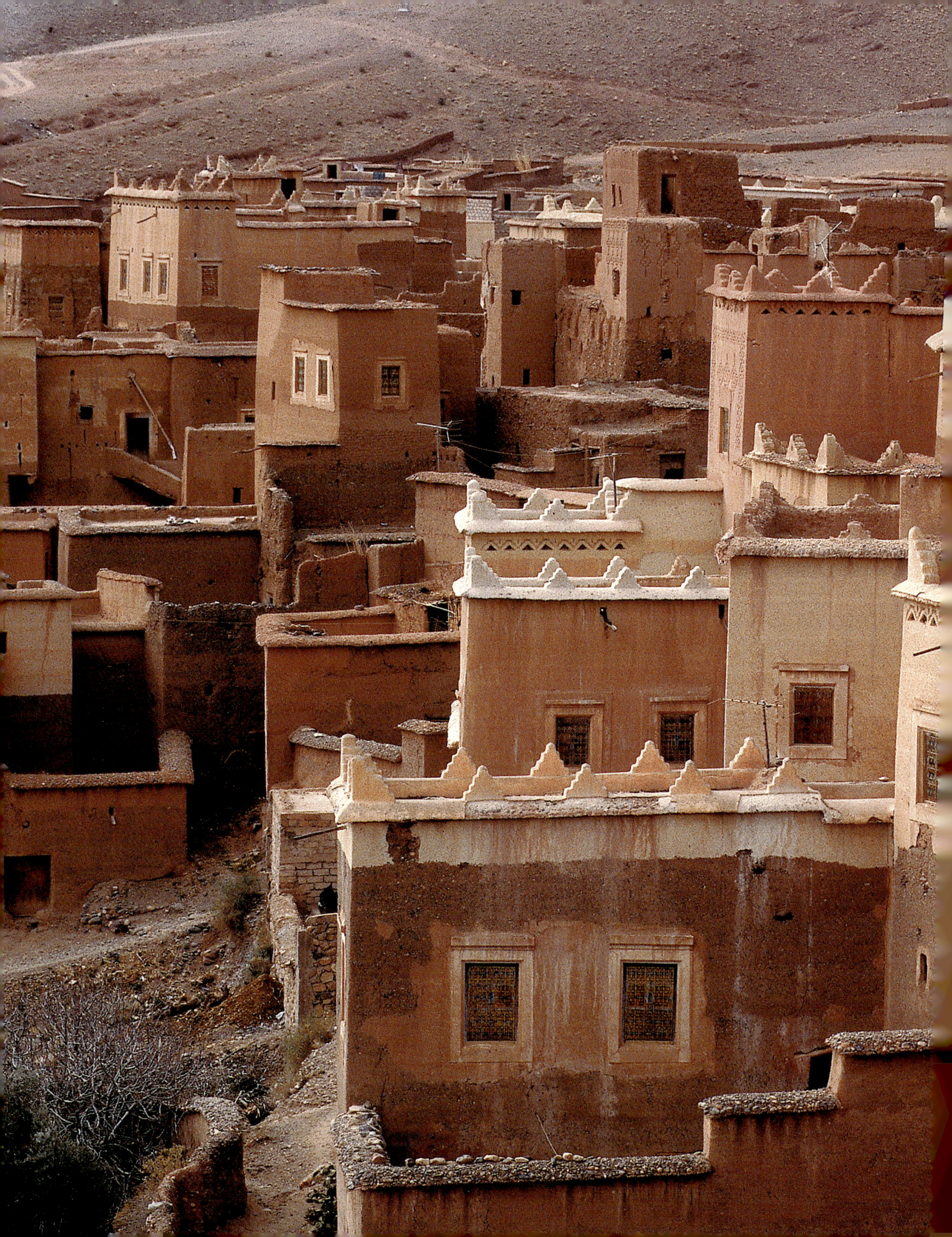

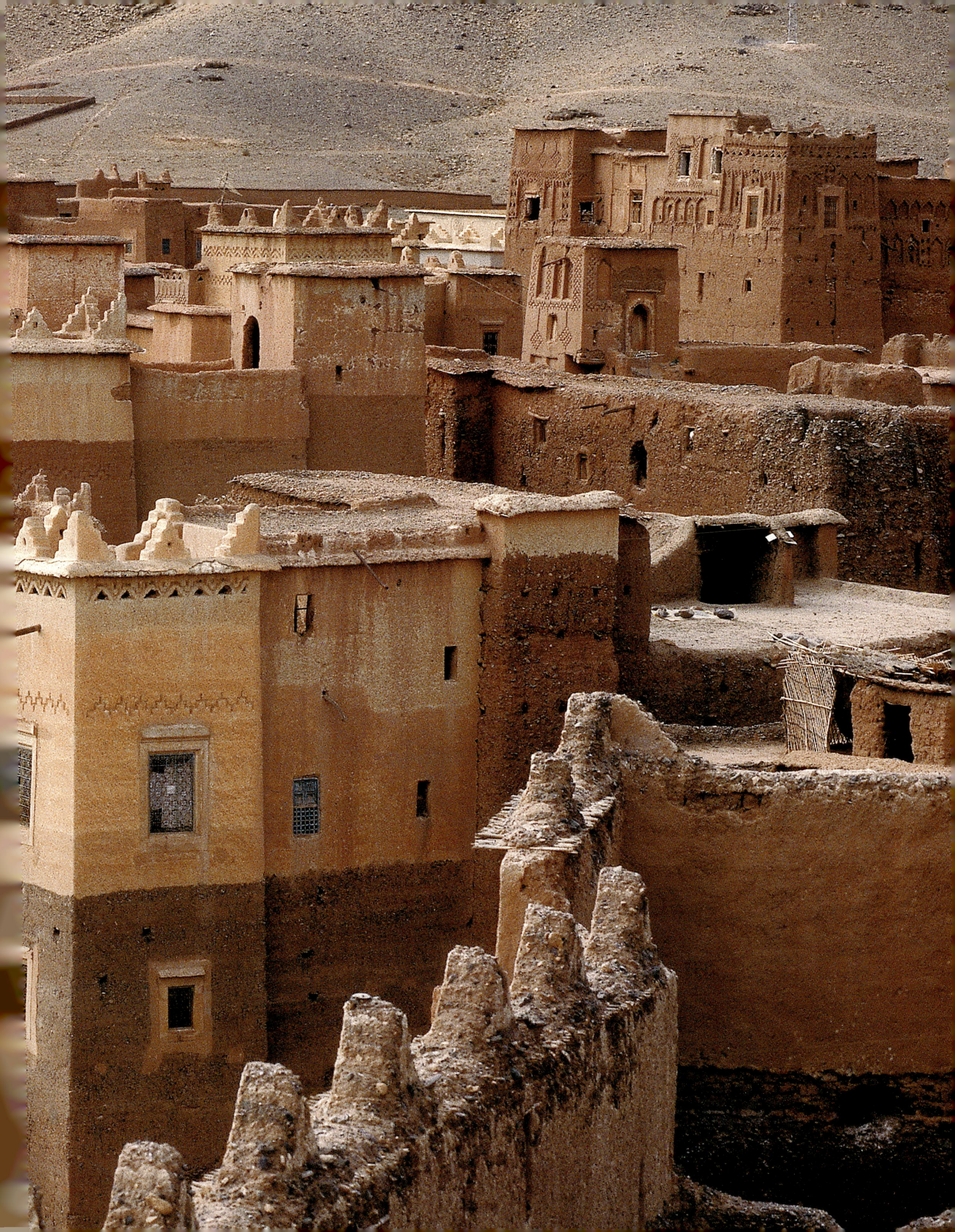

PAGES 160–62:
The village of Toundout is located in the heights of Skoura

RIGHT:
The marmite cooking pots atop the merlons have magical powers: they ward off the evil eye

Kasbahs are built with a single entry that seems exaggerated by its heavy doors made of boards from palm trees and covered with crudely studded pieces of wood. The openings are tiny and are quite a step up. Nevertheless, despite their imposing size and proportions, and their apparent inviolability, kasbahs are fragile structures. Made only of clay, without lime for bonding, they were built according to an outdated method that has largely disappeared.

Adobe and Raw Brick: An Outdated Structure

The aesthetics of the kasbah expresses a desire for elegance as well as for sturdiness. Completely integrated into the natural environment, its proportions are in perfect balance. The method of construction comprises two systems—one of adobe, the other of raw brick. The adobe entails a molding process that employs a wooden frame approximately twenty inches (fifty centimeters) high that is used to build the main walls up to the level of the roof terrace. The bricks, made of mud dried directly on the bare ground, are used for the upper reaches of the walls and for the towers, where they are arranged in decorative carved friezes of arcatures, honeycombs, and diamond motifs. These bricks are also the basic material used for the interior decorations, small partitions, arches, and columns. Work that entails masonry is never undertaken during the winter, but rather before the start of the harvest, when the sunshine and fine weather

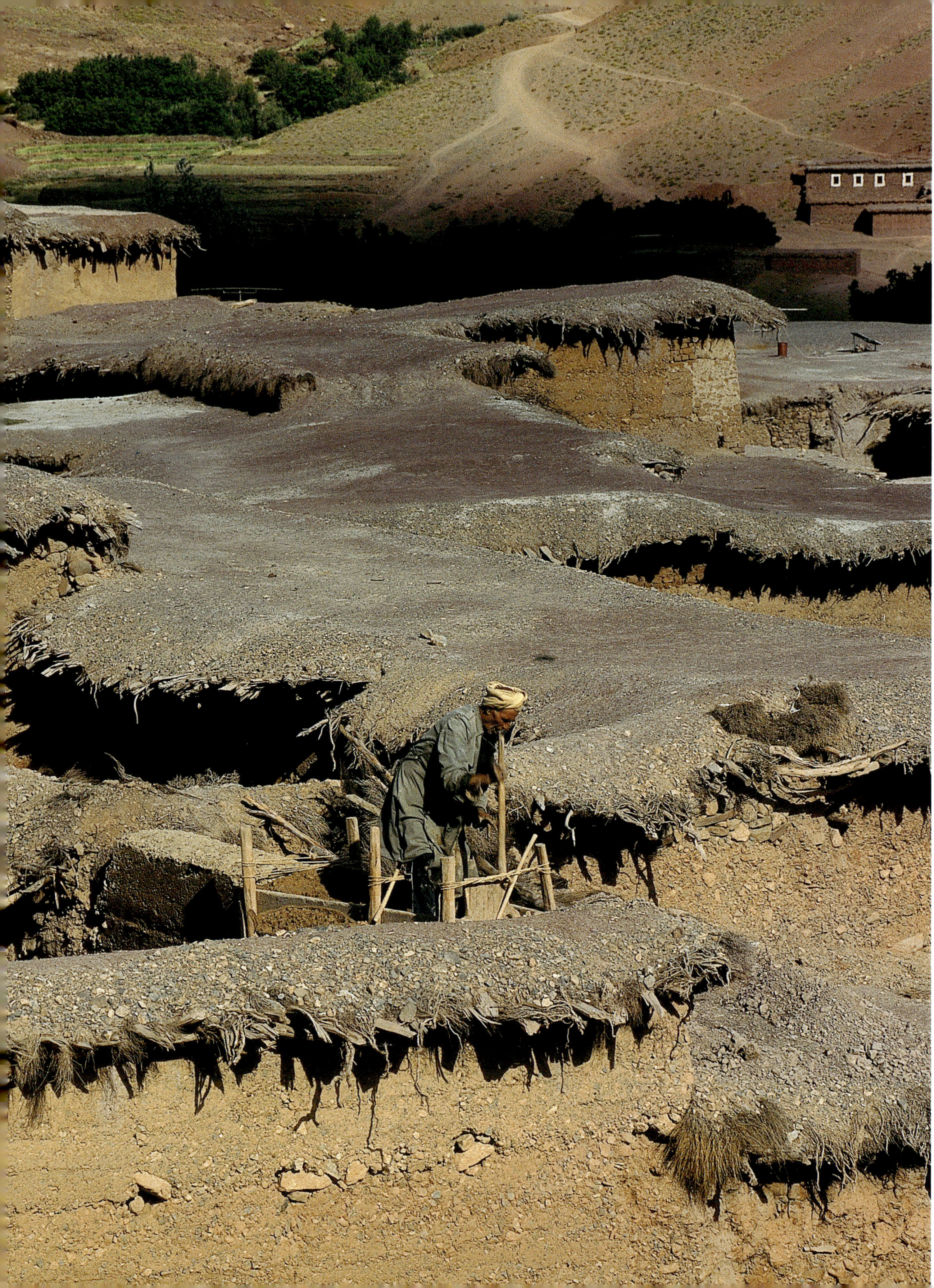

provides sufficient time for drying. The work requires a crew of at least three people—one master adobe mason and two assistants who bring him the clay and the water.

The erection of the peripheral walls always precedes that of the inner walls. Before putting up the frame and the forms, the masons will carve out a small trench where the wall is to be built that they then fill with stones joined together with a mortar made of mud. They erect this base slightly above ground level, just high enough to obtain a continuous low wall that will serve as a foundation. They then pierce semicircular notches into which they will eventually insert pieces of the frame.

The earth used to make the adobe is always taken from the construction site itself and as it is more readily compacted when mixed with gravel, the finest earth is not the most preferable. Accompanied by his mule, one of the workmen fetches water at the nearest *seguia*.

The earth must be continually moistened during the ten days before it is poured into the frame. The responsibility of controlling the amount of water added to obtain the ideal consistency falls to the master adobe mason. He steps inside the form, works the earth with his feet, and then, using a heavy wooden pestle, packs it down, his movements in sync with his rhythmic throaty shouts. Having tamped down one layer of earth after another until all the air has been removed, he finishes by

OPPOSITE AND ABOVE:
Manufacturing adobe entails a molding process using a wooden frame. Bricks of raw earth, or toub, *are made of a mixture of clay and chopped straw*

KASBAHS OF THE OASES 165

leveling the surface of the mold by battering it with a board. Once the mixture has partially dried, he removes the wooden frame. The pieces of wood that had supported the slab leave indentations in the casting. Filled in or not, as deemed necessary, these hollows form small openings in the wall that have often been mistaken for defensive loopholes.

The frame is always moved laterally so as to form an uninterrupted layer that, once sufficiently dry, will be able to support another layer. The bases of the layers are always wider than the height, for stability, so kasbahs taper as they reach to the sky. Their pyramid-like shape, a consequence of the compression that occurs during the molding in the frames, makes it possible for a kasbah to reach exalted heights without risk of collapsing. It takes less than an hour to fill a frame and a master adobe mason can do seven or eight in a day. The exteriors of the peripheral walls, left raw and undecorated so that anyone attempting an attack would not be able to get a foothold, are ordinarily covered with a coat of fine earth mixed with chopped straw. As wood is a rare commodity in pre-Saharan Morocco, workers do not use scaffolding. They just put on the coats as they scale the structure.

At the level of the roof terraces, the low walls and corner towers are constructed of raw bricks (*toub*) and adorned with ornamental carvings that seem all the more intense against the light of the setting sun. The decorations are archetypically Saharan. They are seen only on the southern side of the High Atlas Mountains and then, only on the level of the superstructure.

A good quality clay brick must contain as little sand as possible. The earth is mixed with chopped straw and some water, and then left to set on a bed of straw. The wooden mold, with its twin alveoli that are filled up with clay once the slab is removed, is dampened. The very dry air and the spring sunshine are enough to bake the bricks. Once dry, they are laid out at an angle, forming a zigzag or diamond pattern. More bricks are then superposed, adding several more layers. *Toub*, a more malleable material than adobe, can be carved.

The decorative motifs on the façades of kasbahs are never floral, but rather always geometric—diamonds, chevrons, checkerboards, and arcatures. The same is true of designs seen on woven fabrics, pottery, jewelry, tattoos, and small everyday objects made of leather, wood, or copper, such as spoons, sugar hammers, keys, small chests, and tools.

Here meticulous symmetry does not exist. Each façade has an appearance of its own. Whether influenced by urban aesthetics or out of a concern for

OPPOSITE AND ABOVE:
Motifs, always geometric, are found on many everyday objects in the rural areas

PAGE 168:
The interior walls are covered in a mixture of clay and straw. The ceilings are covered in reeds, held in place by palm tree trunks and tamarisk branches

KASBAHS OF THE OASES 167

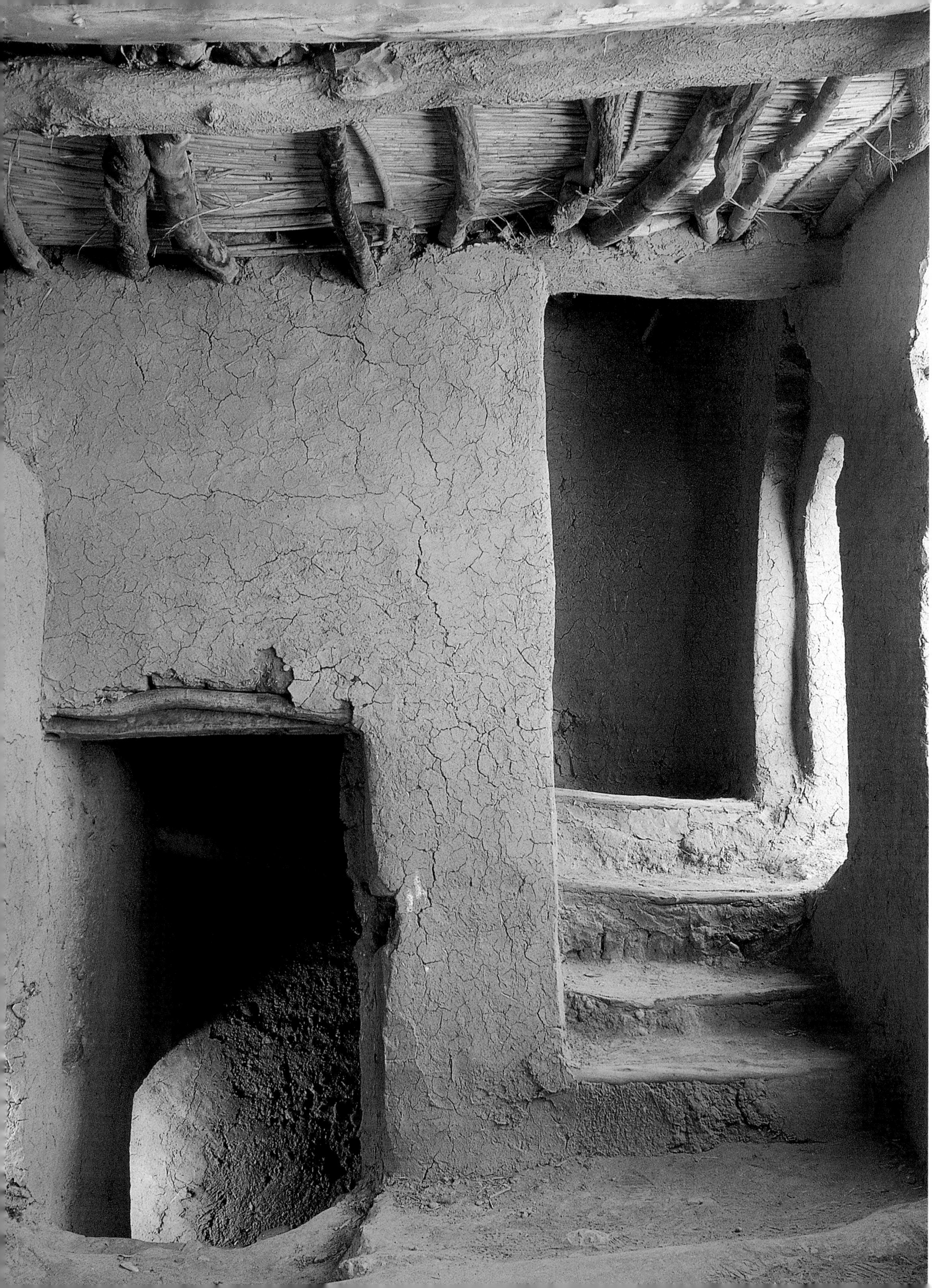

impermeability, some of the upper parts and the window frames of the façades have been whitewashed with lime. The objects (horns, udders, tacks, balls, casseroles) stuck into the walls or at the corners near the merlons are not there for decoration, but rather, serve a magical purpose. They are there to protect the dwelling from nefarious forces, as are the small black stones, shells, and horseshoes that residents embed into the wall just above the door.

★ Rudimentary Interiors

Differing from a *ksar* (*ksour* in the plural), which is a fortified village inhabited by unrelated families, a kasbah is a patriarchic residence; all its inhabitants claim a familial relation based upon a single, shared ancestor. Often, a kasbah will be home to three generations—easily, some twenty people. It is usually the property of a tribal or sub-tribal chief whose authority extends over the neighboring village and its land. The architecture is considered both graceful and warlike. It is here where the women, children, and provisions are housed. But above all, it is where life is lived communally, an aspect of supreme importance among Muslims, for whom nothing is more disturbing than solitude. But the kasbah was also a defensive settlement where the sheik stored his weapons and where the villagers would take refuge when being attacked by outsiders.

Impeccably adapted to the old social structures, kasbahs are also suited to the severe climatic conditions of pre-Saharan Morocco. When the temperature reaches 122 degrees Fahrenheit (50 degrees Celsius) in the shade, and the valleys are battered by winds laden with sand, it feels good to take refuge within the walls and savor the welcomed coolness and shadows. Winters, on the other hand, turn these homes to ice and despite so few openings, the winds still cut through. But the season of intense cold is short and residents climb up to the roof terraces to warm themselves in the sunshine.

Life in the kasbah is as basic as it is in the tents. The furniture is meager and functional. Life is conducted in the shadows, as only oblique rays of light pass through the narrow holes built into the walls. The absence of openings, conceived as a defense tactic, also provides thermal insulation. One gropes one's way through a labyrinth of stairways, zigzagging corridors, and rooms that are utterly indistinguishable from each other. Evenings are illuminated by candlelight, and as farming and herding requires starting the day at sunrise, as does the dawn prayer, people never stay up late.

ABOVE:
The structural elements of rural homes are no different from those of urban ones. As in the cities, doors are clad with large, round-headed nails

KASBAHS OF THE OASES 169

ABOVE AND OPPOSITE:
The interiors of kasbahs are arranged around a small patio illuminated by narrow shafts of light. This way, they retain some coolness

PAGE 172:
The cultivation of roses is a means of subsistence in the Mgoun Valley

PAGE 173:
In Morocco the henna plant grows only in the Dra and Tafilalt Valleys. Once dried, it is tirelessly ground into a fine powder that is mixed with water and a little oil to make expert temporary tattoos

One enters the kasbah through the sole wooden door. Although heavy and massive, the opening is so low that one has to bend down to get in. It is, however, wide enough for a laden beast to pass through. Although crudely made, the door is adorned with round-headed nails and sculpted and painted motifs, often including the fibula, which when fashioned as a piece of jewelry is used to pin closed the traditional garment women wear. It is affixed with a rough-hewn doorknocker that moves on wooden hinges. In the past, the door could only be opened from the inside, making it necessary for a keeper or a resident to be present at all times. Nowadays it usually has a dual system that can be worked from both the inside and outside. The iron lock, introduced at the beginning of the twentieth century, has largely replaced the ancient system of a transverse bar, latch, and wooden dowels.

As with all Moroccan houses, the kasbah is designed around a patio from which radiate narrow, high-ceilinged rooms. The kasbah's patio, however, is much smaller. Dark, its entryway sometimes covered with mats, it keeps the house cool and prevents the scorching, dusty winds from passing through. The galleries are supported by four pillars. Traditionally, this is where guests were received, but this practice has become less common. During the twentieth century kasbah dwellers were influenced by city life and slowly began to add a reception room to their homes. The ground floor became merely a place for storing the harvest, while the rooms on the upper level, although their functions were interchangeable, were primarily used for living. At the homes of herders, the lower parts of the kasbah might also be used to shelter the goats and sheep. A trough carved into the trunk of a palm tree is filled with alfalfa to compensate for the dearth of grazing lands.

Water is drained through open gutters set on the floor, thus preventing the erosion of the foundation.

The interior walls of the kasbah are covered with a mixture of clay and straw. Ornamentation is concentrated on the upper parts of the patio. The arches and galleries are sculpted in geometric patterns and although lumber is in short supply, ceilings are held in place by palm tree trunks or tamarisk branches, and are covered with reeds or stems from pink oleander bushes that have been woven to form small, diamond-shaped coffers (*tataoui*). These stems, approximately twenty inches (fifty centimeters) long but selected for their circumference, are first stripped, then soaked in a dye, and finally dried. The upkeep merely entails some minor adjustments.

The allure of the wood used for the lintels, columns, and capitals depends upon the affluence of the owner and varies, as do all decorations, according to the province

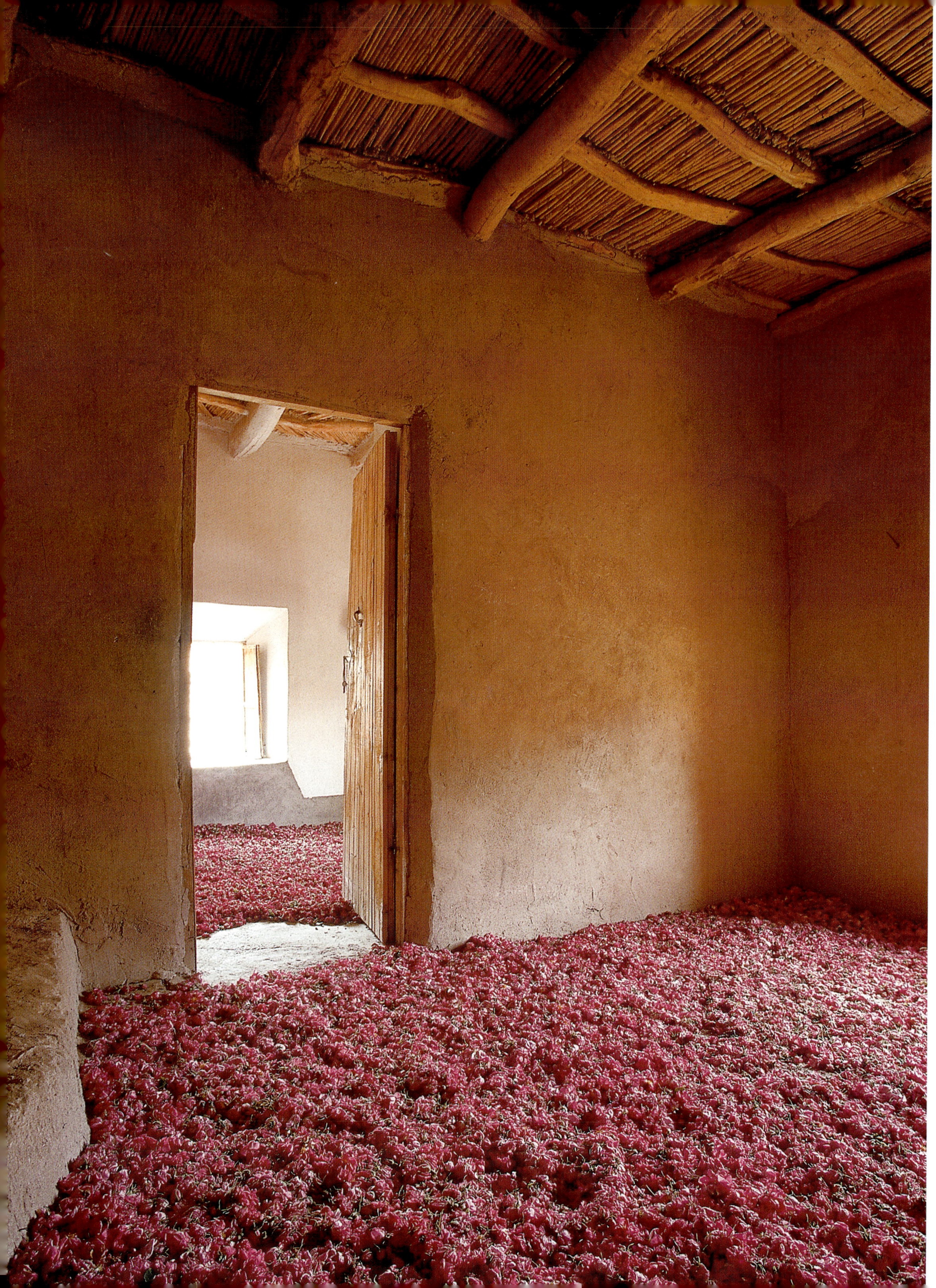

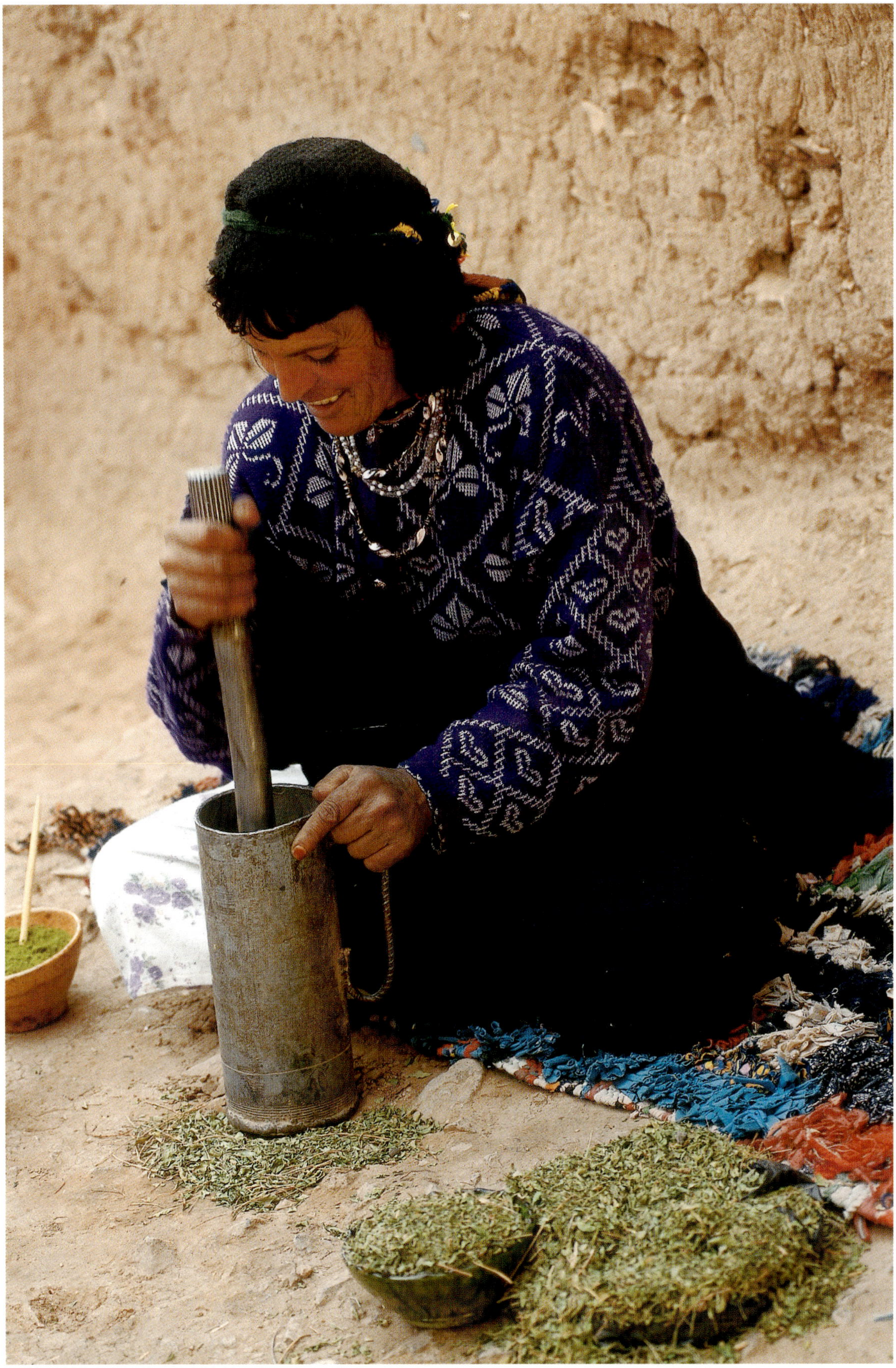

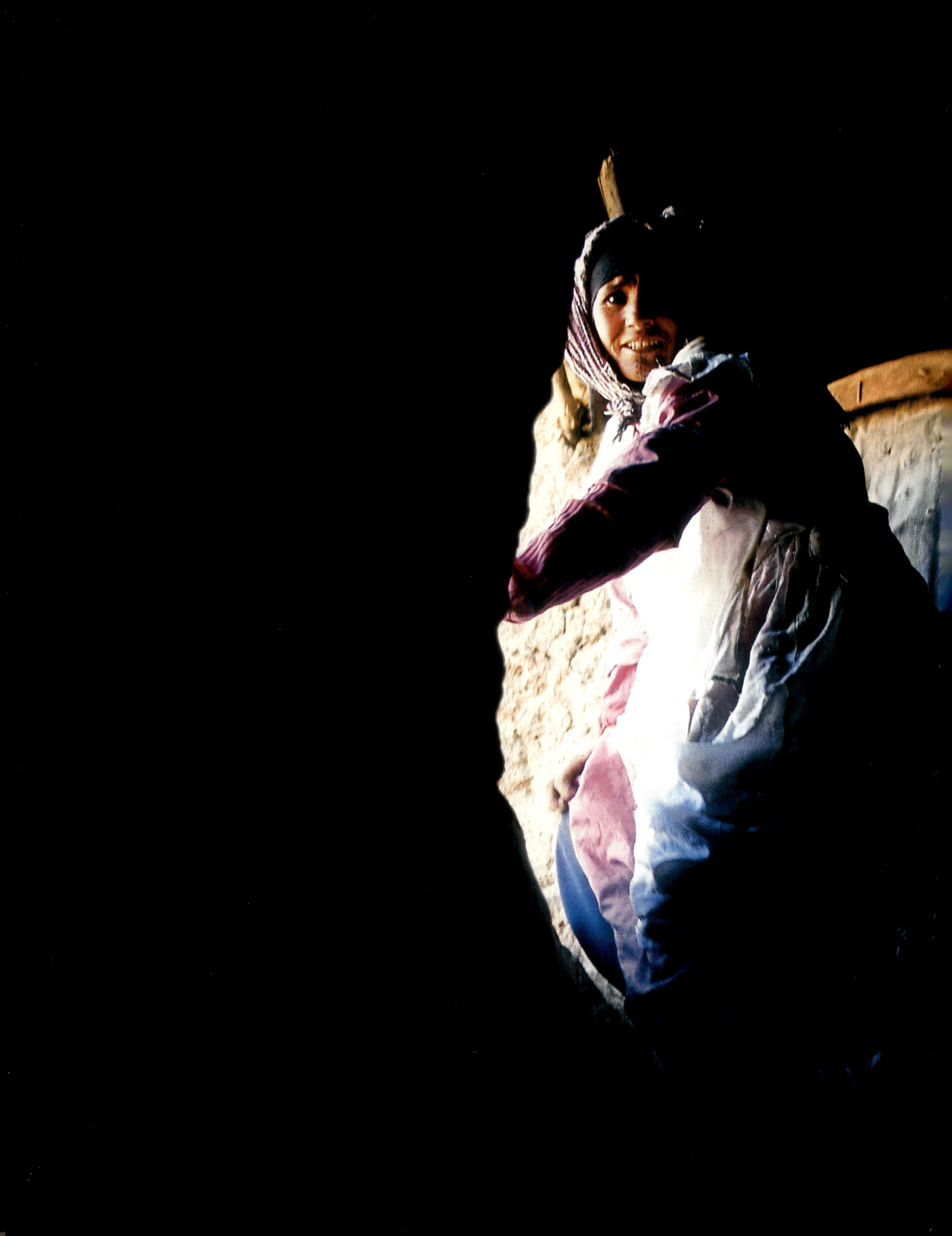

An oasis archetype, the kasbah was a patriarchic residence reserved for kaids. All the same, comforts were as basic as life in a desert tent.

and the traditions of the tribe. Along with the patio, the kitchen is the prime spot where daily life takes place. This is where the wife grinds the grain with a small granite millstone, churns the butter in a goatskin hung on a tripod, kneads the dough, and keeps a fire of palm wood burning in a clay oven. Children play all around her on the earthen floor. Little girls learn how to make bread, couscous, and tagines. Reserved exclusively for women, it is here that the women of the house receive their neighbors and relatives, in this place for chatting and relaxing.

Meals are shared here and when there are no guests, perhaps even in the presence of the father of the family. The ceiling and walls glisten with soot, reinforcing the somber ambience of the room. Kasbahs are tall structures, with some even reaching heights of sixty-five feet (twenty meters) and comprising four to six stories. The stairways are narrow with high rising, uneven steps. A landing with floors that shake beneath one's feet suddenly appears at an unexpected turn. The roofs are open terraces and, as water is the greatest threat to adobe, gutters are essential, despite infrequent rainfall. During the winter residents go up to

KASBAHS OF THE OASES 177

the roof and sit on mats and carpets, warming themselves in the midday sun, and in the summer, they cool off in the first breezes of the evening and sleep beneath a blanket of twinkling stars. Women use the terraces for drying dates, meat, and wool. They also sort the grains, do their sewing, and skein their wool there. From the terraces they can observe the farming and herding life of the valley that seems to have remained utterly untouched by modernity.

Nevertheless, the architecture of the kasbahs has changed over the course of the twentieth century. Adobe has made it easier to enlarge openings, and windows, adorned with foliage motif grilles made in Marrakech, have become a fixture cut into the façades. These windows that ventilate and brighten the upper levels are usually set low, near the floors, and one must crouch down or sit on a chair in order to see out into the distance. They are closed from the inside with wooden shutters or even paned casements. Using city homes as a model, kasbahs now have light and richly decorated reception rooms for which the master of the house is the sole possessor of the key. Their earthen floors are covered with cement, which in turn, is covered with carpets. The walls and ceilings are plastered and brightly painted and often "Allah is the greatest" graces the walls. Depending upon

PAGES 176–77:
Preparing couscous, an essential part of all festive meals, requires many hours of work

OPPOSITE AND ABOVE:
Influenced by city life, the latest kasbah dwellers have added windows to their guest rooms and covered the walls with plaster and vibrant painted motifs

KASBAHS OF THE OASES

PAGES 182–83:
The Ksar Ait Ben Haddou, abandoned by its former residents, has fallen into a state of decay

the wealth of the owner, some kasbahs have added buildings, interior courtyards, and even gardens, which are closed in by a protecting wall. The ceremonial room, which usually is located on the second floor of the main building, might otherwise be situated in a separate house constructed around a *riad* as one would find in the cities.

✦ A Heritage in Peril

Formerly a symbol of security and a mark of prestige, ever since the second half of the twentieth century kasbahs have fallen into a state of decay. From afar they look so majestic that one would think they would be there forever, like European fortresses. From close up, however, they look more like anthills. Eroded by the sand, they have become ruins that are home only to storks. Throughout the ages, kasbahs have always disappeared, whether destroyed by wars, the passage of time, or simply neglect. But the deterioration of these clay castles has accelerated during the past century. When the French Protectorate had pacified the tribes and the oasis dwellers no longer had to protect themselves from raids by the nomads, the climate of fear disappeared and the defensive settlement lost its *raison d'être*. Nevertheless, the residents did not immediately abandon their kasbahs. Without the means to build new housing, they remained attached to their way of life. It was not until after Morocco's independence that the social order of the valley became disrupted. During the 1960s, the valleys of southern Morocco experienced a progressive drought that weakened the region and instigated a massive exodus to the cities in the north, and even to Europe. Today only the older generations live in kasbahs. When former migrants return to their country they no longer want to live in these dark castles made of earth, amid the beasts and the harvest. Influenced by Western consumerism, they have built modern

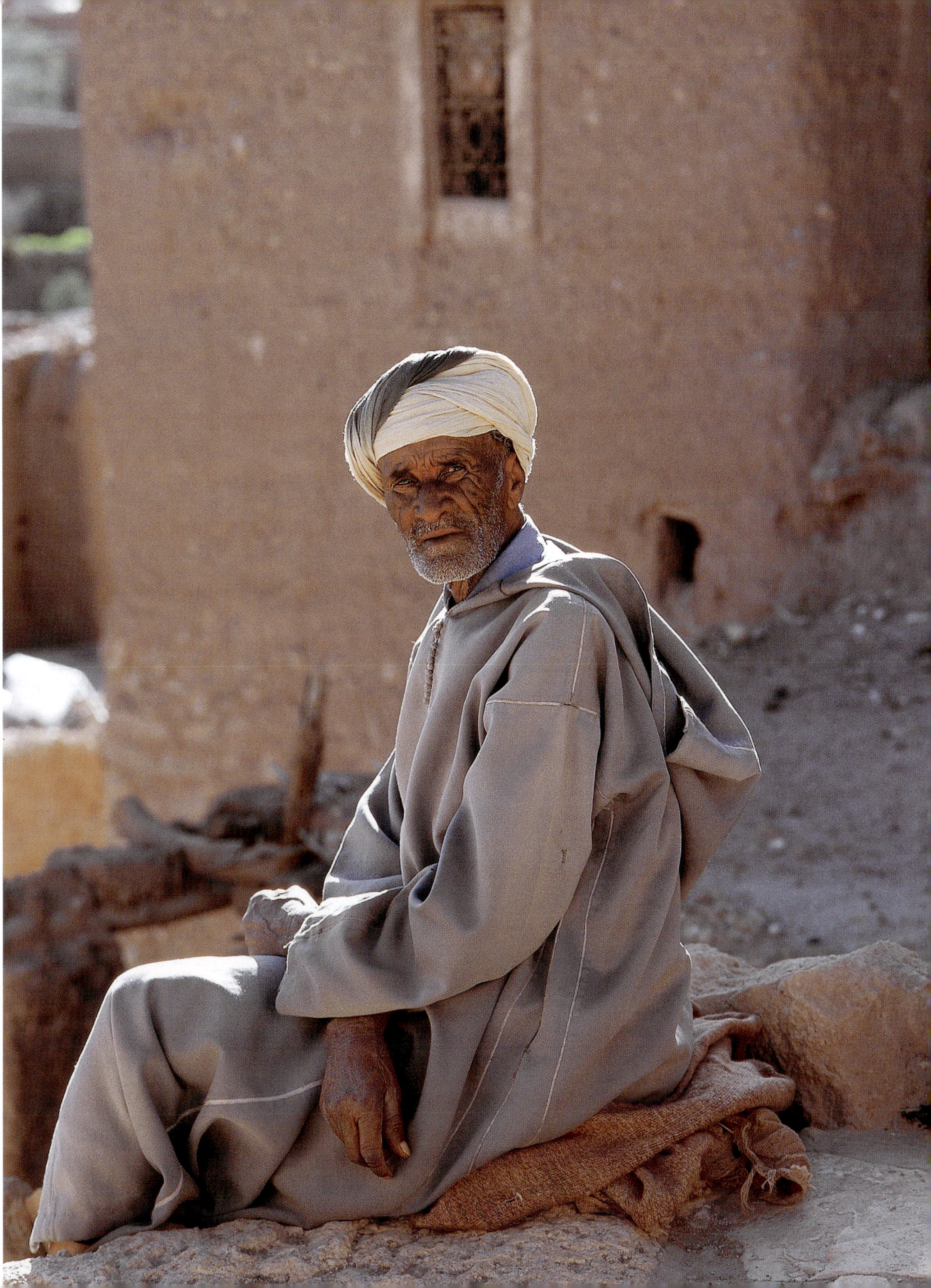

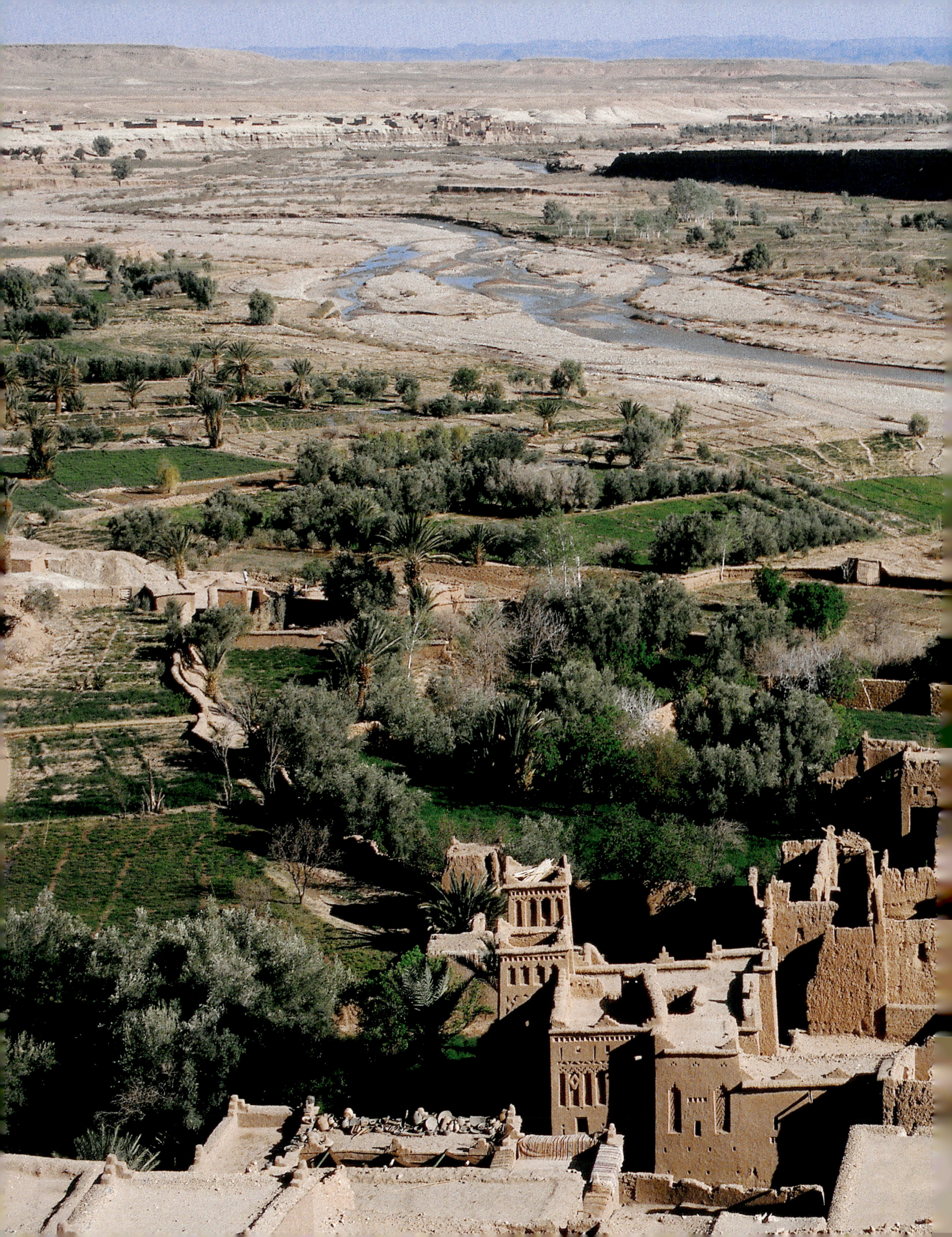

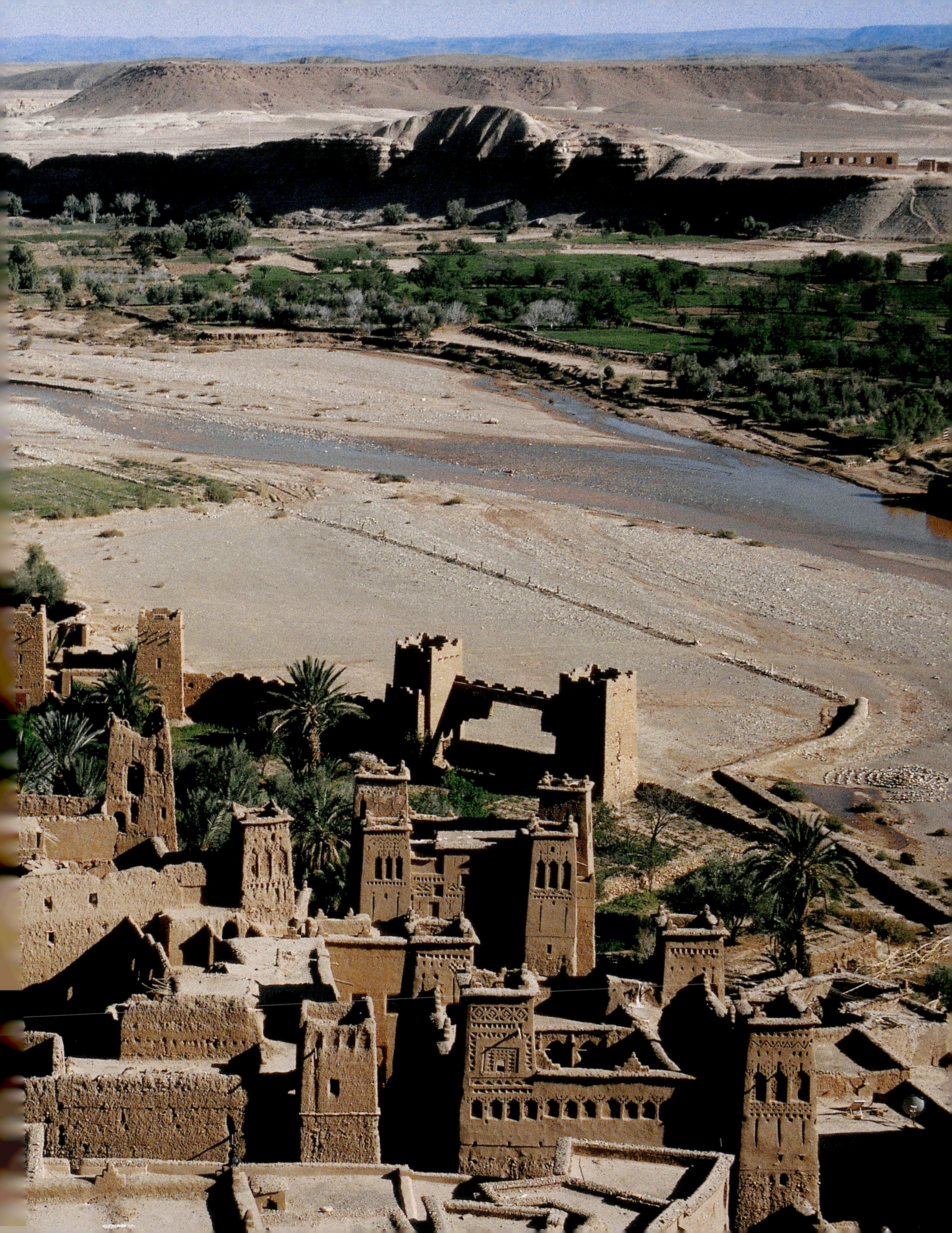

*Kasbahs are so majestic that one would think them unassailable.
But neglected, they are in danger of returning to the earth.*

houses that are sturdier and conform more to their tastes. Their abandoned ancestral homes, not properly maintained, are condemned to return to the earth from which they were made. Today only a few rare, dilapidated kasbahs continue to be inhabited by families attached to their traditional way of life, or too poor to live elsewhere. There are others that have been renovated by private investors with the profits from tourism in mind. But the very complex system of joint ownership of the kasbahs makes the acquisition process long and difficult. Rarely are families in possession of the deeds and it takes months to settle disputes between the heirs. Nevertheless, some restoration initiatives have proven successful and could set an example for ways to safeguard the heritage.

⭐ The Restored Kasbahs of N'Kob and Skoura

Today one-third of all humanity still lives in homes made of raw earth. Architects have rediscovered adobe and note its advantages—excellent thermal insulation, beautiful appearance, and low cost. Adobe does, however, have some drawbacks. It requires regular maintenance and there remain very few artisans who are familiar with the traditional techniques. The last kasbah in the Dra Valley was built in 1955. Thus, elderly *maallems* from the villages who were willing to form a crew and oversee the construction sites would have to be recruited. The restoration projects are truly adventures of human enterprise in which financial stakes play no part.

The most beautiful array of extant earthen architecture is in the Dra and Dades Valleys. Kasbahs abound there, but they are in danger of disappearing if no action is taken to restore them. Private initiatives have been undertaken in N'Kob and Skoura to return these fallen splendors to their exalted state.

LEFT:
An ambitious ecotourism project has worked to restore the earthen architecture. The restoration of Kasbah Baba Baba required five years of work

In the Dades Valley, at the foot of the Hajjaj Wadi, Skoura asserts itself as an oasis of kasbahs. They shoot up from all corners of the palm grove, one more majestic than the next. Their towering silhouettes stand out before the blue-tinted foothills of the Atlas Mountains. Although founded in the seventeenth century during the Alaouite dynasty, the oldest kasbahs in Skoura date back only two hundred years. Despite appearing to soar from time immemorial, many scarcely endure more than half a century.

According to oral history, Kasbah Ait ben Moro was built by a Spaniard, a descendant of generations of Moors expelled from Andalusia at the time of the Spanish reconquest. Ironically, it was restored by a banker from Cádiz who, while spending time in the region, became infatuated with it. Don Juan de Dios Romero Muños has the temperament of an Andalusian. After a year of restoration work assiduously respectful of the local traditions, he transformed the old structures into a charming hotel.

The kasbah was in ruins but still standing. The passage of time had eroded its decorative friezes. A crew of a dozen workers set to the task, perched upon makeshift ladders. Today the building has been returned to its original solidity. Seated on a square base, it is gently tapered and sports four towers, one at each corner, which are crowned with merlons. The upper reaches of the walls are carved with geometric motifs. The interior of the kasbah, dimly lit by a narrow shaft of light, is laid out around a patio that is supported by four massive pillars. The bedrooms in the galleries are spread out on two floors. The walls, recovered in a straw coating, are almost indiscernible. The ceilings are an ensemble of reeds, tamarisk, and stems of pink oleander,

LEFT:
Adobe and raw brick, both attractive and inexpensive, provide excellent thermal insulation. But they are fragile materials that require constant maintenance

ABOVE:
Kasbah Ait ben Moro

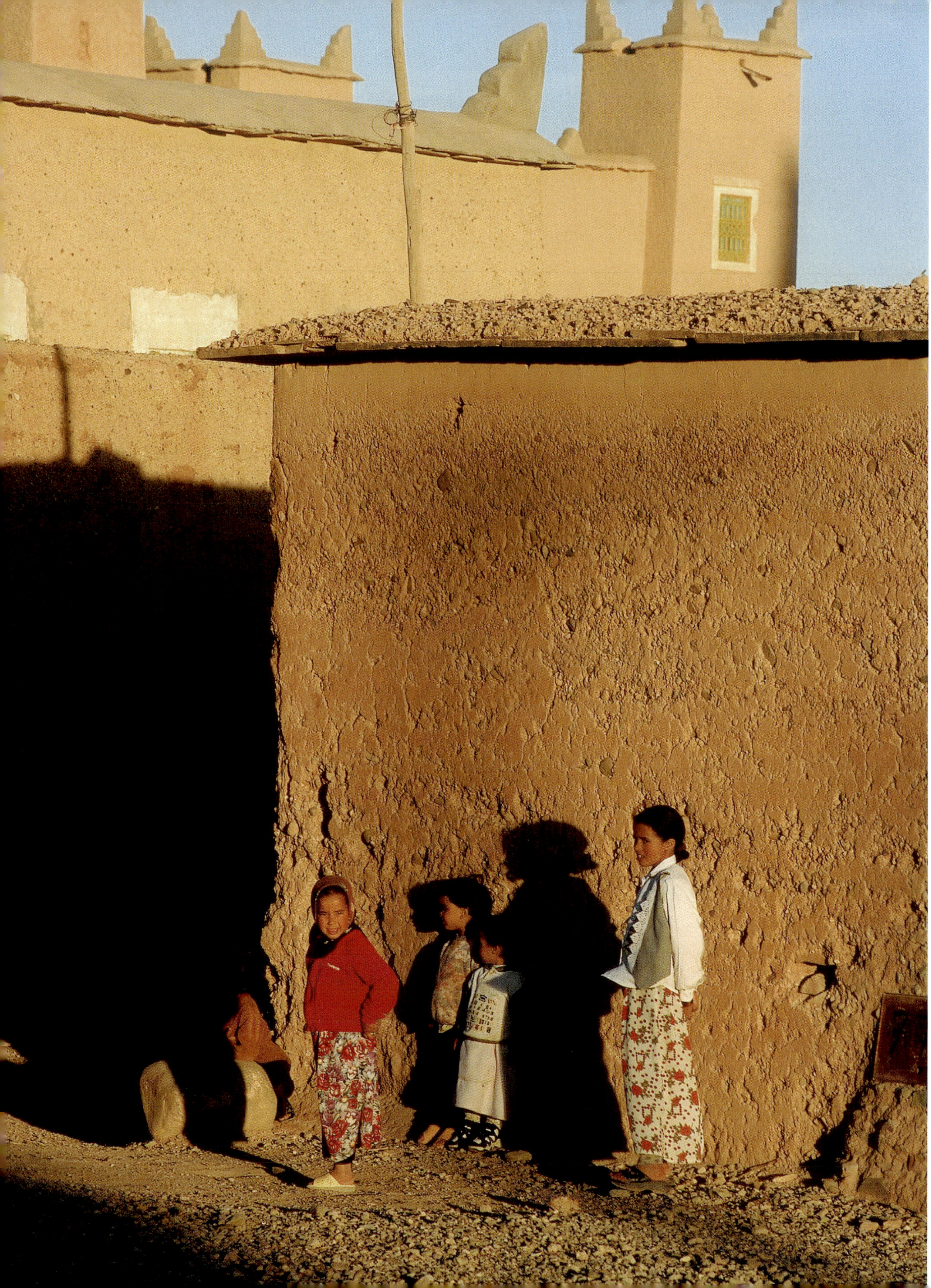

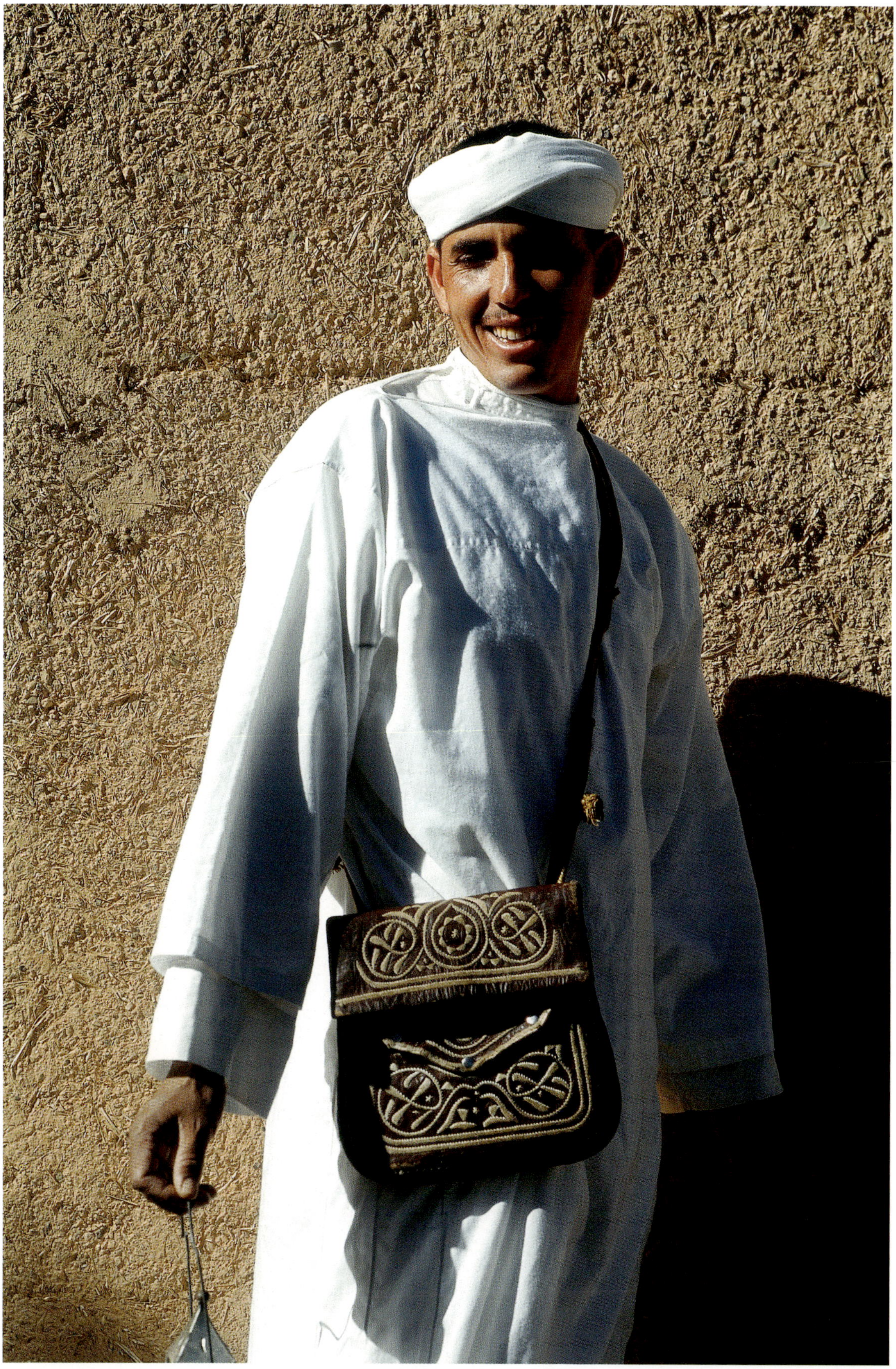

PAGES 188–89:
Will tourism encourage the youth not to flee to the big cities?

RIGHT:
The ceilings of the kasbahs in N'Kob are a weave of pink oleander stems that have been peeled and dyed (tataoui). The patio galleries are supported by four pillars

and the doors hang on their original wooden hinges. As if to emphasize the architecture of the home, the wrought-iron furniture has been designed with right angles.

The village of N'Kob is located in the Dra Valley equidistant from Ouarzazate and Zagora on an ancient transhumant route of the Ait Atta, a large confederation of Sanhaja Berber tribes who, until the 1930s, refused to submit to Glaoui's rule, as he was a French partisan. During the pacification, Haj Bassou Mimoun, an Ait Atta chief of the Ait Ounir tribe, was assigned the role of mediator. Deeming the water supply at N'Kob abundant and the lands fertile, he decided to build a village and ordered the construction of a kasbah for each third of the lineage. Built in 1948, N'Kob comprises no fewer than forty-five kasbahs, each of which serves as an exalted example of earthen architecture. Several years ago Brahim Ouarzazi, the founder's grandson, undertook their restoration and has successfully incorporated them into an ecotourism scheme that not only safeguards the heritage, but has also put a halt to the rural exodus that has so adversely affected the region.

Overhanging the oasis, the Kasbah Baha Baha, which was once the personal residence of Haj Bassou Mimoun, presents a fine example. Restored in adobe following traditional construction techniques, it has been receiving guests since 1999. The original volumes have been retained and it remains astonishingly similar to the neighboring kasbahs. The construction of Baha Baha had required three years; the renovation required five. A search throughout the Dades Valley was made, seeking out those elderly *maallems* who had been the original builders of the N'Kob kasbahs. These men spent a year teaching their young apprentices the techniques of adobe construction so that they would be sufficiently adept and the project a success. To increase the number of people the village can accommodate, a well has been added, enhancing the already efficient system of *khettaras* (the underground canals set at a downward slant from the edge of the mountains). An ambitious purification project is presently under study. A museum of ethnography has been inaugurated. Gardens sprawl, making the most of the dry, rocky, sun-baked soil. It is possible that by welcoming foreign tourists, locals will now be able to make a good life in N'Kob and the youth will no longer need to escape to the big cities. With an eye to safeguarding their heritage and their traditions, they are creating the project of their lives.

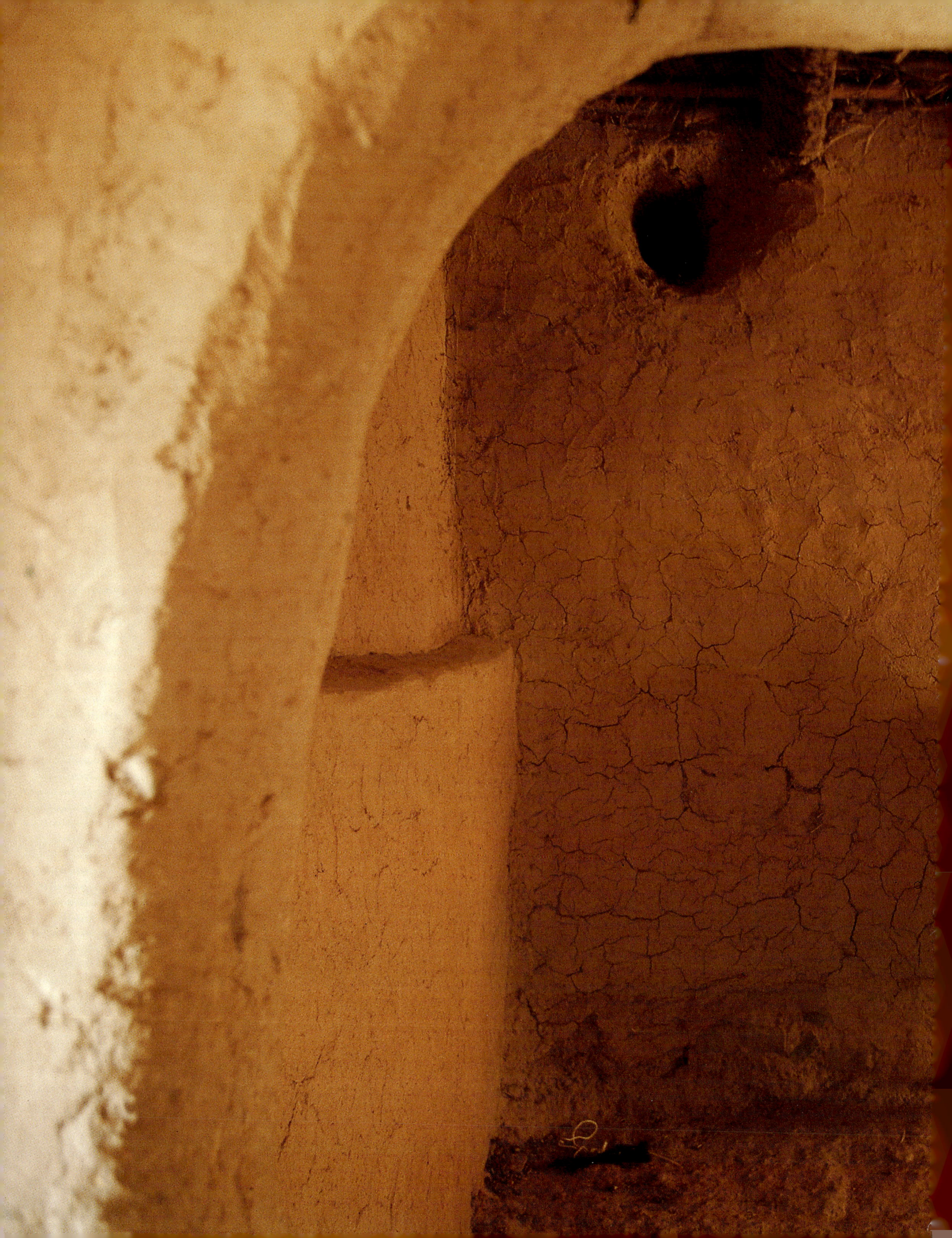

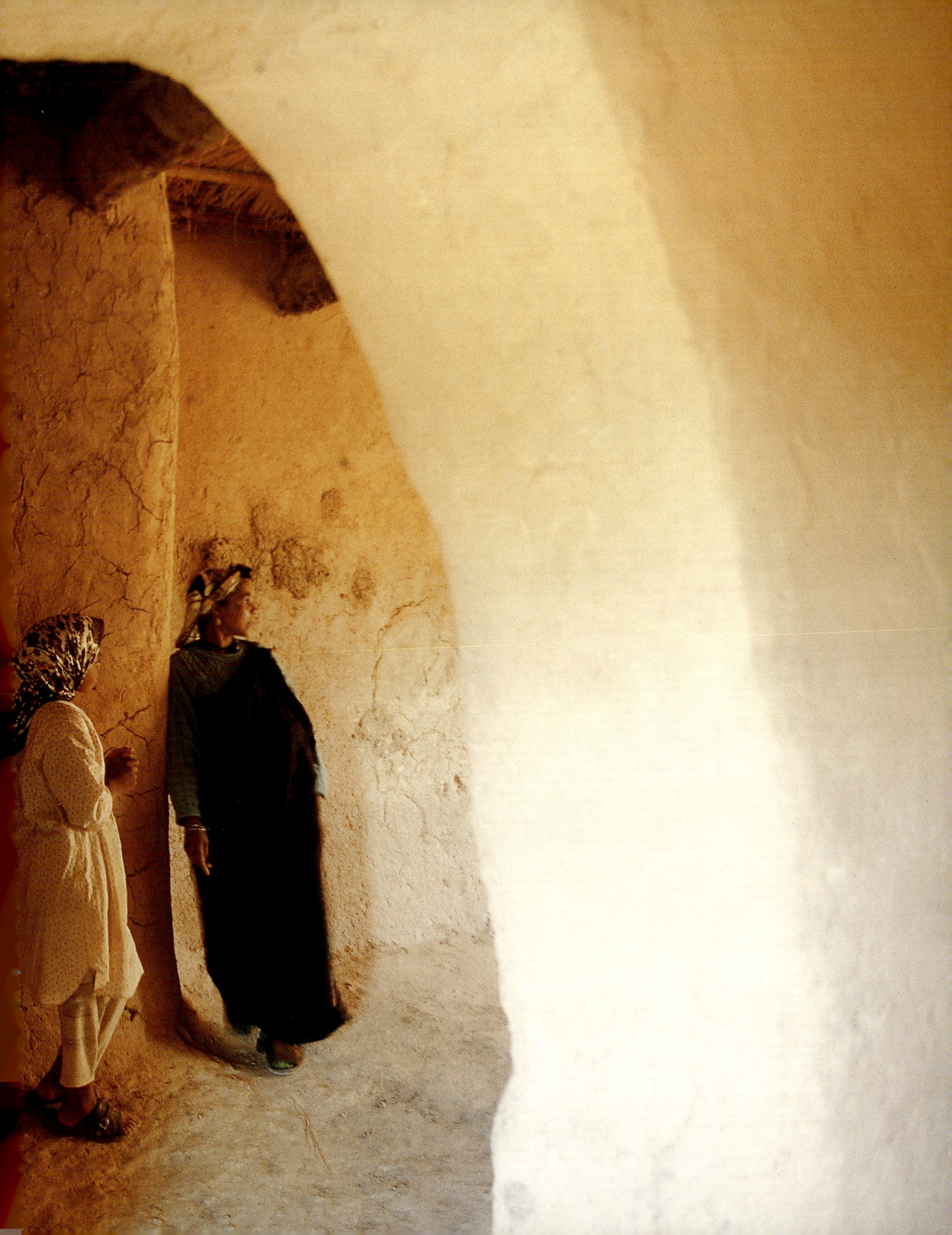

Temples to the Art of Living

There are two kasbahs in Morocco that defy even one's wildest dreams. Both are to be found in the foothills of the High Atlas Mountains, one on the northern slopes in the region of Marrakech, the other, to the south in the palm groves of Skoura. Liberated from the familiar conventions of the art of entertaining, these kasbahs transcend the traditional way of life with their audacious innovations that transport the mind and the senses. Here are homes that evoke Baudelaire, where the scents, colors, and sounds coalesce. Upon their earthen walls the poet might have inscribed, "There is only order and beauty, luxury, quietness, and pleasure."

AGAFAY

Only some twelve miles (twenty kilometers) from Marrakech, the proud silhouette of Kasbah Agafay is visible from far off. As if flaunting its wealth, it sits atop a hill, its terraces descending no less than seven and a half acres (three hectares).
At its feet, on one side lies the desert, on the other, vast olive groves. As the site is still referred to as Agafay ("lake" in Berber), the kasbah naturally adopted the name.

✦ A Kasbah of Lords

The home was owned by a wealthy Sharif family from Tamesloht that held great influence over the Haouz plains beyond Marrakech, thanks to the influence of their *zaouïa*. It is said that they owned more than five thousand acres (two thousand hectares) between Agafay and Marrakech. They built their kasbah so that they might oversee their olive groves, extend their domination over the lowlands, and assure the faithful of the divine authority bestowed upon them by the *zaouïa*.

When Abel Demoussey, a Moroccan businessman based in London, bought the kasbah in 1996, very little of it remained. Wanting to remain faithful to this architecture made of earth, as well as paying it homage, he interviewed the descendants of the family so that he might learn how their grandparents had lived there, and then he contacted the architect Quentin Wilbaux to do the restorations. First, the foundations had to be reinforced, and then a master adobe mason who could erect a series of walls had to be found. Proper building with adobe requires one single expert, as each casting must be tamped down evenly and conform to all the others. To harden the lower levels, clay was added to the lime. The upper floors were built in *toub*, and then the entirety was covered with a coat of lime whitewash tinged with clay.

Renovating kasbahs requires a great deal of time. Erecting an adobe wall takes a year of work and an

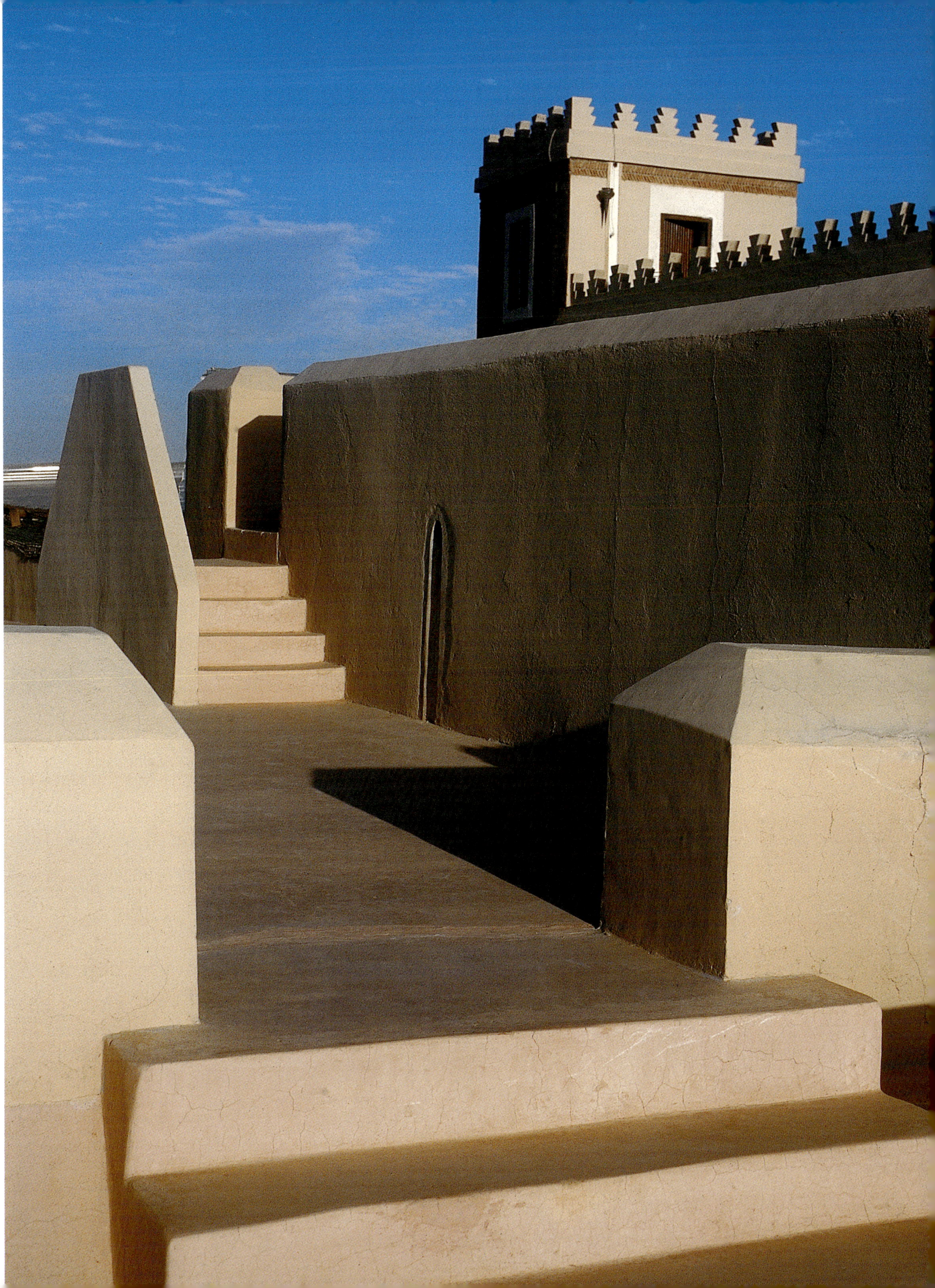

Olive groves, blossoming gardens, fountains, and waterfalls defy the arid steppes.

additional year to dry. The architectural engineers then made studies of the cracks, one by one, filling the key ones with lime. All together, the restoration of Kasbah Agafay took five years to complete and more than a thousand workers and artisans. Some of them, having spent three or four years of their lives there, could no longer even conceive of leaving. But alas, one day, the kasbah was inaugurated.

✦ Usurped Objects

With Abel Demoussy wanting to pay tribute to traditional décor, as well as to the Moroccan artisan, the work never ends. The kasbah has five small houses, all laid out around a central patio that is enlarged by *behous*, and an Andalusian *riad* bordered by four cypresses. Remaining true to custom, the massive doors hang on their wooden hinges, opening onto a labyrinthine entryway. The ceiling joists are made of poplar trunks. The floors are tiled in *bejmat* and the walls have been finished with a coat of dyed plaster. Household objects, usurped of their original purpose, are now scattered throughout the house as decoration. The patio at Dar Ouarda is covered with a glass cupola, which has earned it the name "koubba," and is home to a pulpit, or *minbar*. The tables are in fact old doors, some sculpted wood, others decorated with illuminated paint (*zouaq*). Supporting poles from palanquins frame mirrors, and pillars from Berber houses support the canopies of the beds. Harnesses from *fantasias* have been transformed into curtain tiebacks. Bathrooms have been done in *tadelact* and the bathtubs the size of pools are inlaid with *zellij*. The sinks are fit into wooden plinths and old ladles pruned of their handles serve as soap dishes. Tablecloths are accented with silk-embroidered bridal belts. The walls are bedecked with woven creations made by Soumaya Jalal Mikou of straw and linen. The exterior façades, adorned with leather braids from Mauritania, glow in the broken lantern light.

OPPOSITE AND ABOVE:
An Andalusian riad *and grounds*

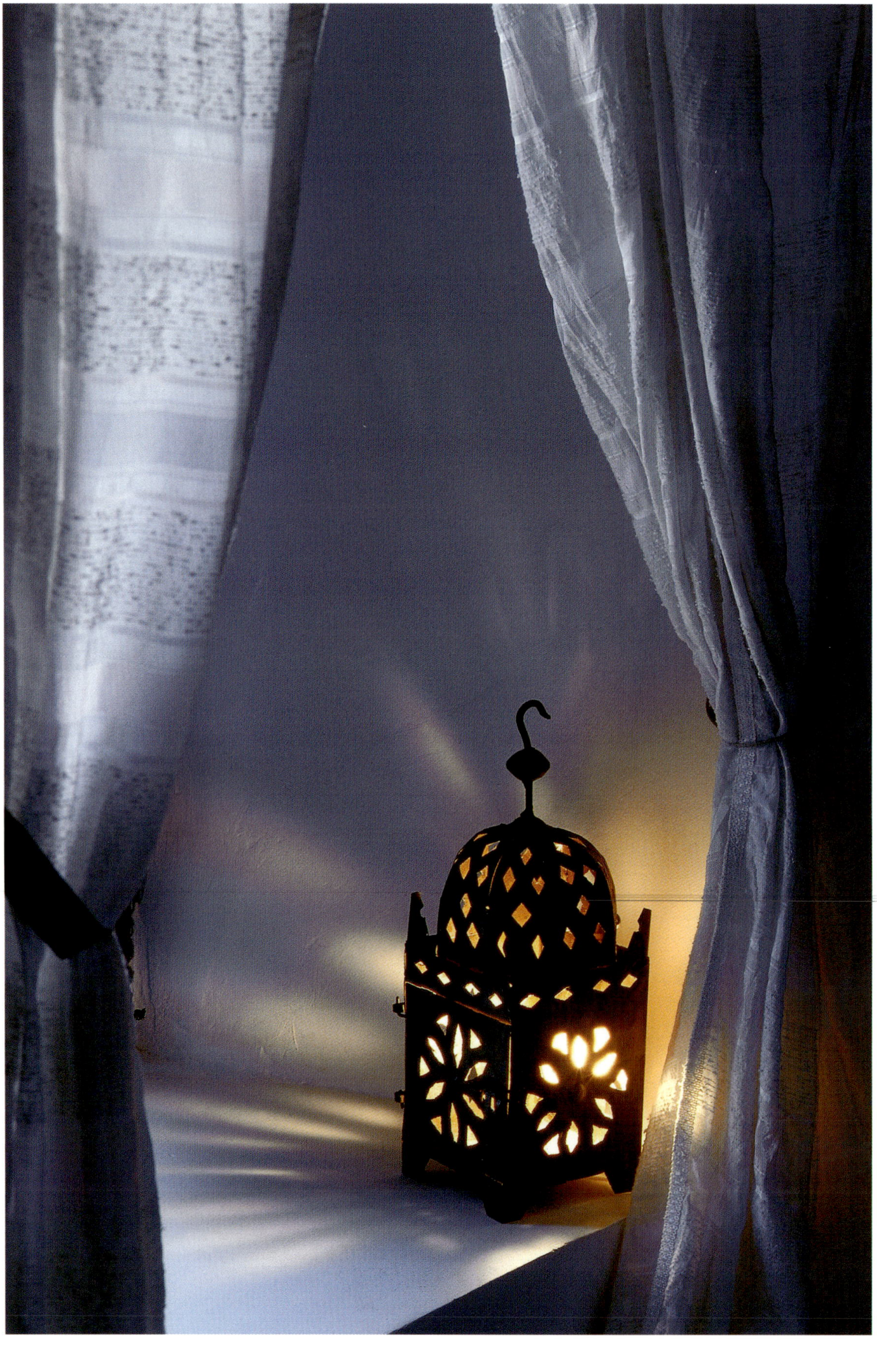

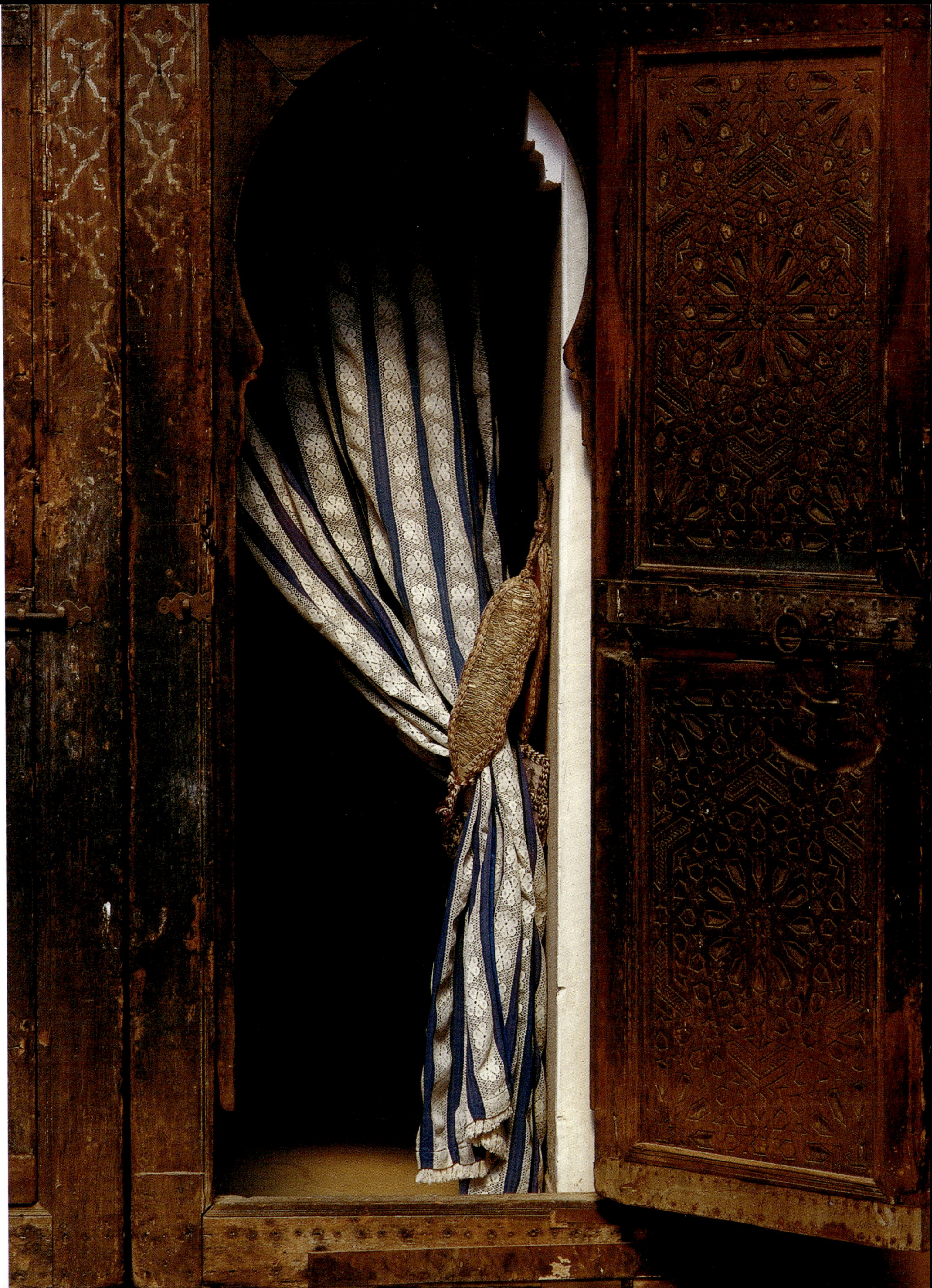

PAGES 200–1:
The embrasures of the drapes borrow motifs from fantasia

ABOVE:
A silk-embroidered wedding belt; a Koranic school tablet

OPPOSITE PAGE:
Joists of poplar replace the more customary palm tree trunks

PAGES 204–5:
The canopy beds use beams from Berber houses for supports

And, as Abel Demoussy has a passion for ancient writings, calligraphy is everywhere. Verses from the Persian poet Omar Khayyam are etched into the mosaics around the fireplaces. Tablets from Koranic schools and notary laws written on small wooden rollers seem to have been left about. In the bedrooms, characters from the Berber alphabet have been painted on the wooden screens. The dark, wine-colored leather furniture bears the seal of the house embroidered in white silk.

✦ Theatrical Décor

Kasbah Agafay also displays some audacious innovations. Modeled after city interiors, the window and door embrasures, as well as the capitals at Dar Ouarda, are decorated in sculpted plaster. On the ceiling is an enormous German silver chandelier that looks like some bizarre sea plant. The colors are vibrant, daring all contrasts. The poplar beams are painted with blue and green flowers on a red background. (It is not easy to convince an artist to paint on a wood less noble than cedar.) A series of embroidered sheer curtains and heavy drapes evoke the baroque ambience of the theaters of yesteryear. Through the large glass doors, the salon looks out over a cascade that starts with the terraces, continues onto the gardens, and finally reaches to the peaks of the Atlas Mountains. A distinctive feature of the kasbah is that it was constructed on a hilltop, so its *riad* and gardens stretch out over several levels, somewhat like the small terraced farms in the upper Atlas Valleys. Below, bordered with olive trees and soft green grass, is the swimming pool, which is decorated in *zellij* motifs designed by Chrissy Piercy, one of the queen of England's preferred artists. For women who wish to dress like queens in this castle made of clay, the Andalusian *riad* offers haute couture creations by the Moroccan designer Kenza Melehi. The desert life lurks about in these haunts. One hundred and twenty palm trees have been transplanted here from the region of Zagora. Across from the olive groves there are tents suited for a kaid, designed as princely suites with all the luxurious amenities found in the house. The open-air health spa,

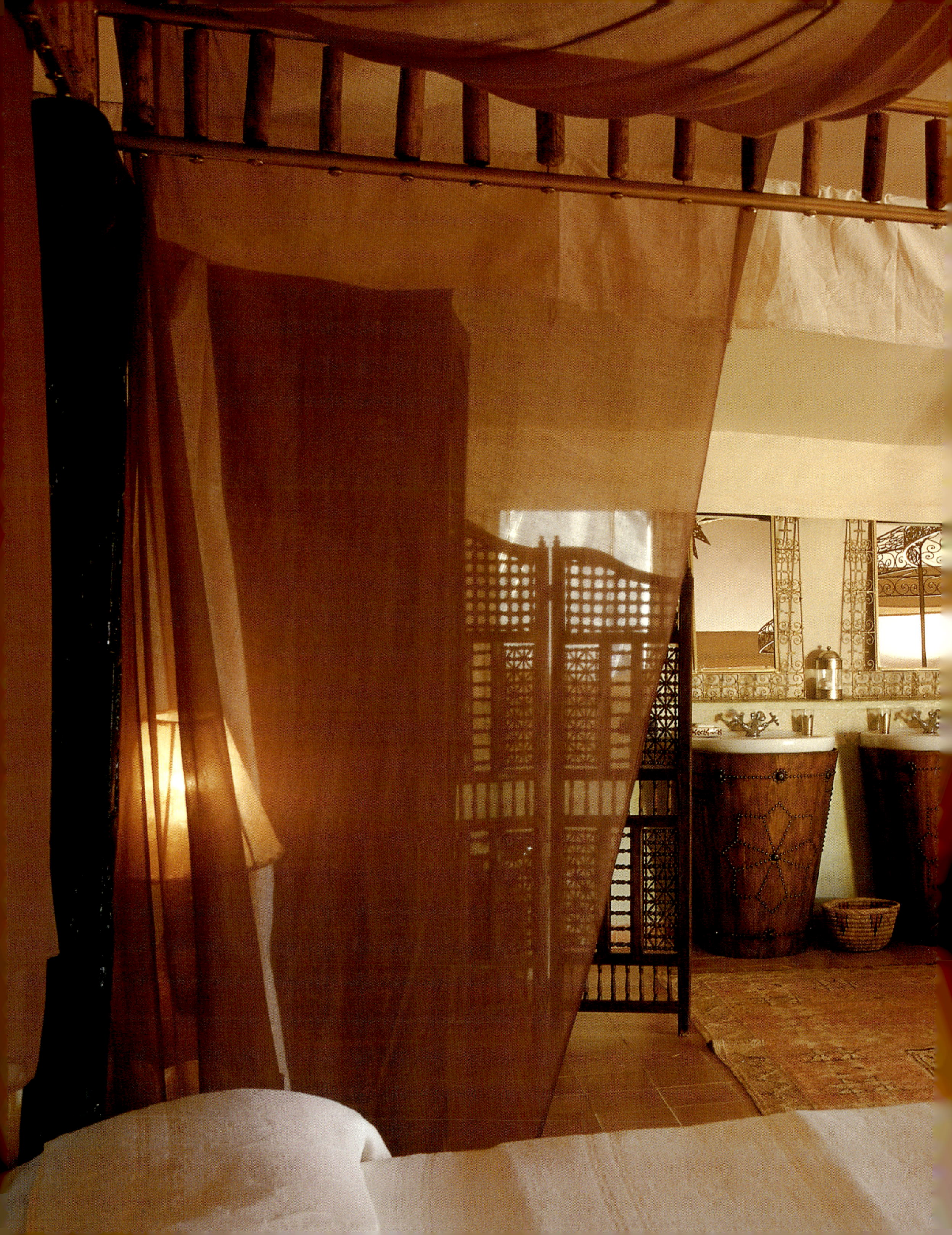

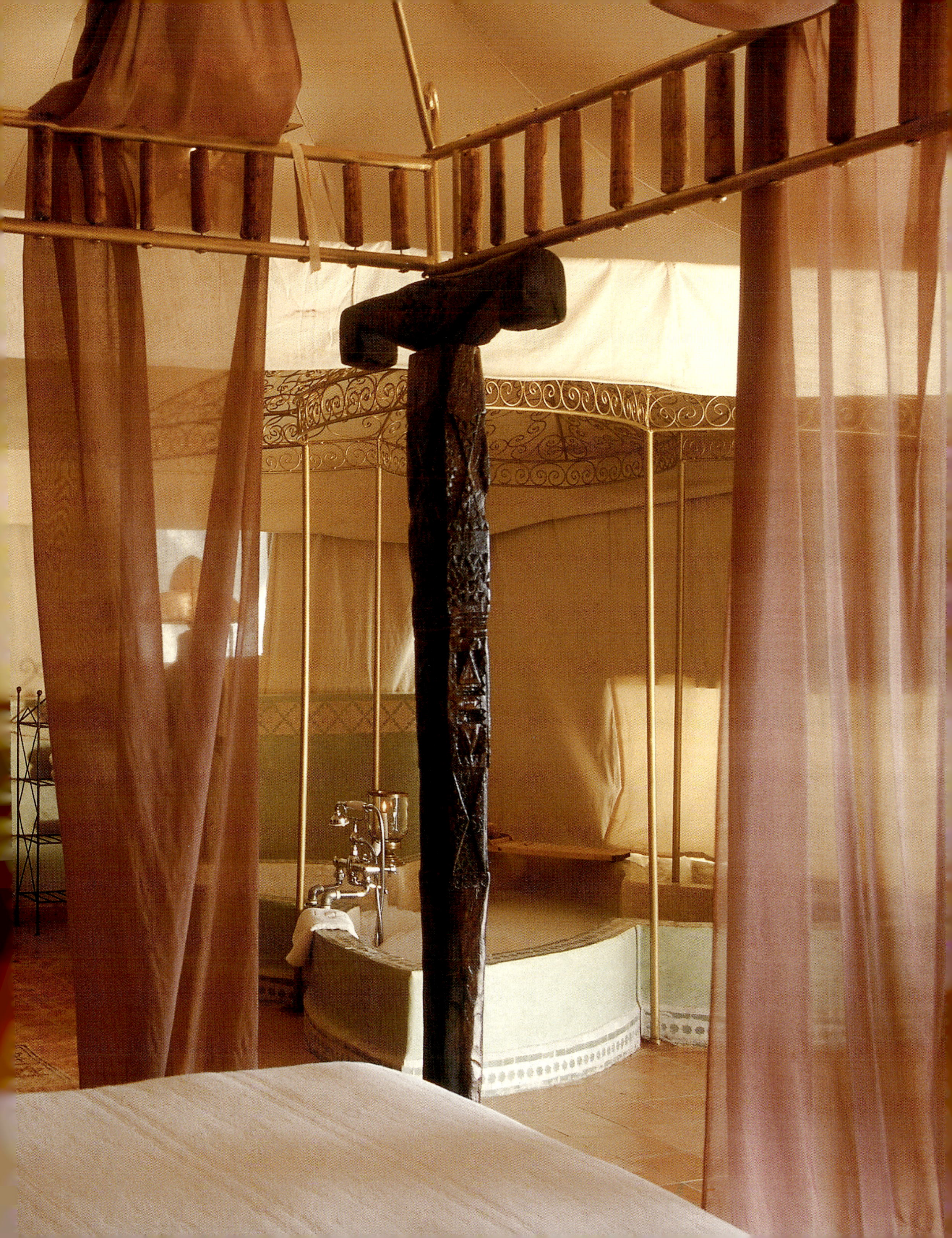

The spirit of the desert is sublimated by the audacious decorations that transform the home into the stage of a vast theater.

enclosed behind hedges of blossoming bougainvillea, is sheltered beneath reed lattices and extends over the aromatic herb garden. Twenty-five different plant species, expressly cultivated at Agafay, compose the essential oils used at the spa. The massage cabanas resemble small gardens—each with its own fountain and plant décor. Here water is the principle of life. It streams down the length of the seguias. It springs forth from the stone and *zellij* waterfalls and shoots up from fountains shaped like jugs. Even a well has been drilled so the villagers can irrigate their fields.

OPPOSITE AND ABOVE:
Interior rooms at Dar Ouarda. The patio is at left

TEMPLES TO THE ART OF LIVING 207

DAR AHLAM

Discreetly tucked away in the palm groves of Skoura, its towers superimposed upon the peaks of the Atlas Mountains, Dar Ahlam shoots up like a mirage amid the dirt roads. The archaism of a kasbah fused with an art of living that boggles the mind, Dar Ahlam offers the quintessential alliance of days past and contemporary style. Here desire is king and sensual transcendence, supreme. Exempt from all hotel norms, the residence is there to be tamed by its guests.

✶ The Enchanted Kasbah

Concealed behind its finely worked adobe walls, Dar Ahlam offers exceptional luxury. Built during the 1920s by a local kaid, the kasbah was dismantled and then re-erected around a cement framework, making it possible to unobtrusively install such infrastructure as air-conditioning and under-floor heating. The interior of the building, nevertheless, has retained the ambience of a traditional kasbah. In the center, glistening in bronze patinas, a narrow shaft of light spreads throughout three levels, seven suites, and three salons, the décors of which respectively call to mind the exoticism of the Sahara, India, and Syria. Although spacious, the rooms have adopted the classic elongated proportions of a Moroccan home. In keeping with the traditional design, the ceilings, which are covered with reeds or stems from pink oleander, are supported by joists made of palm trees or tamarisk branches. Daylight penetrates only through the very small windows and their elegant iron lattices. In concordance with the exterior arcatures, niches carved into the adobe walls are fitted with subdued lights that accentuate the hidden corners of the residence night and day. Zigzagging passageways and concealed doors—collected throughout the countryside— restore the perspectives of Saharan homes. Three

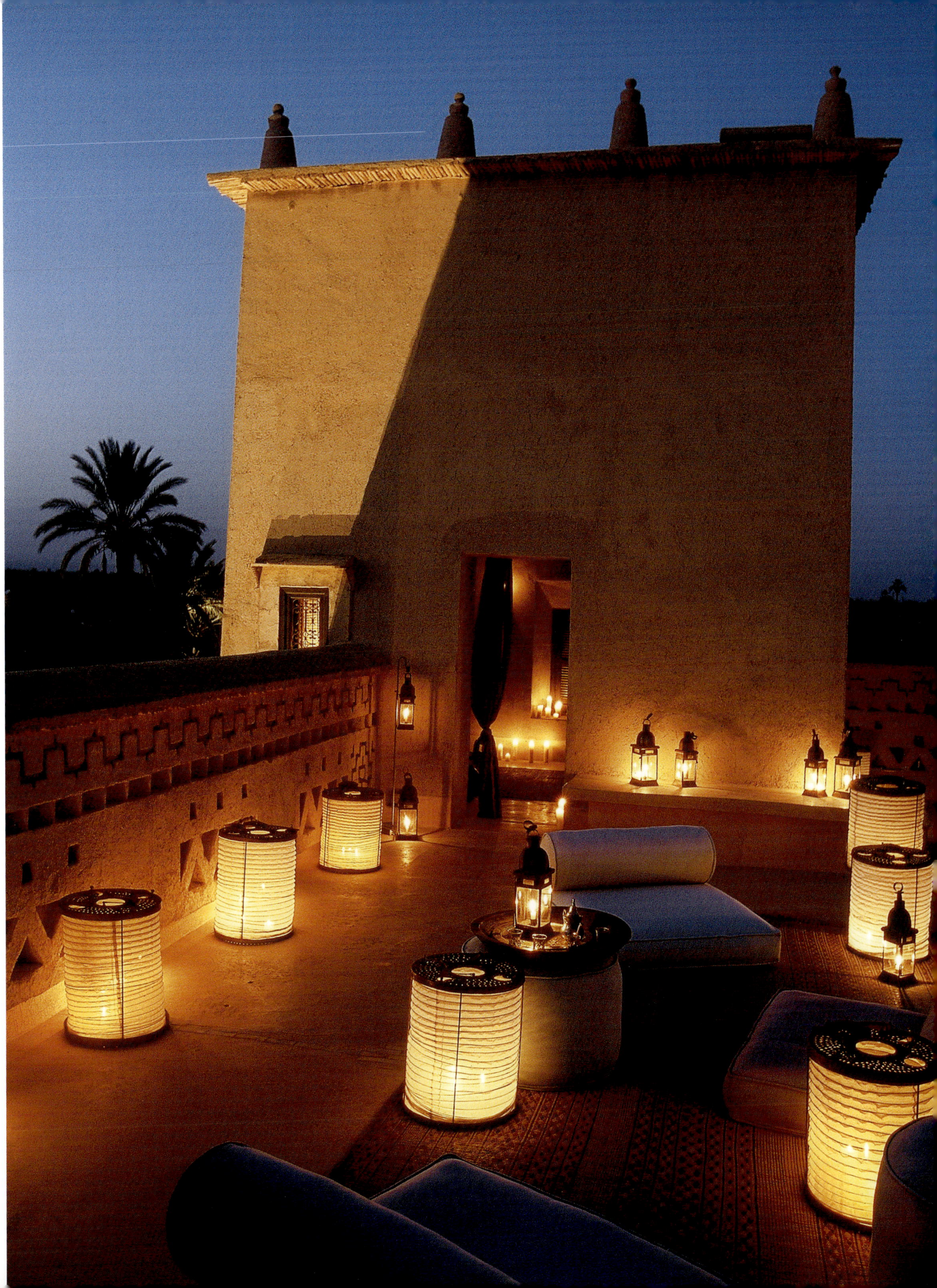

*Rustic and contemporary, Dar Ahlam transcends
the traditional ambience of kasbahs.*

terraces, laid out on several levels, offer a panoramic view over the palm grove, the desert, and the Atlas Mountains, the first foothills of which can be reached in an hour by a sport-utility vehicle. An adjoining *riad* has been retained and it, too, was restored in adobe. Tiled in *bejmat* in the emerald greens of the palm grove, it houses a health spa with a hammam, a jacuzzi, and a perfume parlor that lavishes sultry sensations.

✦ Contemporary Influences

But Dar Ahlam also exudes a contemporary ambience. Galleries and patios effectively extending the kasbah lead to an enormous salon whose bay windows face in the direction of the setting sun and look over the terrace, the swimming pool, and the gardens. Spread out over five acres (two hectares), these gardens, laid out around a central fountain, combine the precision of Persian symmetries with French perspectives. A vegetable garden thrives beneath the shade of the palms and the olive trees. Beyond the lawns and the small wheat fields that surround the swimming pool are three modern villas finished in adobe and endowed with heavy wooden doors. A great tranquility leads one to hear the constant murmur of water. Whether from the fountains or the pools or the *seguias*, each delivers its little sonata punctuated by the cooing of the doves.

Thierry Tessier, the owner of this house of dreams, has attended to even the minutest detail of the art of receiving. The kitchens offer dishes of unknown savors, under the direction of Pierre Hermé, famous for his pastries. Always served in different areas of the kasbah and adapted to the hour and climate of the day, the menus are thematic. There are also light gourmet meals available, accompanied by fruit juices and brioches. Provided by a staff native to the region, the service is pleasant and gracious. Yet, it is so discreet, that above all, one feels at home at Dar Ahlam.

LEFT:
On the upper floors, sunlight streams through ironworks as fine as lace

ABOVE:
The décor of the Sahraouie suite is accented by leather and wood; Mauritanian weavings enliven the floors

TEMPLES TO THE ART OF LIVING 211

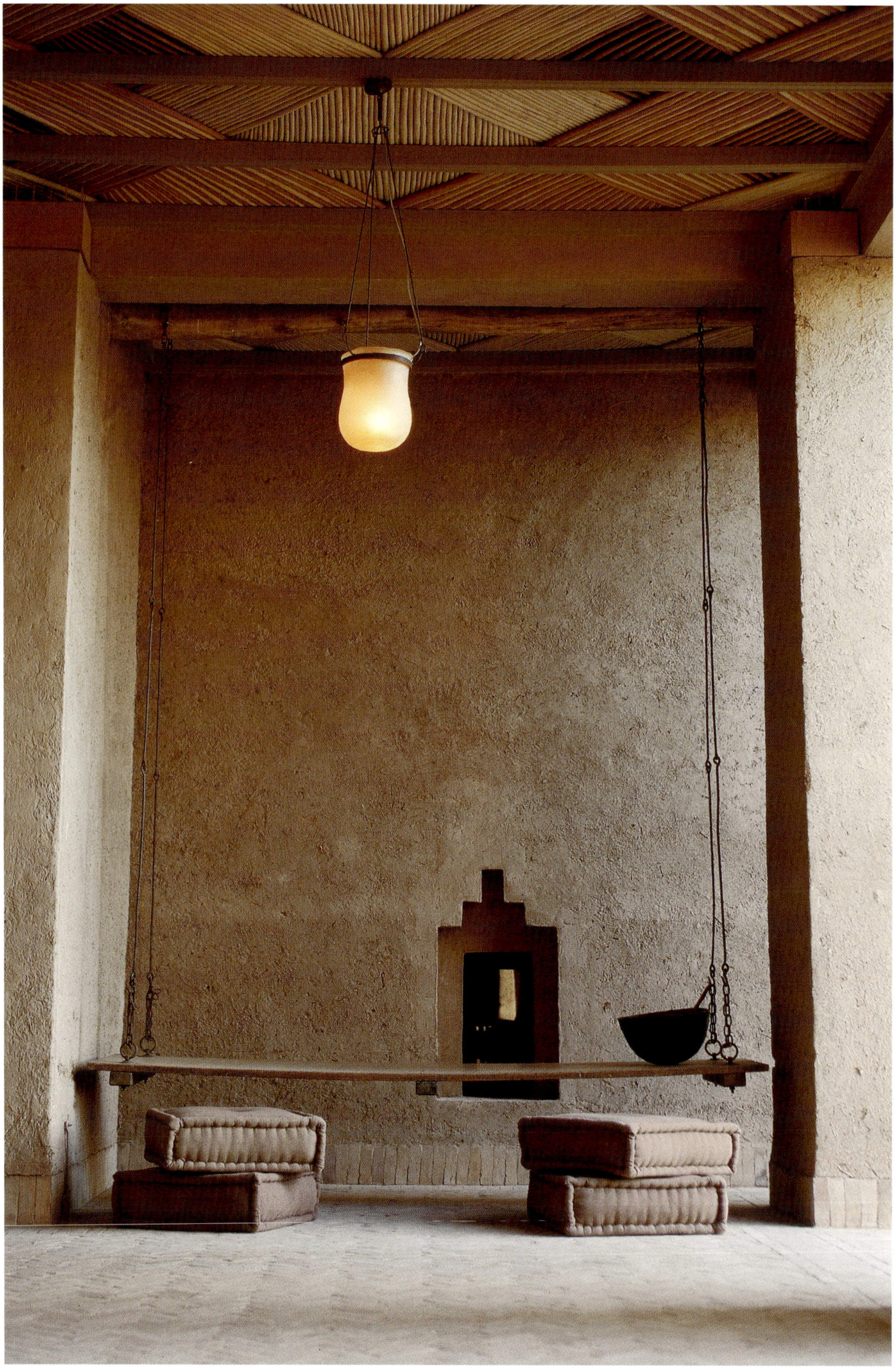

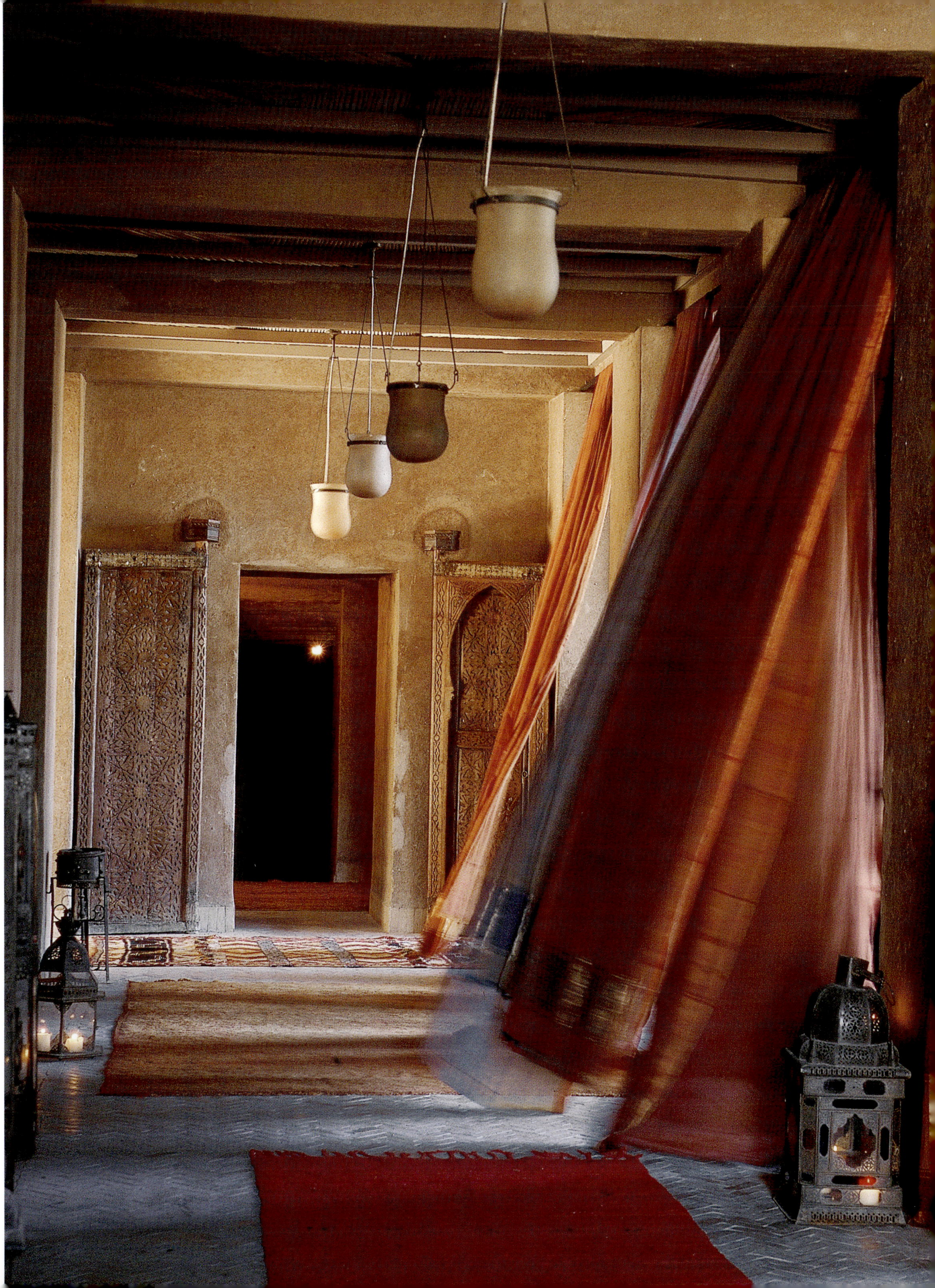

✦ A Universe of Sensations

To the gustatory joys add an olfactory diversity that contributes to the raptures of the home. All along the *bejmat* paths that wind through the garden, the scents of mint, orange blossom, and rosemary become heavy in the cool dampness of the irrigation canals. The delicate perfume of the candles intermingles with the more earthy odors of the omnipresent leather and wood furniture. Guided by the scent, one arrives at the perfume parlor, a magical place where daily hand-cut soaps, body milks, and massage oils are there for the choosing. Crystal flasks display amber-colored essences—musk, jasmine, sandalwood, cedar, geranium, rose, and myrrh. A dazzling array of herbal teas is available to savor while relaxing in the jacuzzi beneath an openwork brick cupola through which some rays of light stream down.

Tactile sensations are also set alight at the health spa through both muscular and relaxing bodyworks. Upon request, massages are given in the gardens, the guest lying upon a nomad palanquin, sheathed behind scrims. Bedrooms and salons harbor materials the hand longs to caress—leather, silk embroideries, linen muslin, or heavy taffetas adorned with traditional jewelry. The heavy and dark winter drapes are exchanged in springtime for a fine gossamer that blows with the slightest breeze. Doors are opened by pulling leather balls or silk braids. Bare feet confirm the warmth of the *tadelact* and the rugged feel of the clay bricks. In winter, one stretches out in

OPPOSITE:
The lantern salon retains the conventional room proportions, which must be narrow due to the short joists

TEMPLES TO THE ART OF LIVING 215

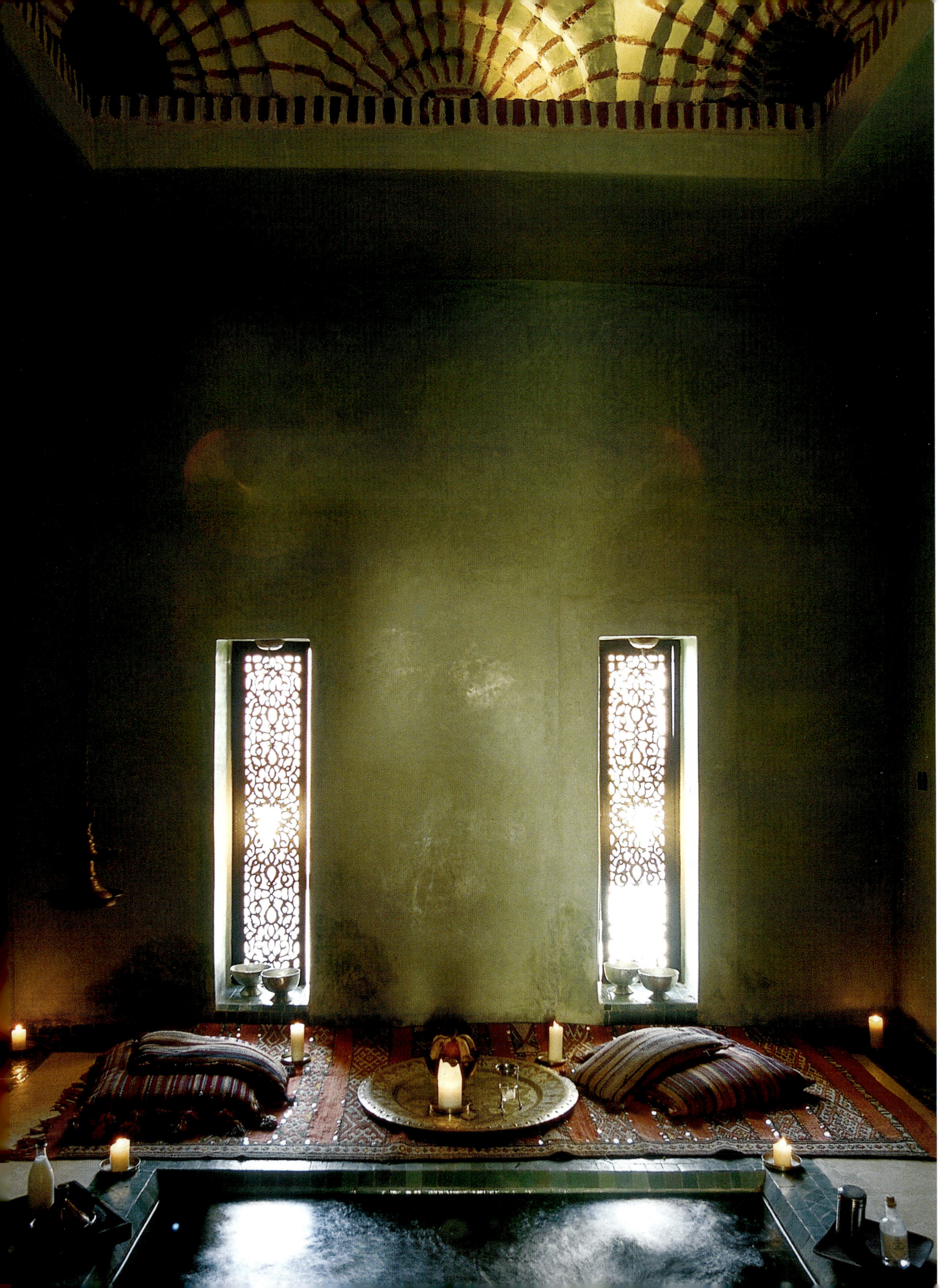

front of the fireplace; each room has its own. And when summer comes, everyone relaxes in the fiery sun, embraced by the cool walls.

And finally, scattered here and there is a plethora of unexpected elegances that enthrall the spirit. At the health spa, the small wooden compartments for placing one's personal paraphernalia are decorated with silver fibulas. The transparent soaps look like the almonds that give them their scent. The mineral water is served in a carafe and, as indicated on the menu, accompanied by rustic wooden spoons crafted with silver. The Mauritanian tablecloths and the ecru cloths hanging from tamarisk perches create an ambience of an African safari that perhaps had been visited upon by the glimmering colors of an Indian sari. Each suite has its own linens, embroidered in accordance with the character of the room. Not remotely discordant, contemporary furniture sits side by side with primitive African art brightening the Herculean-sized rooms. A palace to the art of living, Dar Ahlam makes available to those who might have the talent an easel upon which to set a canvas and submit to the magic of the kasbah.

OPPOSITE PAGE:
Like a traditional hammam, *the jacuzzi has a vaulted roof and is bathed in indirect light*

ABOVE LEFT:
The hand-cut soap made exclusively for the Dar Ahlam has a different scent every day

TEMPLES TO THE ART OF LIVING 217

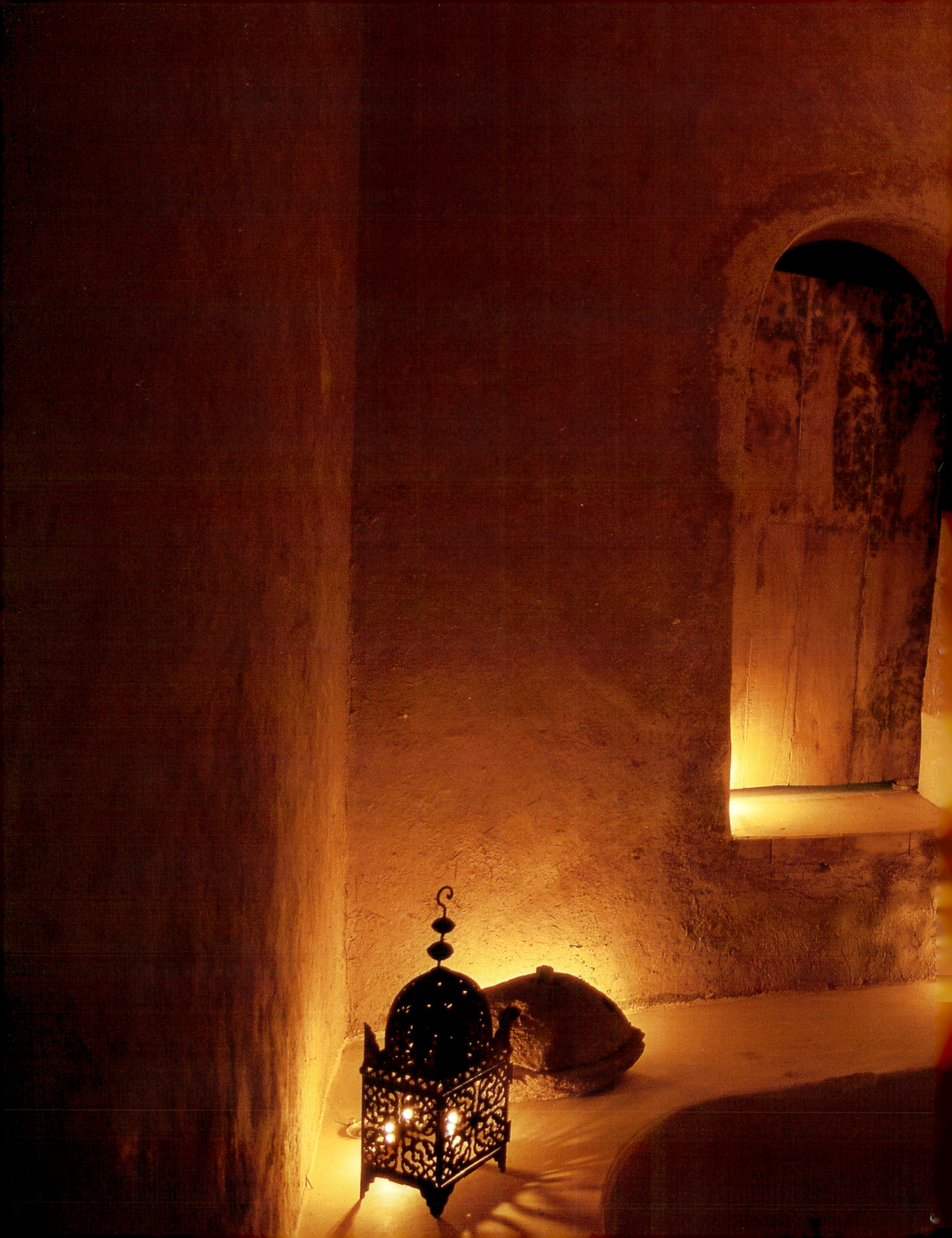

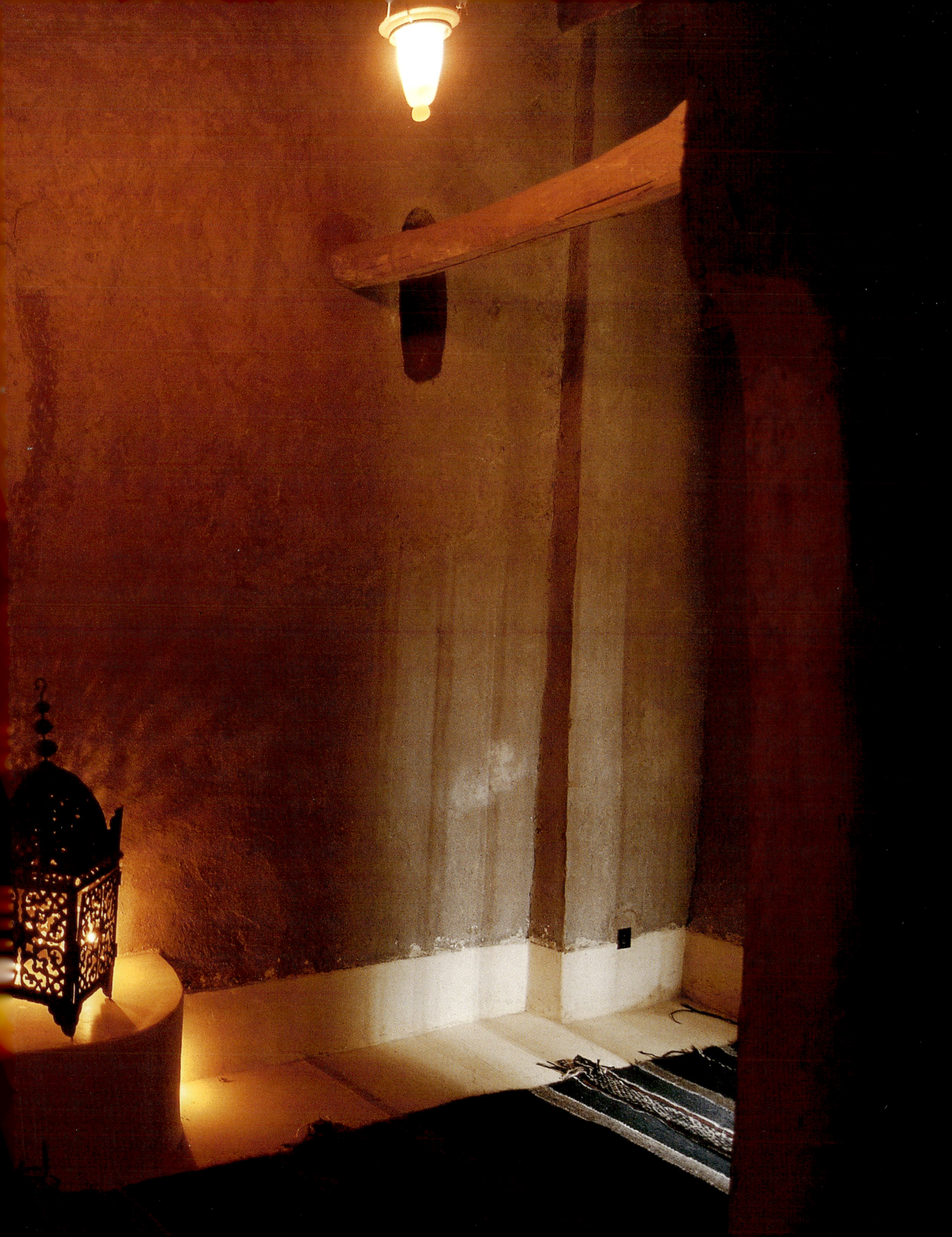

FURTHER READING

BADUEL, Pierre-Robert. *Habitat, état, société au Maghreb*. Paris: CNRS, 1988.

BARRUCAND, Marianne. *Urbanisme princier en Islam*. Paris: Geuthner, 1985.

BEN DRISS OTTMANI, Hamza. *Une cité sous les alizés: Mogador, des origines à 1939*. Rabat: Éditions La Porte, 1997.

BOURQIA, Rahma, and Susan Gilson Miller, eds. *In the Shadow of the Sultan*. Cambridge: Harvard University Press, 1999.

DELABORDE, Michel. *Le Temps d'une ville. Essaouira*. Casablanca: Eddif, 1991.

HUET, Karin, and Titouan Lamazou. *Sous les toits de terre*. Casablanca: Éditions Belvisi, 1988.

http://www.houseinfez.com/Fes-links.htm

JACQUES-MEUNIE, Denise. *Architectures et habitats du Dadès: Maroc présaharien*. Paris: Klincksieck, 1962.

LANDT, Dennis. *New Moroccan Style. Design from Casablanca to Marrakesh*. New York: Thames and Hudson, 2001.

LEWIS, Wyndham. *Journey Into Barbary*. Ed. C. J. Fox. Santa Barbara: Black Sparrow Press, 1983.

LOTI, Pierre. *Morocco*. New York: Columbia University Press, 2002.

Maroc, magie des lieux. L'art de la ville et de la maison. Exh. cat. Paris: Institut du Monde Arabe, 1999.

Maroc, les trésors du royaume. Exh. cat. Paris: Musée du Petit Palais, April 15–July 18, 1999. Paris: Éditions Plume, 1999.

NAJI, Salima. *Art et architectures berbères du Maroc*. Aix-en-Provence: Edisud, Casablanca: Eddif, 2001.

PACCARD, André. *Traditional Islamic Craft in Moroccan Architecture*. Trans. Mary Guggenheim. Paris: Edition Atelier 74, 1980.

PENNELL, C. R. *Morocco since 1830: A History*. New York: New York University Press, 2001.

RAUZIER, Marie-Pascale. *Tableaux du Haut-Atlas marocain*. Paris: Arthaud, 1998.

REVAULT, J., et al. *Palais et demeures de Fès*. 3 volumes. Paris: CNRS, 1992.

SCHROETER, Daniel J., et al., eds. *Merchants of Essaouira: Urban Society and Imperialism in Southwestern Morocco, 1844–1886*. Cambridge: Cambridge University Press, 1988.

SCHROETER, Daniel J. *The Sultan's Jew*. Oxford: Oxford University Press, 2002.

TERRASSE, Henri, and Jean Hainaut. *Les Arts décoratifs au Maroc*. Paris: Henri Laurens, 1925. Reprinted as *Afrique Orient*. Casablanca, 2001.

WHARTON, Edith. "In Morocco." In *Selected Travel Writings, 1888–1920*. New York: St. Martin's Press, 1996.

WILBAUX, Quentin. *Marrakesh: The Secret of Its Courtyard Houses*. London: Art Books International, 2000.

ACKNOWLEDGMENTS

We extend our great thanks for their assistance to the Riad al Bartal, Riad Sheherazade in Fès, Riad Baghdad in Essaouira, Moha and François Villeneuve in Marrakech, Dar Ahlam and Kasbah ben Moro in Skoura, Kasbah Baha Baha in N'Kob, and the Ministers of Communication and Culture.

We also thank all the people who so kindly opened their doors to us and allowed us to photograph their homes. We salute their efforts to bring the traditional Moroccan home to the fore as well as their contributions to the preservation of the national heritage: Martine and Pierre Sageot, Alexandra Lippini, Bernard Sanz, Quentin Wilbaux (architect), the Riad Kaiss, Joël Martial, Yves Dupuis, Clelia, Christian Ferré, Abel Demoussy, Frédéric Damgaard, Nathalie and Philippe Vignal, and Abdou at the Glaoui Palace.

And for all his invaluable help, the author extends special thanks to Alain de Pommereau.

Project Manager, English-language edition: Susan Richmond

Editor, English-language edition: Mary Christian

Jacket design, English-language edition: LeAnna Weller Smith and Christine Knorr

Design Coordinator, English-language edition: Christine Knorr

Production Coordinator, English-language edition: Norman Watkins

Library of Congress Cataloging-in-Publication Data

Verner, Corinne.

  [Maisons & riads du Maroc. English]

  The villas and riads of Morocco / text by Corinne Verner; photographs by Cécile Tréal and Jean-Michel Ruiz; translated from the French by Laurel Hirsch.

    p. cm.

  Translation of: Maisons & riads du Maroc.

  Includes bibliographical references and index.

  ISBN 0-8109-5907-0 (hardcover : alk. paper) 1. Architecture, Domestic--Morocco. 2. Architecture, Islamic--Morocco. I. Title: Villas & riads of Morocco. II. Tréal, Cécile. III. Ruiz, Jean-Michel. IV. Title.

  NA7461.7.A1V4713 2005

  728'.37'0964--dc22

                      2005000277

Copyright © 2004 Aubanel, an imprint of Éditions Minerva, Geneva

English translation copyright © 2005 Harry N. Abrams, Inc.

Published in 2005 by Harry N. Abrams, Incorporated, New York
All rights reserved. No part of the contents of this book may be reproduced without the written permission of the publisher

Printed and bound in France by Pollina s.a. - n° L95476
10 9 8 7 6 5 4 3 2 1

Harry N. Abrams, Inc.
100 Fifth Avenue
New York, N.Y. 10011
www.abramsbooks.com

Abrams is a subsidiary of

LA MARTINIÈRE